SAT Score-Raising Dictionary
Third Edition

PUBLISHING

New York

This publication is designed to provide accurate and authoritative information in regard to the subject matter covered. It is sold with the understanding that the publisher is not engaged in rendering legal, accounting, or other professional service. If legal advice or other expert assistance is required, the services of a competent professional should be sought.

© 2009 by Kaplan, Inc.

Published by Kaplan Publishing, a division of Kaplan, Inc.
1 Liberty Plaza, 24th Floor
New York, NY 10006

Printed in the United States of America

10 9 8 7 6 5 4 3 2

ISBN-13: 978-1-4277-9864-0

Kaplan Publishing books are available at special quantity discounts to use for sales promotions, employee premiums, or educational purposes. Please email our Special Sales Department to order or for more information at kaplanpublishing@kaplan.com, or write to Kaplan Publishing, 1 Liberty Plaza, 24th Floor, New York, NY 10006.

GET READY TO CONQUER THE SAT!

Kaplan's *SAT Score-Raising Dictionary, Third Edition* is designed to help you learn the most frequently tested SAT vocabulary words in a quick, easy, and painless way!

Here's what you'll get:

- 2,000 of the most frequently tested SAT words and their definitions
- The part of speech for each entry to help you master grammar and usage
- A handy pronunciation guide
- A helpful sample sentence that lets you see each word in action
- A list of synonyms, to help you with word association and memorization

A strong vocabulary is crucial for scoring well on every section of the SAT exam. Good luck on your quest for a great SAT score!

ABANDON
noun (uh <u>baan</u> duhn)

total lack of inhibition
restraint

*With her strict parents out of town,
Kelly danced all night with **abandon**.*

Synonyms: exuberance, enthusiasm

. . .

ABASE
verb (uh <u>bays</u>)

to humble, to disgrace

*After his immature behavior, John
abased himself in my eyes.*

Synonyms: demean, humiliate

. . .

ABATE
verb (uh <u>bayt</u>)

to decrease, to reduce

*My hunger **abated** when I saw how
filthy the chef's hands were.*

Synonyms: dwindle, ebb, recede

ABBREVIATE
verb (uh <u>bree</u> vee ayt)

to make shorter

*When the speaker saw that her time
was running short, she decided to
abbreviate her remarks.*

Synonym: decrease

. . .

ABDICATE
verb (<u>aab</u> duh kayt)

to give up a position, right, or power

*With the angry mob clamoring outside
the palace, the king **abdicated** his
throne and fled.*

Synonyms: cede, quit, relinquish,
resign, yield

ABERRANT
adjective (uh <u>ber</u> unt)

deviating from what is normal or expected

*Because he had been a steady, cheerful worker for many years, his fellow postal workers did not expect his **aberrant** burst of rage.*

Synonyms: abnormal, anomalous, deviant, divergent

. . .

ABERRATION
noun (aa buhr <u>ay</u> shuhn)

something different from the usual

*Due to the bizarre **aberrations** in the author's behavior, her publicist decided that the less the public saw of her, the better.*

Synonyms: abnormality, anomaly, deviation, irregularity

. . .

ABET
verb (uh <u>beht</u>)

to aid, to act as an accomplice

*While Derwin robbed the bank, Marvin **abetted** his friend by pulling up the getaway car.*

Synonyms: help, succor, assist

ABEYANCE
noun (uh <u>bay</u> uhns)

temporary suppression or suspension

*Michelle held her excitement in **abeyance** while the college review board considered her application.*

Synonyms: deferral, delay, dormancy, postponement, remission

. . .

ABHOR
verb (ab <u>hor</u>)

to loathe, detest

*George **abhored** his exhausting new job at the supermarket.*

Synonyms: dislike, hate, despise

. . .

ABJECT
adjective (<u>aab</u> jehkt)

miserable, pitiful

*When we found the **abject** creature lying on the ground, we took it inside and tended to its broken leg.*

Synonyms: lamentable, pathetic, sorry

ABJURE
verb (aab joor)

to give up forever [handwritten annotation]

to renounce under oath, to abandon forever, to abstain from

*After having been devout for most of his life, he suddenly **abjured** his beliefs, much to his family's disappointment.*

Synonyms: renounce, disavow

. . .

ABNEGATE
verb (aab nih gayt)

to give up, to deny to oneself

*After his retirement, the former police commissioner found it difficult to **abnegate** authority.*

Synonyms: abjure, surrender, renounce

. . .

ABORTIVE
adjective (uh bohr tihv)

ending without results

*Her **abortive** attempt to swim the full five miles left her frustrated.*

Synonyms: fruitless, futile, unsuccessful

ABRASIVE
adjective (ab ray siv)

harsh and rough in manner

*Ironically, the basketball coach's **abrasive** style really motivated the team to win the game.*

Synonyms: uncompromising, rude, coarse

. . .

ABRIDGE
verb (uh brij)

to condense, shorten

*Chantalle knew she had missed her curfew and hoped her parents would **abridge** her curfew lecture when she got home.*

Synonyms: reduce, abbreviate

. . .

ABROGATE
verb (aab ruh gayt)

to annul, to abolish by authoritative action

*The president's job is to **abrogate** any law that fosters inequality among citizens.*

Synonyms: nullify, revoke, repeal

ABRUPT
adjective (ab rupt)

sudden, curt

*Shanna threw her arms around Paul when he asked her to the prom but **abruptly** pulled back when he announced that he was only kidding.*

Synonyms: unexpected, hasty, quick

. . .

ABSCOND
verb (aab skahnd)

to leave quickly in secret

*The criminal **absconded** during the night with all of his mother's money.*

Synonyms: slip, sneak, flee

. . .

ABSOLVE
verb (ab zolv)

to forgive, free from blame

*Marisol **absolved** her artsy friends for laughing at the preppy sweater her mom made her wear to school—after all, it's not like she wouldn't have done the same thing.*

Synonyms: pardon, clear

ABSORB
verb (ab zorb)

to soak up, to occupy completely

*Jason completely forgot to watch the baseball game, as he was too **absorbed** in his studies.*

Synonym: consume

. . .

ABSTAIN
verb (uhb stayn)

to choose not to do something

*Before the medical procedure, you must **abstain** from eating.*

Synonyms: forbear, refrain, withhold

. . .

ABSTEMIOUS
adjective (aab stee mee uhs)

done sparingly, consuming in moderation

*The spa served no sugar or wheat, but the clients found the retreat so calm that they didn't mind the **abstemious** rules.*

Synonyms: moderate, sparing, abstinent

ABSTRUSE
adjective (<u>aab</u> stroos) (<u>uhb</u> stroos)

difficult to comprehend

*The philosopher's elucidation was so clear that he turned an **abstruse** subject into one his audience could grasp.*

Synonyms: complex, esoteric, profound

. . .

ABYSS
noun (uh <u>bihs</u>)

an extremely deep hole

*The submarine dove into the **abyss** to chart the previously unseen depths.*

Synonyms: chasm, void

. . .

ACCEDE
verb (aak <u>seed</u>)

to express approval, to agree to

*Once the mayor heard the reasonable request, she happily **acceded** to the proposal.*

Synonyms: consent, concur

ACCELERATE
verb (ak <u>sel</u> uh rayt)

to cause to develop or progress more quickly

*When Timmy saw Josh approaching him in the hall, he **accelerated** his pace—he knew Josh would stuff him in a locker if he caught up.*

Synonyms: increase speed, pick up the pace

. . .

ACCENTUATE
verb (ak <u>sen</u> choo ayt)

to stress or emphasize, intensify

*Despite what the fashion magazines said, Ashley was sure that the bright blue eye shadow **accentuated** her blue eyes perfectly.*

Synonyms: emphasize, highlight

. . .

ACCESSIBLE
adjective (ak <u>sess</u> ih bull)

attainable, available

*Poor Shanna forgot to lock her journal, leaving her secrets **accessible** to her nosy little sister.*

Synonym: approachable

ACCLIVITY

noun (uh klihv ih tee)

an incline or upward slope, the ascending side of a hill

*We were so tired from hiking that by the time we reached the **acclivity**, it looked more like a mountain than a hill.*

Synonyms: ascent, upgrade

. . .

ACCOMPLICE

noun (ah komp liss)

an associate in wrongdoing

*Paul had no **accomplice** when he egged the principal's car—he did it all by himself.*

Synonyms: accessory, assistant, collaborator

. . .

ACCORD

verb (uh kord)

to bestow upon

*The bully told Timmy to give up his lunch money or he'd **accord** him a black eye.*

Synonyms: award, present

ACCRETION

noun (uh kree shuhn)

a growth in size, an increase in amount

*The committee's strong fund-raising efforts resulted in an **accretion** in scholarship money.*

Synonyms: buildup, accumulation

. . .

ACERBIC

adjective (uh suhr bihk)

bitter, sharp in taste or temper

*Gina's **acerbic** wit and sarcasm were feared around the office.*

Synonyms: biting, caustic, cutting, tart

. . .

ACIDULOUS

adjective (uh si juh luhs)

sour in taste or manner

*The **acidulous** taste of the spoiled milk made the young boy's lips pucker.*

Synonyms: acerbic, acetose, biting, piquant, pungent, tart

ACME
noun (<u>aak</u> mee)

the highest level or degree attainable

*Just when he reached the **acme** of his power, the dictator was overthrown.*

Synonyms: apex, peak, summit

. . .

ACQUIESCE
verb (<u>aak</u> wee ehs)

to agree, to comply quietly

*The princess **acquiesced** to demands that she marry a nobleman, but she was not happy about it.*

Synonyms: accede, consent, submit

. . .

ACQUIRE
verb (ah <u>kwiyr</u>)

to gain possession of

*George **acquired** a taste for refried beans after eating at the new local Mexican restaurant.*

Synonyms: obtain, get, gain

ACRIMONY
noun (ak ri <u>mow</u> nee)

bitterness, animosity

*The homecoming game ended in **acrimony** after a few of the visiting team members started name-calling on the field.*

Synonyms: animosity, hostility, unfriendliness

. . .

ACTUATE
verb (<u>aak</u> choo ayt)

to put into motion, to activate, to motivate or influence to activity

*The leader's rousing speech **actuated** the crowd into a peaceful protest.*

Synonyms: incite, instigate

. . .

ACUITY
noun (uh <u>kyoo</u> ih tee)

sharp vision or perception character-ized by the ability to resolve fine detail

*With unusual **acuity**, she was able to determine that the masterpiece was a fake.*

Synonyms: acuteness, sharpness

ACUMEN
noun (<u>aak</u> yuh muhn) (uh <u>kyoo</u> muhn)

sharpness of insight, mind, and understanding, shrewd judgment

*The investor's financial **acumen** helped him to select high-yield stocks.*

Synonyms: discernment, shrewdness

• • •

ADAMANT
adjective (<u>aad</u> uh muhnt) (<u>aad</u> uh mint)

stubbornly unyielding

*She was **adamant** about leaving the restaurant after the waiter was rude.*

Synonyms: inflexible, obdurate, inexorable

• • •

ADEPT
adjective (uh <u>dehpt</u>)

extremely skilled

*She is **adept** at computing math problems in her head.*

Synonyms: quick, masterful

ADJOURN
verb (a <u>jern</u>)

to postpone

*The teacher had to **adjourn** the big test when she caught the flu.*

Synonyms: recess, suspend

• • •

ADJUDICATE
verb (uh <u>jood</u> ih kayt)

to hear and settle a matter, to act as a judge

*The principal **adjudicated** the disagreement between two students.*

Synonyms: arbitrate, mediate

• • •

ADJUNCT
verb (<u>a</u> junkt)

something or someone associated with another but in a supplementary position

*When Dave complained about the lousy cafeteria food, Maude added in an **adjunct** of vocal support.*

Synonym: accessory

ADJURE
verb (uh <u>joor</u>)

to appeal to

*The criminal **adjured** to the court for mercy.*

Synonyms: beg, plead

. . .

ADMONISH
verb (aad <u>mahn</u> ihsh)

to caution or warn gently in order to correct something

*My mother **admonished** me about my poor grades.*

Synonyms: berate, rebuke

. . .

ADORN
verb (uh <u>dorn</u>)

to enhance or decorate

*Derek **adorned** the walls of his room with posters of hot girls in bikinis, despite his mother's objections.*

Synonyms: embellish, beautify, garnish

ADROIT
adjective (uh <u>droyt</u>)

skillful, accomplished, highly competent

*The **adroit** athlete completed even the most difficult obstacle course with ease.*

Synonyms: dexterous, proficient

. . .

ADULATION
noun (<u>aaj</u> juh lay shuhn)

excessive flattery or admiration

*The **adulation** she showed her professor seemed insincere, I suspected she really wanted a better grade.*

Synonyms: fawning, buttering up

. . .

ADULTERATE
verb (uh <u>duhl</u> tuhr ayt)

to corrupt or make impure

*The restauranteur made his ketchup last longer by **adulterating** it with water.*

Synonyms: contaminate, dilute

ADUMBRATE

verb (<u>aad</u> uhm brayt) (uh <u>duhm</u> brayt)

to give a hint or indication of something to come

*Her constant complaining about the job **adumbrated** her intent to leave.*

Synonyms: foreshadow, suggest

· · ·

ADVANTAGEOUS

adjective (<u>add</u> van <u>tayj</u> ish)

favorable, useful

*Chantalle found her reasoning skills **advantageous** when convincing her parents to let her go to Mexico for spring break.*

Synonyms: beneficial, helpful, valuable

· · ·

ADVERSARY

noun (<u>add</u> ver <u>seh</u> ree)

opponent, enemy

*Shanna crushed her **adversary** in the race for class president and won the election by a landslide.*

Synonyms: rival, foe, challenger

ADVERSITY

noun (add <u>ver</u> si tee)

a state of hardship or misfortune

*One might say Ashley overcame **adversity** to become head cheerleader despite her lack of flexibility or tumbling skills.*

Synonyms: difficulty, harsh conditions, hard times

· · ·

ADVOCATE

verb (<u>aad</u> vuh kayt)

to speak in favor of

*The vegetarian **advocated** a diet containing no meat.*

Synonyms: back, champion, support

· · ·

AERATE

verb (ayr <u>ayt</u>)

expose to air

*Josh's mom asked him to **aerate** his smelly sneakers outside the house.*

Synonyms: freshen, let breathe

AERIE
noun (<u>ayr</u> ee) (<u>eer</u> ee)

a nest built high in the air, an elevated, often secluded, dwelling

*Perched high among the trees, the eagle's **aerie** was filled with eggs.*

Synonyms: perch, stronghold

• • •

AESTHETIC
adjective (ehs <u>theh</u> tihk)

pertaining to beauty or art

*The museum curator, with her fine **aesthetic** sense, created an exhibit that was a joy to behold.*

Synonyms: artistic, tasteful

• • •

AFFABLE
adjective (<u>a</u> fe bel)

pleasantly easy to get along with, warm and friendly

*Jeremy instantly liked his new English professor, who seemed like an **affable** guy.*

Synonyms: easygoing, amiable, gracious

AFFECTATION
noun (ah feck <u>tay</u> shun)

pretension, false display

*Telling your math teacher how awesome he is just to get a good grade is an **affectation**.*

Synonyms: exaggeration, showing off

• • •

AFFECTED
adjective (uh <u>fehk</u> tihd)

phony, artificial

*The **affected** hairdresser spouted French phrases, though she had never been to France.*

Synonyms: insincere, pretentious, put-on

• • •

AFFILIATION
noun (uh <u>fill</u> ee <u>ay</u> shun)

an association with a group or organization

*Timmy pretended to have an **affiliation** with the tough guys hanging out by the bleachers so that people would think he had cool friends.*

Synonyms: relationship, connection, membership

AGGRANDIZE
verb (uh graan diez) (aa gruhn diez)

to make larger or greater in power

*All the millionaire really wanted was to **aggrandize** his personal wealth as much as possible.*

Synonyms: advance, elevate, exalt, glorify, magnify

. . .

AGHAST
adjective (a gast)

overcome by surprise, disgust, or amazement

*The principal was **aghast** to see the state of the school's gymnasium after the senior prom.*

Synonyms: afraid, shocked

. . .

AGILE
adjective (ah jel)

well-coordinated, nimble

*Ashley picked the most **agile** gymnasts to be on the cheerleading squad.*

Synonyms: supple, lively, sprightly

AGITATE
verb (ah ji tayt)

upset, disturb

*Paul liked to **agitate** his French teacher by speaking English with a French accent.*

Synonyms: excite, rouse, work up

. . .

ALACRITY
noun (uh laak crih tee)

cheerful willingness, eagerness, speed

*The eager dog fetched with **alacrity** the stick that had been tossed for him.*

Synonyms: briskness, celerity, dispatch

. . .

ALGORITHM
noun (aal guh rith uhm)

an established procedure for solving a problem or equation

*The accountant uses a series of **algorithms** to determine the appropriate tax bracket.*

Synonym: calculation

ALLAY
verb (uh lay)

to lessen, ease, reduce in intensity

*Trying to **allay** their fears, the nurse sat with them all night.*

Synonyms: alleviate, soothe

. . .

ALLEGATION
noun (ah leh gay shun)

claim without proof

*Ashley could not prove her **allegations** about her science teacher and her English teacher dating ... she just had a feeling.*

Synonyms: accusation, charge, contention

. . .

ALLEGORY
noun (aa lih gohr ee)

symbolic representation

*The novelist used the stormy ocean as an **allegory** for her life's struggles.*

Synonyms: metaphor, symbolism

ALLEVIATE
verb (uh lee vee ayt)

to relieve, improve partially

*Timmy could do nothing to **alleviate** his embarrassment when he realized his pants zipper had been open all day.*

Synonyms: ease, lessen, lighten

. . .

AMALGAMATE
verb (uh maal guh mayt)

to mix, combine

*Giant Industries **amalgamated** with Mega Products to form Giant-Mega Products Incorporated.*

Synonyms: assimilate, incorporate, integrate, league, merge

. . .

AMALGAMATION
noun (uh mal ga may shun)

consolidation of smaller parts

*Marisol's fashion statement was an **amalgamation** of pieces from different eras.*

Synonyms: mixture, combination, blend

AMBIGUOUS
adjective (am <u>big</u> yoo us)

uncertain, subject to multiple interpretations

*Marisol's painting was so **ambiguous** that none of her classmates could figure out what it was supposed to be about.*

Synonyms: unclear, confusing

. . .

AMBIVALENT
adjective (am <u>biv</u> uh lent)

uncertain, emotionally conflicted

*Shanna is **ambivalent** about using student funds to either buy some teen fiction for the library or to throw a rockin' senior dance.*

Synonyms: undecided, of two minds

. . .

AMELIORATE
verb (uh <u>meel</u> yuhr ayt)

to make better, improve

*Conditions in the hospital were **ameliorated** by the hiring of dozens of expertly trained nurses.*

Synonyms: amend, better, reform

AMIABLE
adjective (A mee uh bull)

friendly, pleasant, likable

*The substitute teacher seemed **amiable** at first ... until he whipped out a pop quiz.*

Synonyms: good-natured, agreeable, kind

. . .

AMICABLE
adjective (<u>am</u> i ka bull)

friendly, agreeable

*Despite the fact that Willow and Marisol were dating the same guy, they tried to maintain an **amicable** relationship while working after school at the Dairy Queen.*

Synonyms: cordial, polite

. . .

AMITY
noun (<u>aa</u> mih tee)

friendship, good will

*Correspondence over the years contributed to a lasting **amity** between the women.*

Synonyms: harmony

AMORPHOUS
adjective (ay mohr fuhs)

having no definite form

*The Blob featured an **amorphous** creature that was constantly changing shape.*

Synonyms: shapeless, indistinct

• • •

AMORTIZE
verb (aam uhr tiiz) (uh mohr tiez)

to diminish by installment payments

*She was able to **amortize** her debts by paying a small amount each month.*

Synonym: extinguish

• • •

AMPLIFY
verb (am pleh fy)

increase, intensify

*Derek **amplified** the sound on his speakers drastically whenever he played his electric guitar.*

Synonyms: strengthen, magnify, enlarge

AMULET
noun (aam yoo liht)

ornament worn as a charm against evil spirits

*Though she claimed it was not because of superstition, Vivian always wore an **amulet** around her neck.*

Synonyms: fetish, talisman

• • •

ANACHRONISM
noun (uh naak ruh nih suhm)

something chronologically inappropriate

*The aged hippie used **anachronisms** like "groovy" and "far out" that had not been popular for years.*

Synonyms: anomalous, inappropriate, inconsistent

• • •

ANACHRONISTIC
adjective (uh nak ru niss tik)

outdated

*Chantalle was horrified when the hair-stylist gave her a puffy, **anachronistic** hairstyle from the 1980s.*

Synonyms: old-fashioned, obsolete

ANALGESIA
noun (aah nuhl jee zhuh)

a lessening of pain without loss of consciousness

*After having her appendix removed, Tatiana welcomed the **analgesia** that the painkillers provided.*

• • •

ANALOGOUS
adjective (uh naal uh guhs)

similar or alike in some way, equivalent to

*His mother argued that not going to college was **analogous** to throwing his life away.*

Synonyms: alike, comparable, corresponding, equivalent

• • •

ANARCHIST
noun (an ar kist)

one who aims for the overthrow of government

*Derek pretended to be an **anarchist** like his friends, but he really thought the student government was doing a great job.*

Synonyms: rebel, radical, revolutionary

ANATHEMA
noun (uh naath uh muh)

ban, curse, something shunned or disliked

*Sweaty, soiled clothing was **anathema** to the elegant Madeleine.*

Synonyms: abomination, aversion, execration, horror

• • •

ANCILLARY
adjective (aan suhl eh ree)

accessory, subordinate, helping

*Reforms were instituted at the main factory, but not at its **ancillary** plants, so defects continued to occur.*

Synonyms: additional, adjunct, auxiliary, supplemental

• • •

ANECDOTE
noun (an ik dote)

short, usually funny, account of an event

*The clarinet players had a good laugh over their bandcamp **anecdotes**.*

Synonyms: story, tale

ANIMOSITY
noun (an i <u>mo</u> si ty)

a feeling of hostility or antagonism

*The argument between Ricardo and Betty left a strong **animosity** between them.*

Synonym: hatred

. . .

ANIMUS
noun (<u>aan</u> uh muhs)

a feeling of animosity or ill will

*Though her teacher had failed her, she displayed no **animus** toward him.*

Synonyms: hostility, animosity

. . .

ANODYNE
noun (<u>aan</u> uh dyen)

a source of comfort, a medicine that relieves pain

*The sound of classical music is usually just the **anodyne** I need after a tough day at work.*

Synonyms: analgesic, painkiller

ANOMALY
noun (uh <u>nahm</u> uh lee)

a deviation from the common rule, something that is difficult to classify

*Among the top-ten albums of the year was one **anomaly**—a compilation of polka classics.*

Synonym: irregularity

. . .

ANONYMOUS
adjective (uh <u>non</u> uh muss)

unknown

*Chantalle found an **anonymous** love note on her locker and vowed to find out who had left it.*

Synonyms: unidentified, unspecified, mysterious

. . .

ANTAGONIST
noun (an <u>tag</u> uh nist)

foe, adversary, opponent

*Willow and Derek have been **antagonists** ever since fifth grade, when he cut off her ponytail.*

Synonyms: rival, enemy competitor

A

ANTAGONIZE
verb (aan <u>taa</u> guh niez)

to annoy or provoke to anger

*The child discovered that he could **antagonize** the cat by pulling its tail.*

Synonyms: clash, conflict, incite

• • •

ANTHOLOGY
noun (an <u>thol</u> uh jee)

collection of literary works

*George hid his **anthology** of Superman comics behind his biology textbook so his teacher wouldn't catch him reading them in class.*

Synonyms: compilation, album

• • •

ANTEDILUVIAN
adjective (aan tih duh <u>loo</u> vee uhn)

prehistoric, ancient beyond measure

*The **antediluvian** fossils were displayed in the museum.*

Synonyms: antique, archaic, old

ANTERIOR
adjective (aan <u>teer</u> ee uhr)

preceding, previous, before, prior (to)

*Following tradition, the couple's wedding was **anterior** to the honeymoon.*

Synonyms: foregoing, previous

• • •

ANTHROPOCENTRISM
noun (an throw po <u>sen</u> chrism)

interpreting reality entirely based on human values

*Willow finds the **anthropocentric** attitudes of her classmates upsetting and plans to start a petition banning people from wearing leather shoes.*

• • •

ANTHROPOMORPHIC
adjective (aan thruh poh <u>mohr</u> fihk)

suggesting human characteristics for animals and inanimate things

*Many children's stories feature **anthropomorphic** animals such as talking wolves and pigs.*

Synonyms: humanlike

ANTIDOTE
noun (an ti <u>dote</u>)

a remedy, an agent used to counteract

*Timmy thinks that dating a popular girl will be the **antidote** to his geek status.*

Synonyms: cure, solution, answer

• • •

ANTIPATHY
noun (aan <u>tih</u> puh thee)

dislike, hostility, extreme opposition or aversion

*The **antipathy** between the French and the English regularly erupted into open warfare.*

Synonyms: antagonism, enmity, malice

• • •

ANTIQUATED
adjective (<u>aan</u> tih kway tihd)

too old to be fashionable or useful

*Next to her coworker's brand-new model, Marisa's computer looked **antiquated**.*

Synonyms: outdated, obsolete

APATHETIC
noun (ap uh <u>thet</u> ik)

indifferent, unconcerned

*Some guys act **apathetic** around a girl they like in order to seem cool.*

Synonyms: uninterested, bored

• • •

APATHY
noun (<u>aa</u> pah thee)

lack of interest or emotion

*The **apathy** of voters is so great that less than half the people who are eligible to vote actually bother to do so.*

Synonyms: coolness, disinterest, disregard, impassivity

• • •

APHORISM
noun (aa fuhr ihz uhm)

a short statement of a principle

*The country doctor was given to such **aphorisms** as "Still waters run deep."*

Synonyms: adage, proverb

A

APLOMB

noun (uh plahm) (uh pluhm)

self-confident assurance, poise

*For such a young dancer, she had great **aplomb**, making her perfect to play the young princess.*

Synonyms: coolness, composure

• • •

APOCRYPHAL

adjective (uh pahk ruh fuhl)

not genuine, fictional

*Sharon suspected that the stories she was hearing about alligators in the sewer were **apocryphal**.*

Synonyms: erroneous, false, fictitious, fraudulent

• • •

APOSTATE

noun (uh pahs tayt)

one who renounces a religious faith

*So that he could divorce his wife, he scoffed at the church doctrines and declared himself an **apostate**.*

Synonyms: traitor, defector, deserter

APOTHEOSIS

noun (uh pahth ee oh sihs) (aap uh thee uh sihs)

glorification, glorified ideal

*In her heyday, many people considered Jackie Kennedy to be the **apotheosis** of stylishness.*

Synonyms: epitome, ultimate

• • •

APPALLING

adjective (uh paw ling)

causing dismay, frightful

*Shanna found George's constant spitting **appalling**.*

Synonyms: awful, dreadful, horrendous

• • •

APPOSITE

adjective (aap puh ziht)

strikingly appropriate or well adapted

*The lawyer presented an **apposite** argument upon cross-examining the star witness.*

Synonyms: apt, relevant, suitable

APPRAISE
verb (uh prayz)

evaluate, estimate the value

*Timmy asked Chantalle to **appraise** his cool factor. She said on a scale of 1 to 10, he was a −4.*

Synonyms: assess, judge, review

. . .

APPRISE
verb (uh priez)

to give notice to, inform

*"Thanks for **apprising** me that the test time has been changed," said Emanuel.*

Synonym: notify

. . .

APPROBATION
noun (aa pruh bay shuhn)

praise, official approval

*Billy was sure he had gained the **approbation** of his teacher when he received a glowing report card.*

Synonyms: acclaim, accolade, applause, encomium, homage

APPROPRIATE
verb (uh proh pree ayt)

to assign to a particular purpose, allocate

*The fund's manager **appropriated** funds for the clean-up effort.*

Synonyms: appoint, earmark

. . .

ARABLE
adjective (aa ruh buhl)

suitable for cultivation

*The overpopulated country desperately needed more **arable** land.*

Synonyms: farmable, fertile

. . .

ARBITRARY
adjective (ahr bih trayr ee)

determined by chance or impulse

*When you lack the information to judge what to do next, you will be forced to make an **arbitrary** decision.*

Synonyms: changeable, erratic, indiscriminate, random, wayward

ARBITRATE
verb (<u>ahr</u> bih trayt)

to judge a dispute between two opposing parties

*Because the couple could not come to an agreement, a judge was forced to **arbitrate** their divorce proceedings.*

Synonyms: adjudge, adjudicate, determine, intermediate

. . .

ARBITRATION
noun (ar bih <u>tray</u> shun)

settlement of a dispute by an outside party

*Shanna wanted **arbitration** between the students and the administration over whether or not the students deserved five extra minutes of lunchtime each day.*

Synonyms: mediation, adjudication

. . .

ARCANE
adjective (ahr <u>kayn</u>)

secret, obscure, known only to a few

*The **arcane** rituals of the sect were passed down through many generations.*

Synonyms: esoteric, mysterious

ARCHAIC
adjective (ar <u>kay</u> ik)

antiquated, from an earlier time, outdated

*Marisol was humiliated when her father displayed his **archaic** dance moves from the 1970s in front of her friends.*

Synonyms: ancient, old, old-fashioned

. . .

ARCHETYPAL
adjective (ark uh <u>ty</u> pul)

an ideal example of a type

*Josh is the **archetypal** jock, playing varsity football in the fall and basketball and baseball in the spring.*

Synonyms: typical, standard, conventional

. . .

ARCHIPELAGO
noun (ahr kuh <u>pehl</u> uh goh)

a large group of islands

*Between villages in the Stockholm **archipelago**, boat taxis are the only form of transportation.*

Synonyms: cluster, scattering

ARCHIVE
verb (<u>ar</u> kiyv)

to place into storage

*At sixteen years old, Ashley finally decided it was time to **archive** her blankie in the attic, along with her collection of stuffed animals.*

Synonyms: files, documents, stores

. . .

ARDENT
adjective (<u>ahr</u> dihnt)

passionate, enthusiastic, fervent

*After a 25-game losing streak, even the Mets' most **ardent** fans realized the team wouldn't finish first.*

Synonyms: fervid, intense, vehement

. . .

ARDOR
noun (<u>ahr</u> duhr)

great emotion or passion

*Bishop's **ardor** for landscape was evident when he passionately described the beauty of the Hudson Valley.*

Synonyms: enthusiasm, zeal

ARDUOUS
adjective (<u>ahr</u> jyoo uhs) (<u>aar</u> dyoo uhs)

extremely difficult, laborious

*Amy thought she would pass out after completing the **arduous** climb up the mountain.*

Synonyms: burdensome, hard, onerous, toilsome

. . .

ARID
adjective (<u>ar</u> id)

extremely dry or deathly boring

*Josh knew it was time to dump his girlfriend when he dozed off during yet another **arid** phone conversation.*

Synonyms: parched, waterless, barren

. . .

ARREARS
noun (uh <u>reerz</u>)

unpaid, overdue debts or bills, neglected obligations

*After the expensive lawsuit, Dominic's accounts were in **arrears**.*

Synonym: balance due

ARROGATE
verb (<u>aa</u> ruh gayt)

claim without justification, to claim for oneself without right

*Lynn watched in astonishment as her boss **arrogated** the credit for her brilliant work on the project.*

Synonyms: take, presume, appropriate

• • •

ARTICULATE
adjective (ahr <u>tih</u> kyuh luht)

able to speak clearly and expressively

*She is extremely **articulate** when it comes to expressing her pro-labor views, as a result, unions are among her strongest supporters.*

Synonyms: eloquent, fluent, lucid

• • •

ASCERTAIN
verb (ah ser <u>tayn</u>)

to find out something by examination

*Ella vowed to **ascertain** whether Peggy's new Prada handbag was real or fake.*

Synonym: discover

ASCETIC
adjective (uh <u>seh</u> tihk)

self-denying, abstinent, austere

*The monk lived an **ascetic** life deep in the wilderness, denying himself all forms of luxury.*

Synonyms: abstemious, continent, temperate

• • •

ASKANCE
adverb (uh <u>skaans</u>)

with disapproval, with a skeptical sideways glance

*She looked **askance** at her son's failing report card as he mumbled that he had done all the schoolwork.*

Synonyms: suspiciously

• • •

ASPERSION
noun (uh <u>spuhr</u> shuhn)

false rumor, damaging report, slander

*It is unfair to cast **aspersions** on someone behind his or her back.*

Synonyms: allegation, insinuation, reproach

ASSAIL
verb (uh sayl)

to attack, assault

*The foreign army will try to **assail** our bases, but they will not be successful in their attack.*

Synonyms: beset, strike, storm

. . .

ASSENT
verb (uh sehnt)

to agree, as to a proposal

*After careful deliberation, the CEO **assented** to the proposed merger.*

Synonyms: accede, yield, concur

. . .

ASSERTION
noun (uh sirshun)

declaration, usually without proof

*Derek thought that Chantalle's **assertion** about getting any guy she wanted was hard to believe.*

Synonyms: claim, allegation, affirmation

ASSESS
verb (uh sess)

to establish a value

*The supermarket manager **assessed** George's job performance and refused to give him a raise.*

Synonyms: evaluate, judge, appraise

. . .

ASSIDUOUS
adjective (uh sih dee uhs)

diligent, persistent, hard-working

*The **assiduous** chauffeur scrubbed the limousine endlessly, hoping to make a good impression on his employer.*

Synonyms: industrious, steadfast, thorough

. . .

ASSUAGE
verb (uh swayj) (uh swayzh) (uh swahzh)

to make less severe, ease, relieve

*Like many people, Philip Larkin used warm milk to **assuage** his sense of sleeplessness.*

Synonyms: alleviate, appease, ease, mitigate, mollify

ASSURANCE
noun (uh <u>shoor</u>)

guarantee, pledge

*Chantalle gave her **assurance** to her parents that she would not have a wild party while they were out of town.*

Synonyms: word, oath, promise

• • •

ASTRINGENT
adjective (uh <u>strihn</u> juhnt)

harsh, severe, stern

*The principal's punishments seemed overly **astringent**, but the students did not dare to complain.*

Synonyms: bitter, caustic, sharp

• • •

ASTUTE
adjective (uh <u>stoot</u>)

having good judgment

*George believed that he was an **astute** driver, but his six speeding tickets proved otherwise.*

Synonyms: perceptive, wise, intelligent

ASYLUM
noun (uh <u>sy</u> lum)

a place offering protection and safety

*After a rough day at school, Ashley seeks **asylum** in her bedroom, curled up with a mug of hot chocolate and a copy of* Teen Cheerleader *magazine.*

Synonyms: safe haven, refuge, santuary

• • •

ATAVISTIC
adjective (aat uh <u>vihs</u> tik)

characteristic of a former era, ancient

*After spending three weeks on a desert island, Roger became a survivalist with **atavistic** skills that helped him endure.*

Synonyms: old-fashioned, outdated

• • •

ATROCIOUS
adjective (uh <u>troh</u> shuhs)

monstrous, shockingly bad, wicked

*The young boy committed the **atrocious** act of vandalizing the new community center.*

Synonyms: appalling, deplorable, direful, horrible

ATROPHY

noun (<u>aa</u> troh fee)

to waste away, wither from disuse

*When Mimi stopped exercising, she started to experience **atrophy** in her muscles.*

Synonyms: degenerate, deteriorate

. . .

ATTAIN

verb (uh <u>tayn</u>)

to accomplish, gain

*Timmy had a fantastic dream about moving away and **attaining** popularity in a brand-new high school.*

Synonyms: reach, achieve, conquer

. . .

ATTENUATE

verb (uh <u>tehn</u> yoo ayt)

to make thin or slender, to weaken

*The Bill of Rights **attenuated** the traditional power of government to change laws at will.*

Synonyms: diminish, raregy, reduce

ATYPICAL

adjective (ay <u>tip</u> ih kul)

unusual, irregular

*Even though they are enemies, Willow thinks Derek's **atypical** purple Mohawk is totally hot.*

Synonyms: different, uncommon, out of the ordinary

. . .

AUDACIOUS

adjective (aw <u>day</u> shis)

bold, daring, fearless

*Ashley thought asking out a guy was totally **audacious**, but Shanna found it pretty easy.*

Synonyms: brave, overconfident, risky

. . .

AUGMENT

verb (awg <u>ment</u>)

to expand, extend

*George wanted to **augment** his salary, but did not want to work the extra hours.*

Synonyms: enhance, increase, boost

AUGURY
noun (<u>aw</u> gyuh ree) (<u>aw</u> guh ree)

prophecy, prediction of events

*Troy hoped the rainbow was an **augury** of good things to come.*

Synonyms: auspices, harbinger, omen, portent, presage

. . .

AUGUST
adjective (aw <u>guhst</u>)

dignified, awe-inspiring, venerable

*The **august** view of the summit of the Grand Teton filled the climbers with awe.*

Synonyms: admirable, awesome, grand, majestic

. . .

AUSPICIOUS
adjective (aw <u>spih</u> shuhs)

having favorable prospects, promising

*Tamika thought that having lunch with the boss was an **auspicious** start to her new job.*

Synonyms: encouraging, hopeful, positive, propitious

AUSTERE
adjective (aw <u>steer</u>)

severe or stern in appearance, undecorated

*The lack of decoration makes Zen temples seem **austere** to the untrained eye.*

Synonyms: bleak, dour, grim, hard, harsh, severe

. . .

AUTHORITARIAN
adjective (aw <u>thar</u> ih <u>tayr</u> ee on)

demanding absolute obedience to authority

*George's **authoritarian** boss did not take kindly to George's napping on the lawn furniture display at work.*

Synonyms: strict, controlling, dictatorial

. . .

AUTOCRAT
noun (<u>aw</u> toh kraat)

a dictator

*Mussolini has been described as an **autocrat** who tolerated no opposition.*

Synonyms: tyrant, despot

AUTONOMOUS
adjective (aw <u>ton</u> uh muss)

separate, independent

*Derek likes to think that his cool, rocker look makes him **autonomous** amidst the average dregs at school.*

Synonyms: self-sufficient, self-ruling

• • •

AVANT-GARDE
adjective (<u>ah</u> vant <u>gard</u>)

radically new or original

*Marisol's **avant-garde** sculpture made with toothpicks and peanut butter was so ahead of its time that her art teacher didn't "get it" and gave her an F on the project.*

Synonyms: ultramodern, ahead of its time, futuristic

• • •

AVARICE
noun (<u>aa</u> vuhr ihs)

greed

*Rebecca's **avarice** motivated her to stuff the $100 bill in her pocket instead of returning it to the man who had dropped it.*

Synonyms: cupidity, rapacity

AVER
verb (uh <u>vuhr</u>)

to declare to be true, to affirm

*"Yes, he was holding a gun," the witness **averred**.*

Synonyms: assert, attest

• • •

AVIAN
adjective (<u>ay</u> vee on)

of, or relating to, birds

*Timmy emitted an **avian** squawk of pain as he tried to pull out the gum that someone had thrown in his hair.*

• • •

AVUNCULAR
adjective (ah <u>vuhng</u> kyuh luhr)

like an uncle in behavior, especially in kindness and warmth

*The coach's **avuncular** style made him well-liked.*

AWE
noun (<u>aw</u>)

reverence, respect, wonder

*Derek watched in **awe** as his favorite rock star jumped from chord to chord on his six-string.*

Synonyms: wonder, admiration

• • •

AWRY
adverb (uh <u>rie</u>)

crooked, askew, amiss

*Something must have gone **awry** in the computer system because some of my files are missing.*

Synonyms: aslant, wrong

AXIOM
noun (<u>aak</u> see uhm)

premise, postulate, self-evident truth

*Halle lived her life based on the **axioms** her grandmother had passed on to her.*

Synonyms: adage, aphorism, maxim, rule

BALEFUL
adjective (<u>bayl</u> fuhl)

harmful, with evil intentions

*The sullen teenager gave his nagging mother a **baleful** look.*

Synonyms: dark, sinister

. . .

BALK
verb (bawk)

to stop short and refuse to go on

*When the horse **balked** at jumping over the high fence, the rider was thrown off.*

Synonyms: flinch, shirk from

. . .

BALLAST
noun (<u>baal</u> uhst)

a structure that helps to stabilize or steady

*Communication and honesty are the true **ballasts** of relationship.*

Synonyms: counterweight, balancer

BANAL
adjective (buh <u>naal</u>) (<u>bay</u> nuhl)
(buh n<u>ahl</u>)

trite, overly common

*He used **banal** phrases like "Have a nice day" or "Another day, another dollar."*

Synonyms: hackneyed, inane, shopworn

. . .

BANALITY
noun (buh <u>nal</u> ih tee)

something that is trite, commonplace, or predictable

*The other kids on the pep squad complained about the **banality** of Ashley's fund-raising idea to hold a bake sale; they wanted something more exciting.*

Synonyms: ordinariness, dullness

BANE
noun (<u>bayn</u>)

cause of harm or ruin, source of annoyance

*Timmy wondered why Josh has to be the **bane** of his existence as the hulking jock shoved him into yet another locker.*

Synonyms: nuisance, pest, irritation

• • •

BANISH
verb (<u>ban</u> ish)

drive away, expel

*Chantalle didn't like the way Shanna was dressing lately, so she **banished** Shanna from her group for three weeks.*

Synonyms: cast out, exile, evict

• • •

BARD
noun (<u>bard</u>)

lyrical poet

*Timmy's friends in the poetry club have called him the **bard** ever since he wrote an inspiring ode to recess.*

Synonyms: rhymester, versifier

BARRICADE
noun (bar ih kayd)

barrier

*During the Revolution, students set up **barricades** to keep the army from moving through the streets.*

Synonym: obstacle

• • •

BASTION
noun (<u>baas</u> chyuhn) (<u>baas</u> tee uhn)

fortification, stronghold

*The club was well known as a **bastion** of conservative values in the liberal city.*

Synonyms: bulwark, defense, haven

• • •

BEATIFIC
adjective (bee uh <u>tihf</u> ihk)

displaying calmness and joy, relating to a state of celestial happiness

*After spending three months in India, she had a **beatific** peace about her.*

Synonyms: angelic, blissful

BECALM
verb (bih <u>kahm</u>)

to stop the progress of, to soothe

*The warm air **becalmed** the choppy waves.*

Synonyms: quiet, allay, still

• • •

BECLOUD
verb (bih <u>klowd</u>)

to make less visible, obscure, or blur

*Her ambivalence about the long commute **beclouded** her enthusiasm about the job.*

Synonyms: muddle, cloud

• • •

BEDRAGGLE
adjective (bih <u>draag</u> uhld)

soiled, wet and limp, dilapidated

*The child's **bedraggled** blanket needed a good cleaning.*

BEGET
verb (bih <u>geht</u>)

to produce, especially as an effect or outgrowth, to bring about

*The mayor believed that finding petty offenders would help reduce serious crime because, he argued, small crimes **beget** big crimes.*

Synonyms: cause, breed

• • •

BEGUILE
verb (<u>be</u> guy el)

to delude or deceive by trickery

*Ella was **beguiled** by her friend's empty promise to pay her back the money she borrowed.*

Synonyms: misguide, mislead

• • •

BEHEMOTH
noun (buh <u>hee</u> muhth)

something of monstrous size or power, huge creature

*The budget became such a **behemoth** that observers believed the film would never make a profit.*

Synonyms: giant, mammoth

BELABOR
verb (bih <u>lay</u> buhr)

to insist repeatedly or harp on

*I understand completely, you do not need to **belabor** the point.*

Synonyms: dwell upon, lambaste

. . .

BELATED
adjective (bee <u>lay</u> tid)

having been delayed, done too late

*Willow's **belated** effort to save the snails was a bust—by the time she got to the French restaurant, the patrons had eaten all the escargot.*

Synonyms: postponed, tardy, deferred

. . .

BELEAGUER
verb (bih <u>lee</u> guhr)

to harass, plague

*Mickey **beleaguered** his parents until they finally gave in to his request for a new computer.*

Synonyms: beset, besiege

BELFRY
noun (<u>behl</u> free)

bell tower, room in which a bell is hung

*The town was shocked when a bag of money was found stashed in the old **belfry** of the church.*

Synonyms: spire, steeple

. . .

BELIE
verb (bih <u>lie</u>)

to misrepresent, expose as false

*The first lady's carefree appearance **belied** rumors that she was on the verge of divorcing her husband.*

Synonyms: distort, refute

. . .

BELLICOSE
adjective (<u>beh</u> lih cohs)

warlike, aggressive

*Immediately after defeating one of his enemies, the **bellicose** chieftain declared war on another.*

Synonyms: belligerent, combative, hostile, pugnacious

BELLIGERENT
adjective (buh lih juhr uhnt)

hostile, tending to fight

The angry customer was extremely **belligerent** *despite the manager's offer to return his money.*

Synonyms: agressive, bellicose, combative, pugnacious

. . .

BENEFACTOR
noun (ben eh fak tur)

someone who helps others financially

Chantalle didn't need to get an after-school job when she already had two **benefactors** *at her disposal—her parents.*

Synonyms: sponsor, supporter, patron

. . .

BENEFICENT
adjective (buh nehf ih sent)

pertaining to an act of kindness

The **beneficent** *man donated the money anonymously.*

Synonyms: charitable, generous

BENEVOLENT
adjective (bu nev uh lint)

friendly and helpful

Even though he's a jokester at school, the ladies at the senior center where Paul volunteers say he's the most **benevolent** *boy they know.*

Synonyms: caring, compassionate, giving

. . .

BENIGHTED
adjective (bih nie tihd)

unenlightened

Ben scoffed at the crowd, as he believed it consisted entirely of **benighted** *individuals.*

Synonyms: ignorant, illiterate, unschooled

. . .

BENIGN
adjective (bi niyn)

gentle, harmless

George's science teacher looked **benign,** *but George knew that she exhibited quite a temper when students were late to class.*

Synonyms: kind, caring, benevolent

BEQUEATH
verb (bih <u>kweeth</u>) (bih <u>kweeth</u>)

to give or leave through a will, to hand down

*Grandpa **bequeathed** the house to his daughter and the car to his son.*

Synonyms: bestow, pass on, transmit

• • •

BERATE
verb (bih <u>rayt</u>)

to scold harshly

*When my manager found out I had handled the situation so insensitively, he **berated** me.*

Synonym: criticize

• • •

BEREFT
adjective (be <u>reft</u>)

deprived of or lacking something

*Even though the diet brownies were **bereft** of anything resembling chocolate, Ashley swore they were tasty.*

Synonym: devoid

BESEECH
verb (bih <u>seech</u>)

to beg, plead, implore

*She **beseeched** him to give her a second chance, but he refused.*

Synonyms: entreat, petition, supplicate

• • •

BETRAY
verb (be <u>tray</u>)

to be false or disloyal to

*Derek's band, Snakebite, felt **betrayed** when, one afternoon, he jammed with the band Venom.*

Synonyms: deceive, let down

• • •

BEVY
noun (<u>beh</u> vee)

group

*As predicted, a **bevy** of teenagers surrounded the rock star's limousine.*

Synonyms: band, bunch, gang, pack, troop

BEWILDER
verb (be <u>will</u> der)

to confuse or puzzle

*Marisol was **bewildered** by Derek's long stare as she walked past him. Did she have something stuck in her teeth?*

Synonyms: baffle, perplex, confound

• • •

BIASED
adjective (<u>by</u> ust)

prejudiced

*Chantalle could not deny that she was **biased** against anyone who wore T-shirts with pictures of cats on them.*

Synonyms: unfair, influenced, subjective

• • •

BIFURCATE
verb (<u>bi</u> fuhr kayt) (bi <u>fuhr</u> kayt)

divide into two parts

*The large corporation just released a press statement announcing its plans to **bifurcate**.*

Synonym: bisect

BILIOUS
adjective (<u>bihl</u> yuhs)

ill-tempered, sickly, ailing

*The party ended early when the **bilious** five-year-old tried to run off with the birthday's girl's presents.*

Synonyms: pale, feeble

• • •

BILK
verb (bihlk)

to cheat, defraud

*Though the lawyer seemed honest, the woman feared he would try to **bilk** her out of her money.*

Synonyms: dupe, fleece, swindle

• • •

BLANDISH
verb (<u>blaan</u> dihsh)

to coax with flattery

*We **blandished** the teacher with compliments until he finally agreed to postpone the exam.*

Synonyms: cajole, charm, wheedle

BLASPHEMOUS
adjective (<u>blaas</u> fuh muhs)

cursing, profane, extremely irreverent

*The politician's offhanded biblical references seemed **blasphemous**, given the context of the orderly meeting.*

Synonym: foul-mouthed

• • •

BLATANT
adjective (<u>blay</u> tnt)

completely obvious and conspicuous, especially in an offensive, crass manner

*Such **blatant** advertising with the bounds of the school drew protest from parents.*

Synonyms: obvious, flagrant

• • •

BLAZE
verb (<u>blayz</u>)

shine brightly, flare up suddenly

*Shanna's newly dyed hair was so red it looked like a **blaze** of fire bobbing through the crowd.*

Synonyms: fire, combustion, burst into flames

BLEMISH
noun (<u>blem</u> ish)

imperfection, flaw

*Ashley couldn't stop staring at the one **blemish** on her otherwise stellar report card—a big fat F in chorus.*

Synonyms: mark, spot, blotch

• • •

BLIGHT
verb (bliet)

to afflict, destroy

*The farmers feared that the previous night's frost had **blighted** the potato crops entirely.*

Synonyms: damage, plague

• • •

BLITHE
adjective (blieth)

joyful, cheerful, or without appropriate thought

*Summer finally came, and the **blithe** students spent their days at the beach.*

Synonyms: carefree, lighthearted, merry

BLITHELY
adverb (<u>blieth</u> lee)

merrily, lightheartedly cheerful,
without appropriate thought

*Wanting to redecorate the office,
she **blithely** assumed her coworkers
wouldn't mind and moved the furniture
in the space.*

Synonym: carefree

. . .

BOAST
verb (<u>bowst</u>)

speak with excessive pride

*Josh **boasted** to his friends that he
would probably get athletic scholar-
ships from every college he applied to.*

Synonyms: brag, show off, swank

. . .

BOLSTER
verb (<u>bohl</u> stuhr)

support, prop up

*The presence of giant footprints
bolstered the argument that Bigfoot
was in the area.*

Synonyms: brace, buttress, crutch,
prop, stay, support

BOMBASTIC
adjective (bahm <u>baast</u> ihk)

high-sounding but meaningless,
ostentatiously lofty in style

*Mussolini's speeches were mostly
bombastic, his outrageous claims had
no basis in fact.*

Synonyms: grandiose, inflated

. . .

BOON
noun (boon)

blessing, something to be thankful for

*Dirk realized that his new coworker's
computer skills would be a real **boon** to
the company.*

Synonyms: benefit, favor, treasure,
windfall

. . .

BONHOMIE
noun (bahn uh <u>mee</u>)

good-natured geniality, atmosphere of
good cheer

*The general **bonhomie** that characterized the party made it a joy to attend.*

Synonym: friendliness

BOOR
noun (bohr)

crude person, one lacking manners or taste

*"That utter **boor** ruined my recital with his constant guffawing!" wailed the pianist.*

Synonyms: clod, lout, oaf, vulgarian, yahoo

. . .

BOURGEOIS
adjective (boor zhwaa) (boo zhwaa) (buh zhwaa)

middle class

*The **bourgeois** family was horrified when the lower-class family moved in next door.*

Synonyms: capitalist, conventional

. . .

BOVINE
adjective (boh vien)

relating to cows, having qualities characteristic of a cow, such as sluggishness or dullness

*His **bovine** demeanor did nothing to engage me.*

Synonyms: dull, placid

BRAGGART
noun (braag uhrt)

a person who brags or boasts in a loud and empty manner

*Usually the biggest **braggart** at the company party, Susan's boss was unusually quiet at this year's event.*

Synonyms: boaster, showoff

. . .

BRANDISH
verb (bran dish)

wave menacingly

*Timmy tried to ward off Josh's taunting in the lunchroom by **brandishing** the only weapon he could find: a hot dog.*

Synonyms: wield, flourish, flaunt

. . .

BREACH
noun (breech)

act of breaking, violation

*The record company sued the singer for **breach** of contract when he recorded for another company without permission.*

Synonyms: contravention, dereliction, gap, lapse, rift

BRIGAND
noun (<u>brihg</u> uhnd)

bandit, outlaw

Brigands held up the bank and made off with the contents of the safe.

Synonym: plunderer

. . .

BROACH
verb (brohch)

to mention or suggest for the first time

Sandy wanted to go to college away from home, but he didn't know how to broach the topic with his parents.

Synonyms: introduce, propose

. . .

BRUSQUE
adjective (bruhsk)

rough and abrupt in manner

The bank teller's brusque treatment of his customers soon evoked several complaints.

Synonyms: blunt, curt, gruff, rude, tactless

BRUTALITY
noun (broo <u>tal</u> ih tee)

ruthless, cruel, and unrelenting acts

Willow was just trying to free the worker bees from the captivity of the farmer's honeycomb, but the brutality of their stings made it clear that they did not want to be saved.

Synonyms: viciousness, violence, rough treatment

. . .

BUCOLIC
adjective (byoo <u>kahl</u> lihk)

pastoral, rural

My aunt likes the hustle and bustle of the city, but my uncle prefers a more bucolic setting.

Synonyms: rustic, country

. . .

BUFFER
noun (<u>buff</u> ur)

something that separates two entities

George used his mashed potatoes as a buffer between the roast beef and lima beans on his lunch plate.

Synonyms: safeguard, shield, defense

BUFFOONERY

noun (bu <u>foo</u> ner ee)

acting like a clown

*Paul knew his **buffoonery** got him a lot of laughs in class, but could it get him a date?*

Synonyms: foolishness

. . .

BURGEON

verb (<u>buhr</u> juhn)

to sprout or flourish

*Because the population of the city is **burgeoning**, we are going to need a major subway expansion.*

Synonyms: blossom, expand, grow, proliferate, thrive

. . .

BURNISH

verb (<u>buhr</u> nihsh)

to polish, to make smooth and bright

*Mr. Frumpkin loved to stand in the sun and **burnish** his luxury car.*

Synonyms: shine, buff

BURSAR

noun (<u>buhr</u> suhr) (<u>buhr</u> sahr)

a treasurer or keeper of funds

*The **bursar** of the school was in charge of allocating all scholarship funds.*

. . .

BUTTRESS

verb (<u>buh</u> trihs)

to reinforce or support

*The construction workers attempted to **buttress** the ceiling with pillars.*

Synonyms: bolster, brace, prop, strengthen

. . .

BYPASS

verb (<u>bi</u> pass)

avoid

*Derek figured he could **bypass** an office job when he grew up by becoming a rock star.*

Synonyms: evade, detour, sidestep

CABAL
noun (kuh <u>bahl</u>)

a secret group seeking to overturn something

*The boys on the street formed a **cabal** to keep girls out of their tree house.*

Synonyms: camp, circle, clan, clique, coterie

· · ·

CACHE
noun (caash)

a hiding place, stockpile

*It's good to have a **cache** where you can stash your cash.*

Synonyms: hoard, reserve

CACOPHONY
noun (kuh <u>kah</u> fuh nee)

a jarring, unpleasant noise

*As I walked into the open-air market after my nap, a **cacophony** of sounds surrounded me.*

Synonyms: clatter, racket

· · ·

CADENCE
noun (<u>kayd</u> ns)

rhythmic flow of poetry, marching beat

*Pierre spoke with a lovely **cadence**, charming all those who heard him.*

Synonyms: inflection, rhythm

· · ·

CAJOLE
verb (kuh <u>johl</u>)

to flatter, coax, persuade

*The spoiled girl could **cajole** her father into buying her anything.*

Synonyms: blandish, wheedle

CALAMITY
noun (ka <u>lam</u> uh tee)

disaster, catastrophe

*Timmy's date was a total **calamity** when he tripped and accidentally pushed the girl into the lake at the park.*

Synonyms: mishap, misfortune, tragedy

. . .

CALCULATING
adjective (<u>kal</u> q lay ting)

shrewd, crafty

*Chantalle was so **calculating** that she developed a plan to convince her parents to let her go skiing in Aspen during Christmas break.*

Synonyms: manipulative, devious, conniving

. . .

CALLOW
adjective (<u>kaa</u> loh)

immature, lacking sophistication

*The young and **callow** fans hung on every word the talk show host said.*

Synonyms: artless, ingenuous, naïve

CALUMNY
noun (<u>kaa</u> luhm nee)

a false and malicious accusation, misrepresentation

*The unscrupulous politician used **calumny** to bring down his opponent in the senatorial race.*

Synonyms: libel, defamation, slander

. . .

CAMARADERIE
noun (kahm <u>rah</u> da ree)

trust, sociability amongst friends

*Timmy likes the **camaraderie** of his friends in the accordion club.*

Synonyms: amity, companionship

. . .

CANARD
noun (kuh <u>nard</u>)

a lie

*That tabloid's feature story about a goat giving birth to a human child was clearly a **canard**.*

Synonyms: falsehood, falsity, fib

CANDID

adjective (kaan did)

impartial and honest in speech

The observations of a child can be charming because they are **candid** *and unpretentious.*

Synonyms: direct, forthright, frank, honest, open

. . .

CANTANKEROUS

adjective (kaan taang kuhr uhs)

having a difficult, uncooperative, or stubborn disposition

The most outwardly **cantankerous** *man in the nursing home was surprisingly sweet and loving with his grandchildren.*

Synonyms: contentious, ornery

. . .

CAPACIOUS

adjective (kuh pay shuhs)

large, roomy, extensive

We wondered how many hundreds of stores occupied the **capacious** *mall.*

Synonyms: ample, commodious

CAPITULATE

verb (kuh pih choo layt)

to submit completely, surrender

After the army was reduced to only five soldiers, there was little choice but to **capitulate**.

Synonyms: acquiesce, succumb, yield

. . .

CAPRICIOUS

adjective (kuh pree shuhs) (kuh prih shuhs)

impulsive, whimsical, without much thought

Queen Elizabeth I was quite **capricious,** *her courtiers could never be sure who would catch her fancy.*

Synonyms: erratic, fickle, flighty, inconstant, wayward

. . .

CAPTIOUS

adjective (kaap shuhs)

marked by the tendency to point out trivial faults, intended to confuse in an argument

I resent the way he asked that **captious** *question.*

Synonyms: critical, censorious

CARNIVOROUS

adjective (kar <u>niv</u> uh riss)

meat-eating

*Willow believes that humans are not supposed to be **carnivorous** because their teeth are not very sharp.*

· · ·

CAROUSE

verb (kuh <u>rowz</u>)

to partake in drunken amusement, drink excessively

*Paul promised his parents that when he turns twenty-one, he will not **carouse** in bars.*

Synonyms: get drunk, party

· · ·

CARTOGRAPHER

noun (kar <u>tog</u> ruh fer)

someone who makes maps

*When George found out a **cartographer** was visiting his social studies class that day to give a lesson on maps, he decided to skip out and take an extra lunch period instead.*

CARTOGRAPHY

noun (kahr <u>tahg</u> ruh fee)

science or art of making maps

*Gail's interest in **cartography** may stem from the extensive traveling she did as a child.*

Synonyms: charting, surveying, topography

· · ·

CASTIGATE

verb (<u>kaa</u> stih gayt)

to punish, chastise, criticize severely

*Authorities in Singapore harshly **castigate** perpetrators of what would be considered minor crimes in the United States.*

Synonyms: discipline, lambaste

· · ·

CATACLYSMIC

adjective (<u>kaat</u> uh <u>klihz</u> mihk)

severely destructive

*By all appearances, the storm seemed **cataclysmic**, though it lasted only a short while.*

Synonyms: catastrophic, tragic

CATALYST
noun (<u>kaat</u> uhl ihst)

something that provokes or speeds up significant change, especially without being affected by the consequences

*Technology has been a **catalyst** for the expansion of alternative education, such as home schooling and online courses.*

Synonym: accelerator

. . .

CATASTROPHIC
adjective (kat uh <u>strof</u> ik)

of, or relating to, a terrible event or complete failure

*In a **catastrophic** turn of events, Marisol left her art portfolio on the bus and had nothing to show the admissions counselors at FIT.*

Synonyms: disastrous, shattering, tragic

. . .

CATHARSIS
noun (kuh <u>thahr</u> sihs)

purification, cleansing

*Plays can be more satisfying if they end in some sort of emotional **catharsis** for the characters involved.*

Synonyms: purgation, release

CATHOLIC
adjective (<u>kaa</u> thuh lihk) (<u>kaa</u> thlihk)

universal, broad and comprehensive

*Hot tea with honey is a **catholic** remedy for a sore throat.*

Synonyms: extensive, general

. . .

CAUCUS
noun (<u>kaw</u> kuhs)

a closed committee within a political party, a private committee meeting

*The president met with the delegated **caucus** to discuss the national crisis.*

Synonyms: assembly, convention

. . .

CAUSTIC
adjective (<u>kah</u> stihk)

biting, sarcastic

*Writer Dorothy Parker gained her reputation for **caustic** wit, and her tombstone is inscribed with a fittingly clever "Excuse my dust."*

Synonyms: sardonic, incisive

CAVALIER
noun (kaav uh <u>leer</u>)

carefree, happy, with lordly disdain

*The nobleman's **cavalier** attitude toward the suffering of the peasants made them hate him.*

Synonym: disdainful

. . .

CEDE
verb (seed)

to surrender possession of something

*Argentina **ceded** the Falkland Islands to Britain after a brief war.*

Synonyms: resign, yield, relinquish

. . .

CELERITY
noun (seh <u>leh</u> rih tee)

speed, haste

*The celebrity ran past his fans with great **celerity**.*

Synonyms: swiftness, briskness

CENSOR
verb (<u>sen</u> sur)

to examine and suppress information

*Willow started a petition to stop the principal from **censoring** controversial books that were in the school library.*

Synonyms: edit, cut, expurgate

. . .

CENSORIOUS
adjective (sehn <u>sohr</u> ee uhs)

critical, tending to blame and condemn

*Closed-minded people tend to be **censorious** of others.*

Synonym: fault-finding

. . .

CENSURE
verb (<u>sen</u> sher)

to find fault with and condemn as wrong, blame

*Madame La Bouche **censured** Derek in front of the class for not doing his French homework.*

Synonyms: criticize, scorn, show disapproval

CENTRIPETAL
adjective (sehn <u>trihp</u> ih tl)

directed or moving toward the center

*It is **centripetal** force that keeps trains from derailing as they round curves.*

Synonym: centralizing

. . .

CEREBRAL
adjective (suh <u>ree</u> brell)

intellectual

*Shanna was looking to date a **cerebral** type who enjoyed conversations about classic literature just as much as she did.*

Synonyms: brainy, clever, logical

. . .

CERTITUDE
noun (<u>suhr</u> tih tood)

assurance, freedom from doubt

*The witness's **certitude** about the night in question had a big impact on the jury.*

Synonyms: certainty, conviction

CESSATION
noun (seh <u>say</u> shuhn)

a temporary or complete halt

*The **cessation** of hostilities ensured that soldiers were able to spend the holidays with their families.*

Synonyms: arrest, termination

. . .

CHAGRIN
noun (shuh grihn)

shame, embarrassment, humiliation

*No doubt, the president felt a good deal of **chagrin** after forgetting the name of the prime minister at the state banquet.*

Synonyms: discomfiture, mortification

. . .

CHALLENGE
verb (<u>chal</u> enj)

take exception to, call into question

*George liked to **challenge** the authority of his boss by goofing off and seeing how much he could get away with.*

Synonyms: confront, defy, face

CHAOS
noun (<u>kay</u> ahs)

great disorder or confused situation

*In most religious traditions, God created an ordered universe from **chaos**.*

Synonyms: clutter, confusion

. . .

CHAPPED
adjective (<u>chap</u> t)

reddened by cold or exposure

*Chantalle's **chapped** hands were a direct result of being too cool to wear gloves during the harsh winter.*

Synonyms: rough, cracked

. . .

CHARLATAN
noun (<u>shahr</u> luh tihn)

quack, fake

*"That **charlatan** of a doctor prescribed the wrong medicine for me!" complained the patient.*

Synonyms: fraud, humbug, imposter

CHARY
adjective (<u>chahr</u> ee)

watchful, cautious, extremely shy

Mindful of the fate of the Titanic, *the captain was **chary** of navigating the iceberg-filled sea.*

Synonyms: wary, careful

. . .

CHAUVINIST
noun (<u>shoh</u> vuh nist).

someone prejudiced in favor of a group to which he or she belongs

*The attitude that men must be obeyed because they are inherently superior to women is common among male **chauvinists**.*

Synonyms: biased, colored, one-sided, partial, partisan

. . .

CHERISH
verb (<u>cher</u> ish)

to remember fondly, treat with affection

*Chantalle gave her boyfriend the line about **cherishing** the good times they'd had together—right before she dumped him.*

Synonyms: treasure, value, prize

CHICANERY

noun (shih kayn ree) (shi kay nuh ree)
("ch" can replace "sh")

trickery, fraud, deception

Dishonest used-car salesmen often use chicanery to sell their beat-up old cars.

Synonyms: deceit, dishonesty, duplicity

. . .

CHIMERICAL

adjective (kie mehr ih kuhl) (kie meer ih kuhl)

fanciful, imaginary, impossible

The inventor's plans seemed chimerical to the conservative businessman from whom he was asking for financial support.

Synonyms: illusory, unreal

. . .

CHOLERIC

adjective (kah luhr ihk)

easily angered, short-tempered

The choleric principal raged at the students who had come late to school.

Synonyms: irate, irritable, surly, wrathful

CHROMOSOME

noun (chro mo some)

a threadlike body that carries genes in an organism

The researcher received funding for his study on chromosomes for the rest of the year.

. . .

CIRCUITOUS

adjective (suhr kyoo ih tuhs)

indirect, roundabout

The venue was only a short walk from the train station, but a roadblock meant I had to take a circuitous route.

Synonyms: lengthy, devious

. . .

CIRCUMLOCUTION

noun (suhr kuhm loh kyoo shuhn)

roundabout, lengthy way of saying something

He avoided discussing the real issues with endless circumlocution.

Synonyms: evasion, wordiness

CIRCUMSCRIBE
verb (<u>suhr</u> kuhm skrieb)

to encircle, set limits on, confine

*Diego Buenaventura's country estate is **circumscribed** by rolling hills.*

Synonyms: limit, surround

• • •

CIRCUMSPECT
adjective (suhr kuhm <u>spehkt</u>)

cautious, wary

*His failures have made Jack far more **circumspect** in his exploits than he used to be.*

Synonyms: careful, chary, prudent

• • •

CIRCUMVENT
verb (suhr kuhm <u>vehnt</u>)

to go around, avoid

*Laura was able to **circumvent** the hospital's regulations, slipping into her mother's room long after visiting hours were over.*

Synonyms: evade, sidestep

CIVILITY
noun (sih <u>vill</u> ih tee)

courtesy, politeness

*Girls like going out on dates with Paul because he treats them with the utmost **civility**.*

Synonyms: respect, graciousness, consideration

• • •

CLAIRVOYANT
adjective (klayr <u>voy</u> nt)

exceptionally insightful, able to foresee the future

*Willow was pumped when the **clairvoyant** psychic told her she was going to meet a hot guy at the Earth Day festival.*

Synonyms: psychic, mind reader, medium

• • •

CLAMP
verb (<u>klamp</u>)

establish by authority

*The principal vowed to **clamp** down on the kids who kept putting "kick me" signs on his back—just as soon as he figured out who they were.*

Synonym: impose

CLANDESTINE
adjective (klaan <u>dehs</u> tien)

secretive, concealed for a darker purpose

The double agent paid many clandestine visits to the president's office in the dead of night.

Synonyms: covert, underground

• • •

CLARITY
noun (<u>klar</u> it ee)

clearness, clear understanding

Shanna told Timmy with the utmost clarity that she would not go out with him.

Synonyms: lucidity, precision, simplicity

• • •

CLEMENCY
noun (<u>kleh</u> muhn see)

merciful leniency

Kyle begged for clemency, explaining that he robbed the bank to pay for his medical bills.

Synonyms: indulgence, pardon

CLICHÉ
noun (klee <u>shay</u>)

overused expression or idea

Derek thought his latest rock song, When Life Gives You Lemons, Make Lemonade, was totally original, but really it was one big cliché.

Synonym: unoriginal

• • •

CLIENTELE
noun (kly en <u>tell</u>)

body of customers or patrons

George always tried to get along with the clientele at the supermarket where he worked.

Synonyms: clients, regulars, consumers

• • •

CLIQUE
noun (<u>klik</u>)

small exclusive group

Chantalle was the leader of the popular clique at school.

Synonyms: circle, gang, elite

CLOYING
adjective (<u>kloy</u> ing)

sickly sweet, excessive

When Dave and Liz got together their **cloying** *affection towards one another often made their friends ill.*

Synonyms: excessive, fulsome

. . .

COAGULATE
verb (koh <u>aag</u> yuh layt)

to clot, to cause to thicken

Hemophiliacs can bleed to death from a minor cut because their blood does not **coagulate**.

Synonyms: jell, congeal

. . .

COALESCE
verb (koh uh <u>lehs</u>)

to grow together or cause to unite as one

The different factions of the organization **coalesced** *to form one united front against their opponents.*

Synonyms: combine, merge

COFFER
noun (<u>kah</u> fuhr)

strongbox, large chest for money

The bulletproof glass of the **coffer** *is what keeps the crown jewels secure.*

Synonyms: treasury, chest, exchequer, war chest

. . .

COGENT
adjective (<u>koh</u> juhnt)

logically forceful, compelling, convincing

Swayed by the **cogent** *argument of the defense, the jury had no choice but to acquit the defendant.*

Synonyms: persuasive, winning

. . .

COGNIZANT
adjective (<u>kog</u> ni zent)

fully informed, conscious

Josh was **cognizant** *of the three girls who had crushes on him and winked at each one as they passed by.*

Synonyms: aware, mindful

COHERENT

adjective (ko hee rent)

intelligible, lucid, understandable

*George wasn't fully **coherent** until third period because he had gone to bed really late the night before.*

Synonyms: logical, rational, consistent

. . .

COHESION

noun (ko hee zhun)

act or state of sticking together, close union

*Derek's band achieved the perfect **cohesion** of music and lyrics as they played a seamless concert.*

Synonyms: unity, organization, structure

. . .

COLLABORATOR

noun (kuh lab uh ray tor)

someone who helps on a task

*Willow's **collaborator** at the animal shelter was a cute boy who held the puppies while she clipped their nails.*

Synonyms: coworker, colleague, partner

COLLAGE

noun (ko lazh)

assemblage of diverse elements

*Marisol's latest project was a **collage** of fashion magazine covers she called Face à La Mode.*

Synonyms: patchwork, random collection, clutter

. . .

COLLATERAL

adjective (kuh laat uhr uhl)

accompanying

*"Let's try to stick to the main issue here and not get into all the **collateral** questions," urged the committee leader.*

Synonym: ancillary

. . .

COLLOQUIAL

adjective (kuh loh kwee uhl)

characteristic of informal speech

*The book was written in a **colloquial** style so it would be user-friendlier.*

Synonyms: conversational, idiomatic

C

COLLOQUY
noun (<u>kahl</u> uh kwee)

dialogue or conversation, conference

*The congressmen held a **colloquy** to determine how to proceed with the environmental legislation.*

Synonym: discussion

. . .

COLLUSION
noun (kuh <u>loo</u> zhuhn)

collaboration, complicity, conspiracy

*The teacher realized that the students were in **collusion** when everyone received the same grade on the test.*

Synonyms: connivance, intrigue, machination

. . .

COLOSSAL
noun (kuh <u>los</u> ul)

immense, enormous

*Chantalle and Shanna realized they made a **colossal** error by not shopping together for dresses to wear to the school dance; they wound up wearing the same one.*

Synonyms: huge massive, oversize

COMBATIVE
adjective (kom <u>bat</u> iv)

eager to fight

*Willow was not usually **combative**, but she couldn't help arguing with a woman on the street who was wearing a fur coat.*

Synonyms: aggressive, belligerent, confrontational

. . .

COMBUSTION
noun (kom <u>bus</u> chen)

the process of burning

*Timmy studied the **combustion** of the marshmallow as he held it over the campfire.*

Synonyms: fire, ignition, incineration

. . .

COMELINESS
noun (<u>kuhm</u> lee nihs)

physical grace and beauty

*Ann's **comeliness** made her perfect for the role of Sleeping Beauty.*

Synonyms: attractiveness, seemliness

COMMEMORATE

verb (kuh <u>mem</u> uh rayt)

to serve as a memorial to

*Shanna bought a pair of earrings every April 22nd to **commemorate** the day she got her ears pierced.*

Synonyms: honor, remember, observe

. . .

COMMENSURATE

adjective (kuh <u>mehn</u> suhr ayt)

proportional

*Steve was given a salary **commensurate** with his experience.*

Synonyms: comparable, corresponding

. . .

COMMENTARY

noun (<u>kom</u> un teh ree)

series of explanations or interpretations

*Chantalle's mother told her to stop gossiping about her classmates, but Chantalle said she was merely giving her **commentary** on the day's events.*

Synonyms: comments, remarks, notes

COMMODIOUS

adjective (kuh <u>moh</u> dee uhs)

roomy, spacious

*Raqiyah was able to stretch out fully in the **commodious** bathtub.*

Synonyms: ample, capacious, extensive

. . .

COMMUTE

verb (kuh <u>myoot</u>)

to change a penalty to a less severe one

*In exchange for cooperating with detectives on another case, the criminal had his charges **commuted**.*

Synonyms: exchange, mitigate

. . .

COMPARABLE

adjective (<u>kom</u> pur uh bul)

similar or equivalent

*Derek liked to think that his band's style was **comparable** to none, but there were tons of rival groups with the same sound.*

Synonym: alike

COMPASSION

noun (kum <u>pash</u> in)

sympathy, helpfulness, or mercy

Willow's **compassion** *led her to take an injured bird to the animal shelter.*

Synonyms: empathy, concern, kindness

. . .

COMPELLING

adjective (kom <u>pell</u> ing)

urgently requiring attention, forceful

Shanna is head of the debate team because she always delivers a **compelling** *argument that drives home the team's objective.*

Synonyms: persuasive, convincing, undeniable

. . .

COMPENSATE

verb (<u>komp</u> en sayt)

to repay or reimburse

Ashley **compensated** *Timmy with a kiss on the cheek for tutoring her in math.*

Synonyms: recompense, recoup, remunerate, requite

COMPLACENCE

noun (kom <u>play</u> senss)

self-satisfaction, lack of concern

George's **complacence** *about studying quickly ended when he realized he was in danger of failing a class.*

Synonyms: conceit, egotism, pompousness, pride

. . .

COMPLACENT

adjective (kuhm <u>play</u> sihnt)

self-satisfied, smug

Alfred always shows a **complacent** *smile whenever he wins the spelling bee.*

Synonyms: contented, unconcerned

. . .

COMPLEMENT

verb (<u>komp</u> leh ment)

to complete, perfect

The fuzzy black tail **complemented** *the cat costume Chantalle would wear to the Halloween party.*

Synonym: supplement

COMPLEX
adjective (kom pleks)

complicated

*Ashley's dance routine for the school talent show was so **complex** that she accidentally fell off the stage while performing it.*

Synonyms: elaborate, intricate, involved

. . .

COMPLIANT
adjective (kuhm plie uhnt)

submissive, yielding

*The boss was unused to an assistant who spoke her mind, but he grew to respect the fact that she wasn't **compliant**.*

Synonyms: malleable, complacent, tractable, acquiescent

. . .

COMPLICITY
noun (kuhm plih sih tee)

knowing partnership in wrongdoing

*The two boys exchanged a look of sly **complicity** when their father shouted "Who broke the window?"*

Synonyms: cahoots, collaboration, involvement

COMPOSED
adjective (kom posd)

serene

*After Willow took a few cleansing breaths, she felt **composed** enough to begin her presentation to her science class.*

Synonym: calm

. . .

COMPREHENSIBLE
adjective (kom pree hen sih bul)

readily understood

*George thought that calculus was too complicated to be **comprehensible** without a tutor.*

Synonym: decipherable

. . .

COMPREHENSIVE
adjective (kom pree hen siv)

very large in scope

*Derek has a **comprehensive** knowledge of music, both popular and obscure.*

Synonyms: exhaustive, complete

COMPULSION
noun (kom <u>pul</u> shin)

an irresistible impulse to act

*Ashley tried to stop her **compulsion** to bite her fingernails by polishing her nails with sour-tasting polish.*

Synonym: force

• • •

COMPUNCTION
noun (kuhm <u>puhnk</u> shuhn)

feeling of uneasiness caused by guilt or regret

*Her **compunction** was intense when she realized that she forgot to send her best friend a birthday card.*

Synonyms: dubiety, qualm, scruple

• • •

COMPUTE
verb (kom <u>pyoot</u>)

to determine by mathematics

*It's odd how Chantalle is failing math, yet she can **compute** 30 percent off a sale item without a calculator.*

Synonym: calculate

CONCEITED
adjective (kon <u>seet</u> id)

holding an unduly high opinion of oneself

*Even Chantalle agreed it was a little **conceited** to check out her reflection in the silverware.*

Synonym: vain

• • •

CONCEIVABLE
adjective (kon <u>seev</u> uh bull)

capable of being understood

*It's **conceivable** that Timmy will go to college after he graduates high school because he is the smartest boy in his class.*

Synonym: feasible

• • •

CONCILIATORY
adjective (kuhn <u>sihl</u> ee uh tohr ee)

overcoming distrust or hostility

*Fred made the **conciliatory** gesture of buying Abby flowers after their big fight.*

Synonym: pleasing

CONCOCT
verb (kon kokt)

to devise using skill and intelligence

George knew he would have to concoct a good reason for skipping social studies class or he would be in big trouble.

Synonym: invent

• • •

CONCOMITANT
adjective (kuh kahm ih tuhnt)

existing concurrently

A double-major was going to be difficult to pull off, especially because Lucy would have to juggle two papers and two exams concomitantly.

Synonyms: coexistent, concurrent

• • •

CONCORD
noun (kahn kohrd)

agreement

The sisters are now in concord about the car they had to share.

Synonyms: accord, concurrence

CONCORDANT
adjective (kon kor dint)

agreeing

The geometry class was concordant on the fact that their teacher gave them too much homework.

Synonym: harmonious

• • •

CONDEMNATION
noun (kon dem nay shun)

an expression of strong disapproval

Shanna's condemnation of four-inch platforms was brought on when she twisted her ankle while wearing a pair.

Synonym: censure

• • •

CONDENSE
verb (kon dens)

to make more concise

Marisol condensed her art portfolio to twenty of her strongest pieces.

Synonym: reduce

CONDESCENDING

adjective (con di <u>sen</u> ding)

possessing an attitude of superiority

*The seniors are always **condescending** to the freshmen because the seniors have been there a lot longer.*

Synonym: patronizing

. . .

CONDOLE

verb (kuhn <u>dohl</u>)

to grieve, to express sympathy

*My hamster died when I was in third grade, and my friends **condoled** with me and helped bury him in the yard.*

Synonyms: console, sympathize

. . .

CONDOLENCE

noun (kon <u>doh</u> lens)

sympathy for a person's misfortune

*Shanna offered her **condolences** to Chantalle when she broke a fingernail.*

Synonyms: commiseration, compassion

CONDONE

verb (kon <u>dohn</u>)

to pardon or forgive

*The principal did not **condone** speaking in homeroom during morning announcements.*

Synonyms: overlook, justify

. . .

CONDUIT

noun (<u>kon</u> doo it)

tube, pipe, or similar passage

*The girls' bathroom was Ashley's **conduit** to gossip about the boys—she could hear them through the air vents.*

Synonym: channel

. . .

CONFIGURATION

noun (kon fig yu <u>ray</u> shun)

arrangement of parts or elements

*Each day Chantalle dictates the seating **configuration** at her lunch table.*

Synonym: format

CONFISCATION
noun (kon fis <u>kay</u> shun)

seizure by authorities

*The **confiscation** of Derek's iPod in class made him so angry he kicked his locker on the way to his next class.*

Synonym: taking

. . .

CONFLAGRATION
noun (kahn fluh <u>gray</u> shuhn)

big, destructive fire

*After the **conflagration** had finally died down, the city center was nothing but a mass of blackened embers.*

Synonyms: blaze, inferno

. . .

CONFLICT
noun (<u>kon</u> flikt)

a clash

*Josh couldn't remember how his **conflict** with Timmy began, but he continued to torture him anyway.*

Synonym: battle

CONFLUENCE
noun (<u>kahn</u> floo uhns)

the act of two things flowing together, the junction or place where two things meet

*At the political meeting, while planning a demonstration, there was a moving **confluence** of ideas between members.*

Synonyms: junction, merging

. . .

CONFORMITY
noun (kon <u>form</u> ih tee)

similarity in form or character

*Marisol is totally against **conformity** when it comes to her style.*

Synonyms: accord, accordance, agreement

. . .

CONFOUND
verb (kun <u>fownd</u>)

to baffle, perplex

*Josh, **confounded** by the complicated football play, threw a pass that was intercepted by the opposing team.*

Synonym: confuse

CONFRONTATIONAL
adjective (kon fron <u>tay</u> shun al)

eager to come face-to-face with

*Timmy was not a **confrontational** kind of guy, instead choosing to avoid conflict.*

Synonym: adversarial

. . .

CONGEAL
verb (kun <u>jeel</u>)

to become thick or solid as a liquid freezing

*Marisol watched the gravy **congeal** on her mashed potatoes and decided to head back to the lunch line to grab a PB&J sandwich.*

Synonyms: harden, coagulate

. . .

CONGENITAL
adjective (kuhn <u>jehn</u> ih tl)

existing since birth

*The infant's **congenital** health problem was corrected through surgery.*

Synonym: innate

CONGRUITY
noun (kuhn <u>groo</u> ih tee)

correspondence, harmony, agreement

*There was an obvious **congruity** between Marco's pleasant personality and his kind actions towards others.*

Synonym: accord

. . .

CONJECTURE
noun (kuhn <u>jehk</u> shuhr)

speculation, prediction

*The actor refused to comment, forcing gossip columnists to make **conjectures** on his love life.*

Synonyms: hypothesis, postulation, supposition

. . .

CONJURE
verb (<u>kahn</u> juhr) (kuhn <u>joor</u>)

to evoke a spirit, cast a spell

*The cotton candy **conjured** up the image in Arthur's mind of the fairgrounds he used to visit as a child.*

Synonym: summon

CONNOISSEUR

noun (kah nuh <u>suhr</u>)

a person with expert knowledge or discriminating tastes

*Dr. Crane was a **connoisseur** of fine food and wine, drinking and eating only the best.*

Synonyms: authority, epicure, expert, gastronome, gourmet

• • •

CONSANGUINEOUS

adjective (kahn saang <u>gwihn</u> ee uhs)

having the same lineage or ancestry, related by blood

*After having a strange feeling about our relationship for years, I found out that my best friend and I are **consanguineous**.*

Synonyms: kin, cognate

• • •

CONSECRATE

verb (<u>kon</u> si krayt)

to declare sacred, dedicate to a goal

*Josh **consecrated** his purple underwear and wore them at every home football game whether they were clean or not.*

Synonyms: devote, bless

CONSENSUS

noun (kon <u>sen</u> suss)

agreement of opinion or attitude

*After much debate, Shanna and the rest of the student council reached a **consensus** and decided to have a car wash as a senior-trip fundraiser.*

Synonym: unanimity

• • •

CONSERVATISM

noun (kon <u>sur</u> va tizm)

inclination to maintain traditional values

*Marisol knew her new nose ring was going to clash with her parents' **conservatism**.*

Synonym: traditionalism

• • •

CONSERVE

verb (kon <u>serv</u>)

use sparingly, protect from loss or harm

*Willow decided to take a shower only once a week to **conserve** water.*

Synonym: maintain

CONSOLATION
noun (kon so <u>lay</u> shun)

something providing comfort or solace for a loss or hardship

*The twenty bucks Timmy found on the floor was a small **consolation** for tripping and splitting his pants in front of a large crowd.*

Synonym: comfort

• • •

CONSONANT
adjective (<u>kahn</u> suh nuhnt)

consistent with, in agreement with

*The pitiful raise Ingrid received was **consonant** with the low opinion her manager had of her performance.*

Synonyms: accordant, compatible, congruous

• • •

CONSTELLATION
noun (kon stuh <u>lay</u> shun)

a collection of stars with a perceived design

*When her date told her she was as beautiful as the **constellation** Orion, Ashley realized he was a little too corny for her to go out with again.*

CONSTERNATION
noun (kahn stuhr <u>nay</u> shuhn)

an intense state of fear or dismay

*One would never think that a seasoned hunter would display such **consternation** when a grizzly bear lumbered too close to camp.*

Synonyms: cowardice, fear

• • •

CONSTITUENT
noun (kuhn <u>stih</u> choo uhnt)

component, part, citizen, voter

*A machine will not function properly if one of its **constituents** is defective.*

Synonyms: element, factor

• • •

CONSTRAINT
noun (kuhn <u>straynt</u>)

something that restricts or confines within prescribed bounds

*Given the **constraints** of the budget, it was impossible to accomplish my goals.*

Synonyms: limitation, check

CONSTRUE
verb (kuhn <u>stroo</u>)

to explain or interpret

*"I wasn't sure how to **construe** that last remark he made," said Delia, "but I suspect it was an insult."*

Synonyms: analyze, translate

. . .

CONSUMMATE
adjective (kahn suh muht) (kahn soo miht)

accomplished, complete, perfect

*The skater delivered a **consummate** performance, perfect in every aspect.*

Synonyms: exhaustive, flawless, ideal, thorough

. . .

CONSUMPTION
noun (kon <u>sump</u> shun)

the act of eating or taking in

*Ashley's **consumption** of five cans of soda before bed kept her awake all night.*

Synonym: digestion

CONTAGIOUS
adjective (kon <u>tay</u> jus)

spreading from one to another

*The supermarket manager said that George's laziness was **contagious** and was spreading to the rest of the employees.*

Synonyms: catching, infectious, spreading

. . .

CONTAMINATE
verb (kon <u>tam</u> uh nayt)

to make impure by contact

*Despite his parents' warning that television **contaminates** the mind, George had no problem watching twenty hours of TV every weekend.*

Synonyms: foul, pollute, taint

. . .

CONTEMPLATE
verb (<u>kon</u> tem playt)

to consider carefully

*Timmy had to seriously **contemplate** where he wanted to apply to college.*

Synonym: ponder

C

CONTEMPORARY
adjective (kon <u>temp</u> uh rery)

belonging to the same period of time

*Chantalle vowed to get Marisol to wear **contemporary** clothes one day instead of the vintage styles she always had on.*

Synonym: current

. . .

CONTEMPTUOUS
adjective (kuhn <u>tehmp</u> choo uhs)

scornful, expressing contempt

*The diners were intimidated by the waiter's **contemptuous** manner.*

Synonyms: derisive, disdainful, supercilious

. . .

CONTENT
adjective (kon <u>tent</u>)

satisfied

*Josh is **content** to be known in school as a jock. After all, he does play three varsity sports.*

Synonyms: gratified, happy, pleased

CONTENTIOUS
adjective (kuhn <u>tehn</u> shuhs)

quarrelsome, disagreeable, belligerent

*The **contentious** gentleman in the bar ridiculed anything anyone said.*

Synonyms: argumentative, fractious, litigious

. . .

CONTIGUOUS
adjective (kuhn <u>tihg</u> yoo uhs)

sharing a boundary, neighboring

*The two houses had **contiguous** yards, so the families shared the landscaping expenses.*

Synonyms: bordering, adjoining

. . .

CONTINENCE
noun (<u>kahn</u> tih nihns)

self-control, self-restraint

*Lucy exhibited impressive **continence** in steering clear of fattening foods, and she lost fifty pounds.*

Synonyms: discipline, moderation

CONTRACT
verb (kon <u>trakt</u>)

acquire

*Willow thinks she **contracted** a cold waiting in the rain for the bus.*

Synonym: incur

• • •

CONTRADICTION
noun (kon tra <u>dik</u> shun)

statement opposite to what was already said

*Timmy corrected the teacher when he noticed what she said was a **contradiction** to what was in the textbook.*

Synonyms: incongruity, paradox

• • •

CONTRAVENE
verb (kahn truh <u>veen</u>)

to contradict, deny, act contrary to

*The watchman **contravened** his official instructions by leaving his post for an hour.*

Synonyms: disobey, transgress, violate

CONTRITE
adjective (kon <u>tryt</u>)

deeply sorrowful and repentant for a wrong

*Shanna felt **contrite** for making fun of Timmy after she saw the sad expression on his face.*

Synonyms: apologetic, penitent, regretful

• • •

CONTUMACIOUS
adjective (kahn tuh <u>may</u> shuhs)

rebellious

*The **contumacious** teenager ran away from home when her parents told her she was grounded.*

Synonyms: factious, insubordinate, insurgent, mutinous

• • •

CONUNDRUM
noun (ka <u>nun</u> drum)

riddle, puzzle, or problem with no solution

*Josh found himself with a **conundrum** when he realized that his upcoming baseball game overlapped with his basketball game—how would he play at both?*

Synonym: mystery

CONVALESCE

verb (kahn vuhl _ehs_ uhns)

to gradually recover from an illness

*After her bout with malaria, Tatiana needed to **convalesce** for a whole month.*

Synonyms: heal, recuperate

• • •

CONVENTION

noun (kon _ven_ shen)

general acceptance of practices or attitudes

*Shanna followed the **convention** of a typical overachiever. She excelled in all her classes and joined as many extracurricular activities as humanly possible.*

Synonym: tradition

• • •

CONVENTIONAL

adjective (kon _ven_ sheh nell)

typical, customary

***Conventional** fast-food restaurants have a drive-thru window so customers can order and pick up their food without getting out of their cars.*

Synonym: commonplace

CONVERGENCE

noun (kuhn _vehr_ juhns)

the state of separate elements joining or coming together

*A **convergence** of factors led to the tragic unfolding of World War I.*

Synonyms: union, concurrence, coincidence

• • •

CONVEY

verb (kon _vay_)

to transport, to make known

*Unfortunately, George **conveyed** his appreciation for pretty girls by making kissing noises at them.*

Synonyms: carry, communicate

• • •

CONVICT

verb (kon _vict_)

to find guilty of a crime

*Madame La Bouche, the French teacher, **convicted** Paul of shooting the spitball when she found him hiding a straw under his desk.*

Synonym: condemn

CONVICTION
noun (kon VIC shin)

fixed or strong belief

*Shanna spoke with **conviction** when she addressed the student body—it was one of the things that made her a good class president.*

Synonym: confidence

• • •

CONVIVIAL
adjective (kuhn vihv ee uhl)

sociable, fond of eating, drinking, and people

*The restaurant's **convivial** atmosphere contrasted starkly with the gloom of Maureen's empty apartment.*

Synonym: companionable

• • •

CONVOKE
verb (kuhn vohk)

to call together, summon

*The president **convoked** a group of experts to advise him on how to deal with the crisis.*

Synonyms: assemble, convene, gather

CONVOLUTED
adjective (kahn vuh loo tehd)

twisted, complicated, involved

*Although many people bought A Brief History of Time, few could follow its **convoluted** ideas and theories.*

Synonyms: baroque, elaborate, intricate

• • •

COPIOUS
adjective (koh pee uhs)

abundant, plentiful

*The hostess had prepared **copious** amounts of food for the banquet.*

Synonyms: abounding, ample

• • •

COQUETTE
noun (koh keht)

a flirtatious woman

*The librarian could turn into a **coquette** just by letting her hair down and changing the swing of her hips.*

Synonym: flirt

CORDIAL
adjective (<u>kor</u> jel)

warm and sincere

*Chantalle offered Derek a **cordial** smile in the hallway even though the two rarely spoke to each other.*

Synonym: friendly

. . .

CORPOREAL
adjective (kohr <u>pohr</u> ee uhl)

having to do with the body, tangible, material

*Makiko realized that the problem was **corporeal** in nature, it was not just an intangible issue.*

Synonyms: concrete, physical, somatic

. . .

CORPULENCE
noun (<u>kohr</u> pyuh luhns)

obesity, fatness, bulkiness

*Egbert's **corpulence** increased as he spent several hours each day eating and drinking.*

Synonyms: plumpness, portliness, rotundity, stoutness

CORRECTIVE
adjective (koh <u>rek</u> tiv)

intended to fix, remedy

*Marisol hardly wore her **corrective** glasses even though she could barely see without them.*

Synonyms: rectifying, reformative

. . .

CORROBORATE
verb (kuh <u>rahb</u> uhr ayt)

to confirm, verify

*Roberto was able to **corroborate** his friend's story by showing the receipt that proved they were indeed at a restaurant all night.*

Synonyms: confirm, prove, warrant

. . .

CORROSIVE
adjective (ku <u>row</u> siv)

gradually destructive

*The dentist told George that soda was **corrosive** to his teeth.*

Synonym: harmful

COSMOPOLITAN
adjective (kos muh <u>pol</u> i tun)

pertinent or common to the whole world

*Chantalle considers herself quite **cosmopolitan** because she's already been to Europe twice.*

Synonym: worldly

. . .

COSSET
verb (<u>kahs</u> iht)

to pamper, treat with great care

*Mimi **cosseted** her toy poodle, feeding him gourmet meals and buying it a silk pillow to sleep on.*

Synonym: spoil

. . .

COTERIE
noun (<u>koh</u> tuh ree)

an intimate group of persons with a similar purpose

*Judith invited a **coterie** of fellow stamp enthusiasts to a stamp-trading party.*

Synonyms: clique, set

COUNTENANCE
noun (<u>kown</u> tuh nuhns)

facial expression, look of approval or support

*Jeremy was afraid of the new music appreciation instructor because she had such an evil **countenance**.*

Synonyms: face, expression

. . .

COUNTENANCE
verb (<u>kown</u> tuh nuhns)

to favor, support

*When the girls started a pillow fight, the baby-sitter warned them, "I will not **countenance** such behavior."*

Synonyms: approve, tolerate

. . .

COUNTERACT
verb (kown ter <u>act</u>)

to oppose the effects by contrary action

*Ashley started spreading rumors about Shanna to **counteract** the rumors Shanna was telling about her.*

Synonym: offset

COUNTERMAND
verb (<u>kown</u> tuhr maand)

to annul, cancel, make a contrary order

*Residents were relieved when the councilmembers **countermanded** the rule of thirty-minute parking on all city streets.*

Synonym: revoke

• • •

COUNTERVAIL
verb (kown tuhr <u>vayl</u>)

to act or react with equal force

*In order to **countervail** the financial loss the school suffered after the embezzlement, the treasurer raised the price of room and board.*

Synonyms: counteract, compensate, offset

• • •

COVERT
adjective (koh <u>vuhrt</u>)

secretive, not openly shown

*The **covert** military operation wasn't disclosed until weeks later after it was determined to be a success.*

Synonym: veiled

CRAFTY
adjective (kraf tee)

underhanded, devious, or deceptive

*Timmy devised a **crafty** plan to give Josh at least one supersonic wedgie before graduation.*

Synonym: artful

• • •

CRASS
adjective (<u>krass</u>)

crude, unrefined

*George couldn't believe that Shanna had called him **crass,** he belched only once during lunch.*

Synonym: coarse

• • •

CRAVEN
adjective (<u>kray</u> vuhn)

cowardly

*The **craven** lion cringed in the corner of his cage, terrified of the mouse.*

Synonyms: faint-hearted, spineless, timid

CREDENCE

noun (<u>kreed</u> ns)

acceptance of something as true or real

*Mr. Bagley couldn't give any **credence** to the charge that his darling son had cheated on his test.*

Synonym: credibility

• • •

CREDO

noun (<u>kree</u> doh)

system of principles or beliefs

*Paul's **credo** is "Do unto others as you would have them do unto you."*

Synonym: creed

• • •

CREDULOUS

adjective (<u>kreh</u> juh luhs)

gullible, trusting

*Although some four-year-olds believe in the Easter Bunny, only the most **credulous** nine-year-olds do.*

Synonyms: naïve, uncritical

CRESCENDO

noun (kruh <u>shehn</u> doh)

gradual increase in volume of sound

*The **crescendo** of tension became unbearable as Evel Knievel prepared to jump his motorcycle over the school buses.*

Synonym: progressively greater

• • •

CRUDE

adjective (<u>krood</u>)

unrefined, natural, blunt, offensive

*Ashley thought Josh's remark about their teacher's hairy legs was totally **crude**.*

Synonyms: unrefined, untreated

• • •

CUE

noun (q)

reminder, prompt

*Marisol shone the spotlight on Derek, center stage, giving him the **cue** to sing.*

Synonym: hint

CULL
verb (kuhl)

to select, weed out

*You should **cull** the words you need to study from all the flash cards.*

Synonyms: pick, extract

. . .

CULPABLE
adjective (kuhl puh buhl)

guilty, responsible for wrong

*The CEO is **culpable** for the bankruptcy of the company, he was, after all, in charge of it.*

Synonyms: answerable, blameworthy

. . .

CUMULATIVE
adjective (kyoom yuh luh tihv)

increasing, collective

*The new employee didn't mind her job at first, but the daily petty indignities had a **cumulative** demoralizing effect.*

Synonyms: added up, gradual

CUNNING
adjective (kun ing)

given to artful deception

*Chantalle, as **cunning** as she is beautiful, thinks she would make the perfect spy.*

Synonym: artful

. . .

CUPIDITY
noun (kyoo pih dih tee)

greed

*The poverty-stricken man stared at the shining jewels with **cupidity** in his gleaming eyes.*

Synonyms: avarice, covetousness, rapacity

. . .

CURATOR
noun (q ray ter)

overseer of an exhibition, especially in a museum

*The **curator** of the museum yelled at Marisol to stop touching the famous painting.*

Synonym: caretaker

CURMUDGEON
noun (kuhr <u>muh</u> juhn)

cranky person

The old man was a notorious **curmudgeon** *who snapped at anyone who disturbed him for any reason.*

Synonyms: coot, crab, grouch

. . .

CURRICULUM
noun (cur <u>ric</u> u lum)

the syllabus for a particular class or the courses offered by a school

When Mr. Jennings handed out his chemistry **curriculum,** *there were moans and groans throughout the room!*

. . .

CURSORY
adjective (<u>kuhr</u> suh ree)

hastily done, superficial

The copyeditor gave the article a **cursory** *once-over, missing dozens of errors.*

Synonyms: careless, shallow

CURT
adjective (kuhrt)

abrupt, short with words

The grouchy shop assistant was **curt** *with one of her customers, which resulted in a reprimand from her manager.*

Synonyms: terse, rude

. . .

CURTAIL
verb (ker <u>tayl</u>)

to shorten

Willow **curtailed** *the time she spent on her date because the guy kept talking about how he thought vegetarians were narrow-minded.*

Synonym: shorten

. . .

CYLINDRICAL
adjective (cy <u>lin</u> dri cal)

having the form of a cylinder

The vase he created was blue and had a **cylindrical** *shape.*

DANGLE
verb (<u>dang</u> gul)

to hang loosely and swing

*George laughed as he **dangled** a piece of candy in front of a baby, then pulled it away, making the baby cry.*

Synonym: hang

• • •

DATED
adjective (<u>day</u> tid)

old-fashioned, out of style

*Shanna wore her mother's neon-pink sweatshirt and a pair of matching leg warmers over her jeans; the look was totally **dated** but perfect for a Halloween costume.*

Synonym: obsolete

DAUNT
verb (dawnt)

to discourage, intimidate

*She tried hard not to let the enormity of the situation **daunt** her.*

Synonyms: consternate, demoralize, dishearten

• • •

DAUNTING
adjective (<u>dawn</u> ting)

discouraging

*Living in a tree for three weeks might be a **daunting** task for some, but Willow was determined to do it to become one with nature.*

Synonym: dismaying

DEARTH
noun (duhrth)

lack, scarcity, insufficiency

*The **dearth** of supplies in our city made it difficult to survive the blizzard.*

Synonyms: absence, shortage

. . .

DEBACLE
noun (dih baa kuhl)

a sudden, disastrous collapse or defeat, a total, ridiculous failure

*It was hard for her to show her face in the office after the **debacle** of spilling coffee on her supervisor—three times.*

Synonyms: crash, wreck

. . .

DEBASE
verb (dih bays)

to degrade or lower in quality or stature

*The president's deceitful actions **debased** the stature of his office.*

Synonyms: adulterate, defile, demean, denigrate

DEBILITATE
verb (dih bih lih tayt)

to weaken, enfeeble

*The flu **debilitated** the postal worker, she was barely able to finish her rounds.*

Synonyms: devitalize, drain, enervate, exhaust, sap

. . .

DEBILITATING
adjective (dee bil uh tay ting)

impairing the strength or energy of

*Timmy's fear of public speaking was so **debilitating** that he couldn't even practice in front of his goldfish.*

Synonym: weaken

. . .

DEBRIS
noun (de bris)

broken or destroyed remains

*The janitor swept up the **debris** left behind by the construction crew.*

Synonym: garbage

DEBTOR
noun (<u>det</u> ur)

someone that owes something to someone else

*Shanna is Chantalle's **debtor** because Shanna so owes her for getting her a date.*

. . .

DEBUNK
verb (dih <u>buhnk</u>)

to discredit, disprove

*It was the teacher's mission in life to **debunk** the myth that females are bad at math.*

Synonyms: belie, confute, contradict, controvert, explode

. . .

DEBUTANTE
noun (<u>dehb</u> yoo tahnt)

young woman making debut in high society

*The **debutante** spent hours dressing for her very first ball, hoping to catch the eye of an eligible bachelor.*

Synonyms: lady, maiden

DECEIVE
verb (de <u>seev</u>)

give false impression

*Chantalle has **deceived** her classmates into thinking that she's a tough cookie, but in reality she is very sensitive.*

Synonym: mislead

. . .

DECIBEL
noun (<u>deh</u> sib ul)

unit of sound intensity

*Derek's mom told him to turn down the **decibel** level on his amplifier because the neighbors were complaining about the noise.*

. . .

DECIDUOUS
adjective (dih <u>sih</u> joo uhs)

losing leaves in the fall, short-lived, temporary

***Deciduous** trees are bare in winter, which is why coniferous trees, such as evergreens, are used during winter holidays.*

Synonym: ephemeral

DECISIVE
adjective (de siy siv)

capable of determining outcome

*Grades, extracurricular activities, and SAT score are **decisive** factors in college admissions.*

Synonym: conclusive

. . .

DECLAIM
verb (dih klaym)

to speak loudly and vehemently

*At Thanksgiving dinner, our grandfather always **declaims** his right, as the eldest, to sit at the head of the table.*

Synonyms: perorate, rant, rave

. . .

DECLIVITY
noun (dih klih vih tee)

downward slope

*Because the village was situated on the **declivity** of a hill, it never flooded.*

Synonyms: decline, descent, grade, slant, tilt

DECOROUS
adjective (deh kuhr uhs) (deh kohr uhs)

proper, tasteful, socially correct

*The socialite trained her daughters in the finer points of **decorous** behavior, hoping they would make a good impression at the debutante ball.*

Synonyms: appropriate, courteous, polite

. . .

DECORUM
noun (deh kohr uhm)

appropriateness of behavior or conduct, propriety

*The countess complained that the vulgar peasants lacked the **decorum** appropriate for a visit to the palace.*

Synonyms: correctness, decency, etiquette, manners

. . .

DECRY
verb (dih crie)

to belittle, to openly condemn

*Governments all over the world **decried** the dictator's vicious massacre of the helpless citizens.*

Synonyms: depreciate, deride

DEDUCTION
noun (dee duk shin)

the drawing of a conclusion through logic

*It was simple **deduction** that led Shanna to the conclusion that her sister was reading her journal.*

Synonym: determination, inference

. . .

DEFACE
verb (dih fays)

to mar the appearance of, vandalize

*After the wall was torn down, the students began to **deface** the statues of Communist leaders of the former Eastern bloc.*

Synonyms: disfigure, impair, spoil

. . .

DEFAMATORY
adjective (dih faam uh tohr ee)

injurious to the reputation

*The tabloid was sued for making **defamatory** statements about the celebrity.*

Synonyms: libelous, slanderous

DEFECTIVE
adjective (dee fek tiv)

faulty

*Shanna realized that her new iPod was **defective** when it wouldn't turn on.*

Synonyms: flawed, imperfect

. . .

DEFERENCE
noun (deh fuh ruhn(t)s) (def ruhn(t)s)

respect, courtesy

*The respectful young law clerk treated the Supreme Court justice with the utmost **deference**.*

Synonyms: courtesy, homage

. . .

DEFERENTIAL
adjective (dehf uh rehn shuhl)

respectful and polite in a submissive way

*The respectful young law clerk was **deferential** to the Supreme Court justice.*

Synonyms: courteous, obsequious

DEFERMENT
noun (de _fur_ ment)

the act of delaying

Chantalle asked her parents for a **deferment** *from being grounded because of a party she wants to attend.*

Synonyms: detainment, holdup

• • •

DEFIANTLY
adverb (de _fi_ ant lee)

boldly resisting

Marisol **defiantly** *told her parents that she would apply to her dream art school.*

Synonym: disobediently

• • •

DEFICIT
noun (_def_ ih sit)

inadequacy, disadvantage

Timmy is at a bit of a **deficit** *when it comes to social skills.*

Synonym: deficiency

DEFT
adjective (dehft)

skillful, dexterous

It was a pleasure to watch the **deft** *carpenter as he repaired the furniture.*

Synonyms: adept, adroit, expert

• • •

DEGRADATION
noun (deh gruh _day_ shun)

reduction in worth or dignity

Shanna was fired from her job, but she hid her **degradation** *by saying that she had resigned.*

Synonyms: corruption, decline

• • •

DELEGATE
verb (_del_ uh gayt)

to give powers to another

Chantalle planned to have a party at her house, but she **delegated** *all of the setup to her friends.*

Synonym: commission, deputize

DELETERIOUS
adjective (dehl ih <u>teer</u> ee uhs)

harmful, destructive, detrimental

*If we put these defective clocks on the market, it could be quite **deleterious** to our reputation.*

Synonyms: adverse, hurtful, inimical

. . .

DELIBERATION
noun (de lib uh <u>ray</u> shun)

careful consideration of an issue

*After much **deliberation**, Josh's parents agreed to let him use the car on Saturday.*

Synonym: discussion

. . .

DELINEATE
verb (de <u>lin</u> ee ayt)

to portray, depict

*Shanna **delineated** to her parents her plan to become president of the United States one day.*

Synonyms: outline, describe

DELINEATION
noun (dih lihn ee <u>ay</u> shuhn)

depiction, representation

*Mrs. Baxter was very satisfied with the artist's **delineation** of her new mansion.*

Synonyms: figuration, illustration, picture, portraiture

. . .

DELUGE
verb (<u>dehl</u> yooj) (<u>dehl</u> yoozh) (<u>day</u> looj) (<u>day</u> loozh) (dih <u>looj</u>) (dih <u>loozh</u>)

to submerge, overwhelm, flood

*The popular actor was **deluged** with fan mail.*

Synonyms: engulf, immerse, inundate, swamp, whelm

. . .

DEMAGOGUE
noun (<u>deh</u> muh gahg) (<u>deh</u> muh gawg)

leader, rabble-rouser, usually using appeals to emotion or prejudice

*Hitler began his political career as a **demagogue**, giving fiery speeches in beer halls.*

Synonyms: agitator, inciter, instigator

DEMEAN
verb (di <u>meen</u>)

to degrade, humiliate, humble

*Derek believes that singing cover songs would **demean** his band.*

Synonym: debase

• • •

DEMEANOR
noun (de <u>mee</u> ner)

the way a person behaves

*Jana's patient **demeanor** was a real asset as a teacher.*

Synonym: behavior

• • •

DEMOLISH
verb (de <u>mol</u> ish)

destroy, damage severely

*Josh roused his teammates by saying that they were going to **demolish** the other team.*

Synonyms: raze, tear down

DEMOLITION
noun (de muh <u>lish</u> un)

the act of destroying

*Timmy believed that the **demolition** of his science project was sabotage.*

Synonyms: decimation, annihilation

• • •

DEMONIZE
verb (<u>dee</u> mun iyz)

to represent as evil

*George **demonized** his English teacher after getting a bad grade.*

Synonym: vilify

• • •

DEMUR
verb (dih <u>muhr</u>)

to express doubts or objections

*When scientific authorities claimed that all the planets revolved around the Earth, Galileo, with his superior understanding of the situation, was forced to **demur**.*

Synonyms: expostulate, dissent, protest, remonstrate

DENIGRATE
verb (<u>deh</u> nih grayt)

to slur or blacken someone's reputation

*The people still loved the president, despite his enemies' attempts to **denigrate** his character.*

Synonyms: belittle, disparage, malign, slander, vilify

. . .

DENIZEN
noun (<u>dehn</u> ih zihn)

inhabitant, a resident

*The **denizens** of the state understandably wanted to select their own leaders.*

Synonyms: dweller, occupant

. . .

DEPOSE
verb (dih <u>pohs</u>)

to remove from a high position, as from a throne

*After he was **deposed** from his throne, the king spent the rest of his life in exile.*

Synonyms: dethrone, displace, overthrow, topple, unseat

DEPRAVITY
noun (dih <u>praav</u> ih tee)

sinfulness, moral corruption

*The **depravity** of the actor's Hollywood lifestyle shocked his traditional parents.*

Synonyms: corruption, debauchery, decadence, degradation, enormity

. . .

DEPRECATE
verb (<u>dehp</u> rih kayt)

to belittle, disparage

*Ernest **deprecated** his own contribution, instead praising the efforts of his coworkers.*

Synonyms: denigrate, discount, minimize

. . .

DEPRECIATE
verb (dih <u>pree</u> shee ayt)

to lose value gradually

*The Barrettas sold their house, fearful that its value would **depreciate** due to the nuclear reactor being built around the corner.*

Synonym: lessen

DERELICT
adjective (<u>der</u> uh likt)

neglectful of one's obligations, abandoned

*George was fired for being **derelict** in his job duties at the supermarket.*

Synonym: negligent

. . .

DERIDE
verb (dih <u>ried</u>)

to laugh at contemptuously, to make fun of

*As soon as Jorge heard the others **deriding** Anthony, he came to his defense.*

Synonym: ridicule

. . .

DERIVATIVE
adjective (di <u>riv</u> uh tiv)

copied or adapted

*Chantalle and Shanna both had on an outfit **derivative** of what the other had worn the day before.*

Synonym: unoriginal

DEROGATE
verb (<u>dehr</u> uh gayt)

to belittle, to disparage

*The sarcastic old man never stopped **derogating** the efforts of his daughter, even after she won the Nobel Prize.*

Synonym: detract

. . .

DESECRATE
verb (<u>dehs</u> ih krayt)

to abuse something sacred

*The archaeologist tried to explain to the explorer that he had **desecrated** the temple by spitting in it.*

Synonyms: defile, degrade, profane

. . .

DESICCATE
verb (<u>deh</u> sih kayt)

to dry completely, dehydrate

*The hot desert sun will **desiccate** anyone who dares spend the day there without any source of water.*

Synonyms: evaporate, exsiccate, parch

DESOLATE
adjective (<u>des</u> uh lit)

lifeless, barren

*The school was **desolate** after all the students had left for the weekend.*

Synonym: deserted

• • •

DESPONDENT
adjective (dih <u>spahn</u> duhnt)

discouraged, dejected

*Mr. Baker was lonely and **despondent** after his wife's death.*

Synonyms: dejected, depressed, desolate, forlorn, sad

• • •

DESPOT
noun (<u>dehs</u> puht) (<u>dehs</u> paht)

tyrannical ruler

*The **despot** banished half the nobles in his court on a whim.*

Synonyms: authoritarian, autocrat, dictator, totalitarian

DESPOTISM
noun (<u>des</u> puh tizm)

dominance through threat of violence

*Josh's **despotism** occurs not because he's a tough guy, but because he is insecure.*

Synonyms: totalitarianism, tyranny

• • •

DESTITUTE
adjective (<u>dehs</u> tih toot)
(dehs tih <u>tyoot</u>)

very poor, poverty-stricken

*After the stock market crash, Jeanette was **destitute**, forced to beg on the streets in order to survive.*

Synonyms: broke, impecunious, insolvent, needy, penurious

• • •

DESTITUTION
noun (<u>des</u> tih TOO shun)

complete poverty

*If Willow could have only one wish granted it would be to abolish **destitution**.*

Synonyms: impoverishment, indigence

DESULTORY

adjective (<u>dehs</u> uhl tohr ee) (<u>dehz</u> uhl tohr ee)

at random, rambling, unmethodical

Diane had a desultory academic record; she had changed majors twelve times in three years.

Synonym: chaotic

• • •

DETERMINE

verb (di <u>tur</u> min)

to decide

*Ashley was unable to **determine** what she should wear to the party.*

Synonyms: establish, judge

• • •

DETRACTOR

noun (di <u>trak</u> tur)

someone who belittles something else

*Chantalle's **detractors** noted that although she's popular, she isn't that smart.*

Synonym: critic

DEVIOUS

adjective (<u>dee</u> vee us)

shifty, not straightforward

*Ashley felt a little **devious** as she snuck into the kitchen and ate the last cupcake.*

Synonyms: sly, beguiling

• • •

DEVOUR

verb (di <u>vowr</u>)

eat greedily

*Paul stared, amazed, as George **devoured** his entire bowl of spaghetti in one gulp.*

Synonym: consume

• • •

DEXTEROUS

adjective (<u>dehk</u> stuhr uhs) (<u>dehk</u> struhs)

skilled physically or mentally

*The gymnast who won the contest was far more **dexterous** than the other competitors were.*

Synonyms: adept, adroit, deft, nimble

DIABOLICAL
adjective (die uh bahl ih kuhl)

fiendish, wicked

Sherlock Holmes's archenemy is the **diabolical** *Professor Moriarty.*

Synonym: evil

• • •

DIAMETRICALLY
adjective (di a met ri cally)

in direct opposition

The candidate was **diametrically** *opposed to her opponent's views.*

Synonym: opposite

• • •

DIAPHANOUS
adjective (die aaf uh nuhs)

allowing light to show through, delicate

Ginny's **diaphanous** *gown failed to disguise the fact that she was wearing ripped panty hose.*

Synonyms: gauzy, tenuous, translucent, transparent, sheer

DIATRIBE
noun (die uh trieb)

bitter verbal attack

During the CEO's lengthy **diatribe,** *the board members managed to remain calm and self-controlled.*

Synonyms: fulmination, harangue, jeremiad, philippic, tirade

• • •

DICHOTOMY
noun (die kah tuh mee)

division into two parts

Westerns often feature a simple **dichotomy** *between good guys and bad guys.*

Synonyms: bifurcation, distinction, opposition, split

• • •

DICTUM
noun (dihk tuhm)

authoritative statement, popular saying

Chris tried to live his life in accordance with the **dictum** *"Two wrongs don't make a right."*

Synonyms: adage, aphorism, apothegm, decree, edict

DIDACTIC
adjective (die <u>daak</u> tihk)

excessively instructive

*The father was overly **didactic** with his children, turning every activity into a lesson.*

Synonyms: educational, improving, moralistic

. . .

DIFFIDENCE
noun (<u>dih</u> fih duhns) (<u>dih</u> fih dehns)

shyness, lack of confidence

*Steve's **diffidence** during the job interview stemmed from his nervous nature and lack of experience.*

Synonyms: reticence, timidity

. . .

DIFFIDENT
adjective (<u>dif</u> ih dint)

shy, lacking confidence

*Something about the pretty new girl in school made Josh feel **diffident**.*

Synonym: unassertive

DIFFUSE
verb (dih <u>fyooz</u>)

to spread out widely, to scatter freely, to disseminate

*They turned on the fan, but all that did was **diffuse** the cigarette smoke throughout the room.*

Synonyms: disperse, soften

. . .

DIGNITY
noun (<u>dig</u> nih tee)

self-respect

*Shanna conducted herself with **dignity** when her date canceled on her at the last minute.*

Synonym: poise

. . .

DIGRESS
verb (die <u>grehs</u>)

to turn aside, especially from the main point, to stray from the subject

*The professor repeatedly **digressed** from the topic, boring his students.*

Synonyms: deviate, wander

DIGRESSION
noun (di <u>gresh</u> un)

the act of straying, an instance of straying

*Ashley found it tiring that every time she mentioned their World War II project Edward would go into a **digression** about his parents' divorce.*

Synonym: tangent

• • •

DILAPIDATED
adjective (dih <u>laap</u> ih dayt ihd)

in disrepair, run down

*Rather than get **discouraged**, the architect saw great potential in the dilapidated house.*

Synonyms: decayed, fallen into partial ruin

• • •

DILATE
verb (<u>die</u> layt) (die <u>layt</u>)

to make larger, expand

*When you enter a darkened room, the pupils of your eyes **dilate** so as to let in more light.*

Synonyms: amplify, develop, elaborate, enlarge, expand, expatiate

DILATORY
adjective (<u>dihl</u> uh tohr ee)

slow, tending to delay

*The congressman used **dilatory** measures to delay the passage of the bill.*

Synonyms: sluggish, tardy, unhurried

• • •

DILETTANTE
noun (<u>dih</u> luh tahnt)

someone with an amateurish and superficial interest in a topic

*Jerry's friends were such **dilettantes** they seemed to have new jobs and hobbies every week.*

Synonyms: amateur, dabbler, tyro

• • •

DILUVIAL
adjective (dih <u>loo</u> vee uhl)

pertaining to a flood

*After she left the water running in the house all day, it looked simply **diluvial**.*

Synonym: waterlogged

DIMINISH
verb (di <u>min</u> ish)

to make smaller

No matter how much zit cream Timmy used, he was not able to diminish the bulbous pimple on his nose.

Synonym: decrease

• • •

DIMINUTIVE
adjective (dih <u>mihn</u> yuh tihv)

small

Napoleon made up for his diminutive stature with his aggressive personality, terrifying his courtiers.

Synonyms: minscule, short, tiny, wee

• • •

DINGY
adjective (<u>din</u> gee)

shabby, drab

Chantalle thought that her nail polish was looking a little dingy, so she got a manicure.

Synonym: dirty

DIRGE
noun (duhrj)

a funeral hymn or mournful speech

Melville wrote the poem "A Dirge for James McPherson" for the funeral of a Union general who was killed in 1864.

Synonyms: elegy, lament

• • •

DISABUSE
verb (dih suh <u>byuze</u>)

set right, free from error

Galileo's observations disabused scholars of the notion that the Sun revolved around the Earth.

Synonyms: correct, undeceive

• • •

DISAVOW
verb (dis uh <u>vow</u>)

to refuse to acknowledge

Ashley disavowed any knowledge of her surprise birthday party.

Synonym: disclaim

DISCERN
verb (di surn)

to perceive something

*George wondered if his boss could **discern** that he was lying about why he was late.*

Synonym: distinguish

• • •

DISCLOSE
verb (dis cloz)

to make known, expose

*Marisol refused to **disclose** the identity of the cute boy who was hugging her in the photo.*

Synonym: reveal

• • •

DISCOMFIT
verb (dihs kuhm fiht)

to disconcert, to make one lose one's composure

*The class clown enjoyed **discomfiting** her classmates whenever possible.*

Synonym: embarrass

DISCONCERT
verb (dis kuhn surt)

ruffle, upset one's self-possession

*The coach was **disconcerted** when the star player of the football team was*

Synonym: discomfit

• • •

DISCONCERTING
adjective (dihs kuhn suhr tihng)

bewildering, perplexing, slightly disturbing

*Brad found his mother-in-law's hostile manner so **disconcerting** that he acted like a fool in her presence.*

Synonym: upsetting

• • •

DISCORD
noun (dis kord)

lack of agreement, inharmonious combination

*The **discord** between Chantalle and Shanna was evident when they didn't sit together during lunch.*

Synonyms: dissent, friction, strife

DISCORDANT
adjective (dihs <u>kohr</u> duhnt)

disagreeing, at variance

*The feelings about the child's education were becoming more and more **discordant**.*

Synonyms: cacophonous, dissonant, inharmonious

• • •

DISCOURSE
noun (<u>dis</u> kors)

verbal exchange, conversation

*Timmy wanted to settle his argument with Josh through polite **discourse**.*

Synonym: discussion

• • •

DISCOURTEOUS
adjective (dis <u>kur</u> tee us)

rude

*Paul bumped into a girl at the mall and quickly apologized, not wanting to seem **discourteous**.*

Synonym: impolite

DISCREDIT
verb (diss <u>kred</u> it)

to harm the reputation of

*Willow hoped to **discredit** the journalist for his article's false claims.*

Synonyms: dishonor, disgrace

• • •

DISCREPANCY
noun (dis <u>krep</u> un see)

difference between

*George was outraged to find a **discrepancy** between the number of hours he worked and what he was paid for.*

Synonyms: contrast, disagreement

• • •

DISCRETE
adjective (dih <u>skreet</u>)

individually distinct, separate

*What's nice about the CD is that each song functions as a **discrete** work and also as part of the whole compilation.*

Synonyms: unconnected, distinct

DISCRETION
noun (dis <u>kresh</u> in)

ability to judge on one's own

*Marisol's mom said she could decorate her room at her own **discretion**.*

Synonym: choice

• • •

DISCRETIONARY
adjective (dis <u>kresh</u> uh ner ee)

subject to one's own judgment

*As student body president, Shanna has a great deal of **discretionary** power.*

Synonym: optional

• • •

DISCURSIVE
adjective (dih <u>skuhr</u> sihv)

wandering from topic to topic

*The professor, known for his **discursive** speaking style, covered everything from armadillos to zebras in his zoology lecture.*

Synonym: rambling

DISDAIN
verb (diss <u>dayn</u>)

to regard with contempt

*Josh felt **disdain** for the inferior dodgeball players on the opposing team.*

Synonym: scorn

• • •

DISHEVELED
adjective (di <u>shev</u> uld)

marked by disorder, untidy

*Shanna neatened her hair between classes because she didn't like to look **disheveled**.*

Synonyms: messy, scruffy

• • •

DISINGENUOUS
adjective (<u>dihs</u> ihn <u>jehn</u> yoo uhs)

giving a false appearance of simple frankness, misleading

*It was **disingenuous** of him to suggest that he had no idea of the requests made by his campaign contributors.*

Synonyms: insincere, tricky

DISINTERESTED

adjective (dihs <u>ihn</u> trih stihd) (dihs <u>ihn</u> tuh reh stihd)

fair-minded, unbiased

*A fair trial is made possible by the selection of **disinterested** jurors.*

Synonyms: impartial, unprejudiced

. . .

DISMISSAL

noun (dis <u>mis</u> ul)

act of being fired or let out

*The seniors were psyched about their early **dismissal** from school.*

Synonyms: discharge, release

. . .

DISPARAGE

verb (dih <u>spaar</u> ihj)

to belittle, speak disrespectfully about

*Gregorio loved to **disparage** his brother's dancing skills, pointing out every mistake he made on the floor.*

Synonyms: denigrate, deride, derogate

DISPARATE

adjective (dis <u>par</u> it)

dissimilar, different in kind

*Marisol broke up with her boyfriend because they had **disparate** personalities, she had a sense of humor and he didn't.*

Synonyms: unlike, unequal

. . .

DISPASSIONATE

adjective (dihs <u>paash</u> ih niht)

unaffected by bias or strong emotions, not personally or emotionally involved in something

*Ideally, photographers should be **dispassionate** observers of what goes on in the world.*

Synonyms: disinterested, impartial

. . .

DISPEL

verb (dis <u>pell</u>)

to drive out or scatter

*George's rocking SAT score **dispelled** any remarks about him being stupid.*

Synonyms: dismiss, disperse

DISPLAY
verb (dis play)

to show, to exhibit, to present

*Marisol was psyched to get a chance to **display** her artwork in the school's auditorium.*

Synonyms: put on view, demonstrate

. . .

DISPUTANT
noun (dis pyoo tent)

someone in an argument

*Paul is rarely a **disputant**, because he's a cheerful, outgoing guy.*

Synonym: debater

. . .

DISREGARD
verb (dis rih gard)

ignore

*Shanna told the driving instructor that she did not **disregard** the stop sign, she just didn't see it.*

Synonyms: take no notice of, pay no attention to

DISSEMBLE
verb (dihs sehm buhl)

to pretend, disguise one's motives

*The villain could **dissemble** to the lawyers no longer—he finally had to confess to the forgery.*

Synonyms: camouflage, cloak, conceal, feign

. . .

DISSEMINATE
verb (dih sehm uh nayt)

to spread far and wide

*The wire service **disseminates** information so rapidly that events get reported shortly after they happen.*

Snonyms: circulate, diffuse, disperse

. . .

DISSENSION
noun (dih sehn shunhn)

difference of opinion

*The government was forced to abandon the extensive reforms it had planned, due to continued **dissension** within its party ranks about the form these changes should take.*

Synonym: disagreement

DISSIDENT
adjective (<u>dihs</u> ih duhnt)

disagreeing with an established religious or political system

*The **dissident** had been living abroad and writing his criticism of the government from an undisclosed location.*

Synonym: heretical

• • •

DISSIPATE
verb (<u>dihs</u> uh payt)

to scatter, to pursue pleasure to excess

*The fog gradually **dissipated**, revealing all the ships docked in the harbor.*

Synonyms: carouse, consume, disperse, dissolve, squander

• • •

DISSONANCE
noun (<u>dihs</u> uh nuhns)

a harsh and disagreeable combination, especially of sounds

*Cognitive **dissonance** is the inner conflict produced when long-standing beliefs are contradicted by new evidence.*

Synonyms: clash, contention, discord

DISTAFF
noun (<u>dis</u> taf)

the female branch of a family

*The lazy husband refused to cook dinner for his wife, joking that the duty belongs to the **distaff's** side.*

• • •

DISTANT
adjective (<u>dis</u> tent)

separate, far apart

*Last summer, Chantalle visited her **distant** relatives in France.*

Synonyms: remote, isolated

• • •

DISTEND
verb (dih <u>stehnd</u>)

to swell, inflate, bloat

*Her stomach **distended** after she gorged on the six-course meal.*

Synonyms: broaden, bulge

D

DISTINCTIVE

adjective (dis <u>tink</u> tiv)

distinguishing characteristic

*Paul's piercing blue eyes are his most **distinctive** feature.*

Synonym: unique

. . .

DISTORTION

noun (dis <u>tor</u> shun)

misrepresentation, the act of twisting out of shape

*Shanna told Chantalle that her ugly haircut looked awesome, which was a major **distortion** of the truth.*

Synonyms: warp, deformation

. . .

DISTRACT

verb (dis <u>trakt</u>)

to cause to lose focus, to divert attention

*Timmy tried studying in a coffee shop, but the noise **distracted** him and he couldn't concentrate.*

Synonyms: sidetrack, engross

DITHER

verb (<u>dihth</u> uhr)

to act indecisively

*Ellen **dithered** around her apartment, uncertain how to tackle the family crisis.*

Synonyms: falter, hesitate, vacillate, waffle, waver

. . .

DIURNAL

adjective (die <u>uhr</u> nuhl)

daily

***Diurnal** creatures tend to become inactive during the night.*

Synonyms: daylight, daytime

. . .

DIVERT

verb (di <u>vurt</u>)

to turn aside, to distract

*Shanna slipped unseen into her bedroom after curfew, while her sister **diverted** her mom's attention.*

Synonyms: redirect, deflect

DIVINATION

noun (div uh _nay_ shin)

foretelling the future using supernatural means

Marisol thought it would be fun to use **_divination_** _to predict whether or not she'd get a date for the dance, so she pulled out her Ouija board._

Synonyms: prediction, forecast

• • •

DIVINE

verb (dih _vien_)

to foretell or know by inspiration

The fortune-teller **_divined_** _from the pattern of the tea leaves that her customer would marry five times._

Synonyms: auger, foresee, intuit, predict, presage

• • •

DIVISIVE

adjective (dih _vie_ sihv) (dih _vih_ sihv) (dih _vih_ zihv)

creating disunity or conflict

The leader used **_divisive_** _tactics to pit his enemies against each other._

Synonyms: controversial, disruptive, sensitive

DIVULGE

verb (di _vulj_)

to make known

Paul was embarrassed when Marisol walked by just as he was **_divulging_** _to his friend his secret crush on her._

Synonyms: reveal, disclose

• • •

DOCTRINAIRE

adjective (dahk truh _nayr_)

rigidly devoted to theories without regard for practicality, dogmatic

The professor's manner of teaching was considered **_doctrinaire_** _for such a liberal school._

Synonyms: inflexible, dictatorial

• • •

DOGGED

adjective (_daw_ guhd)

stubbornly persevering

The police inspector's **_dogged_** _determination helped him catch the thief._

Synonyms: tenacious, obstinate

D

D

DOGMA
noun (<u>dahg</u> muh) (<u>dawg</u> muh)

a firmly held opinion, especially a religious belief

*Linus's central **dogma** was that children who believed in The Great Pumpkin would be rewarded.*

Synonyms: creed, doctrines, teaching, tenet

. . .

DOGMATIC
adjective (dahg <u>maat</u> ihk) (dawg <u>maat</u> ihk)

rigidly fixed in opinion, opinionated

*The dictator was **dogmatic**—he, and only he, was right.*

Synonyms: authoritative, doctrinaire, inflexible, obstinate

. . .

DOLEFUL
adjective (<u>dohl</u> fuhl)

sad, mournful

*Looking into the **doleful** eyes of the lonely pony, the girl decided to take him home with her.*

Synonyms: dejected, woeful

DOMINANT
adjective (<u>dom</u> uh nent)

most prominent, exercising the most control

*The **dominant** reason for the track star winning the 100-meter dash was not her talent, but her extreme competitiveness.*

Synonyms: leading, main

. . .

DOUR
adjective (<u>doo</u> uhr) (<u>dow</u> uhr)

sullen and gloomy, stern and severe

*The **dour** hotel concierge demanded payment for the room in advance.*

Synonyms: austere, strict, grave

. . .

DRAB
adjective (<u>jrab</u>)

faded, dull, dreary

*Marisol thought her living room walls were a bit **drab**, so she painted them bright pink—a gesture her parents did not appreciate.*

Synonyms: plain, dingy

DRAWBACK
noun (jraw back)

disadvantage, inconvenience

*Timmy thought the fact that he was really scrawny was another **drawback** he didn't want to deal with, so he decided to start working out.*

Synonyms: **downside, shortcoming**

. . .

DROLL
adjective (drohl)

amusing in a wry, subtle way

*Although the play couldn't be described as hilarious, it was certainly **droll**.*

Synonyms: **comic, entertaining, funny, risible, witty**

. . .

DROUGHT
noun (jrowt)

long period of abnormally low rainfall

*Willow saved her sunflowers from the **drought** by watering them three times a day.*

Synonyms: **lack, famine**

DRUB
verb (jrub)

defeat soundly, beat

*The crowd went crazy as Josh stole the football and made a touchdown, **drubbing** the visiting team in the last minutes of the game.*

Synonyms: **hammer, whip**

. . .

DUAL
adjective (doo ul)

having two parts, double

*Some say that Chantalle has a **dual** personality because she's really nice some days and not so nice other days.*

Synonyms: **twin, twofold**

. . .

DUBIOUS
adjective (doo bee iss)

arousing doubt, doubtful

*The teacher knew that George's excuse about a dog eating his homework was **dubious**, but gave him an extra day to hand it in anyway.*

Synonyms: **uncertain, unsure**

DULCET
adjective (<u>duhl</u> suht)

pleasant sounding, soothing to the ear

*The **dulcet** tone of her voice lulled me to sleep.*

Synonyms: agreeable, harmonious, melodious, sweet

. . .

DUPE
verb (doop)

to deceive or a person who is easily deceived

*Bugs Bunny was able to **dupe** Elmer Fudd by dressing up as a lady rabbit.*

Synonyms: beguile, betray, bluff

. . .

DUPLICATE
noun (<u>doo</u> plih kit)

an exact copy

*Timmy made a **duplicate** of his home-work assignment just in case a bully stole his on the way to school.*

Synonyms: replacement, spare

DUPLICITY
noun (doo <u>pliss</u> ih tee)

deception, dishonesty, double-dealing

*Ashley was engaging in an act of **duplicity** when she told Shanna she didn't think Derek was hot ... because she does.*

Synonyms: deceit, disloyalty

. . .

DURATION
noun (doo <u>ray</u> shun)

period of time that something lasts

*After Timmy got slammed in the face with a volleyball during gym, the teacher allowed him to spend the **duration** of the class in the nurse's office.*

Synonyms: length, extent

. . .

DURESS
noun (duhr <u>ehs</u>)

threat of force or intimidation, imprisonment

*Under **duress**, the political dissident revealed the names of others in her organization to the secret police.*

Synonyms: coercion, compulsion, constraint, pressure

DYSPEPTIC
adjective (dihs <u>pehp</u> tihk)

suffering from indigestion, gloomy and irritable

*The **dyspeptic** young man cast a gloom over the party the minute he walked in.*

Synonyms: melancholy, morose, solemn, sour

EBB
verb (ehb)

to fade away, recede

*From her beachside cottage, Melissa **enjoyed** watching the tide ebb and flow.*

Synonyms: abate, retreat, subside, wane, withdraw

. . .

EBULLIENT
adjective (<u>ih</u> byool yuhnt) (<u>ih</u> buhl yuhnt)

exhilarated, full of enthusiasm and high spirits

*The **ebullient** child exhausted the baby-sitter, who lacked the energy to keep up with her.*

Synonyms: ardent, avid, bubbly, zestful

ECCENTRIC
adjective (ek <u>sen</u> trik)

abnormal, unconventional

*Some say that Marisol is a bit **eccentric** because sometimes she likes to paint with her own hair.*

Synonyms: unusual, peculiar

. . .

ECLECTIC
adjective (ee <u>klek</u> tik)

made up of elements from different sources

*Chantalle's closet was an **eclectic** array of clothing, including pieces inspired by the 1980s to the present.*

Synonyms: assorted, miscellaneous

ECSTASY
noun (<u>ek</u> stuh see)

intense joy or delight

*George was filled with **ecstasy** as he participated in a test at the sleep disorder research center—they were actually paying him to sleep!*

Synonyms: elation, bliss

· · ·

ECSTATIC
adjective (ek <u>stat</u> ik)

joyful

*Ashley was **ecstatic** when the captain of the football team asked her out in front of the whole senior class.*

Synonyms: delighted, thrill

· · ·

EDICT
noun (<u>ee</u> dihkt)

law, command, official public order

*Pedestrians often disobey the **edict** that they should not jaywalk.*

Synonyms: decree, dictum, directive, fiat, ukase

EDIFY
verb (<u>eh</u> duh fie)

to instruct morally and spiritually

*The guru was paid to **edify** the actress in the ways of Buddhism.*

Synonyms: enlighten, educate, guide, teach

· · ·

EFFACE
verb (ih <u>fays</u>) (eh <u>fays</u>)

to erase or make illegible

*Benjamin attempted to **efface** all traces of his troubled past by assuming a completely new identity.*

Synonyms: expunge, obliterate

· · ·

EFFICACIOUS
adjective (ef ih <u>kay</u> shus)

effective, efficient

*Shanna's **efficacious** study system helped her ace the test.*

Synonyms: effectual, successful

EFFICACY

noun (<u>eh</u> fih kuh see)

effectiveness

The efficacy of penicillin was unsurpassed when it was first introduced, completely eliminating almost all bacterial infections.

Synonyms: dynamism, effectiveness, efficiency, force

• • •

EFFICIENT

adjective (ee <u>fish</u> int)

effective with a minimum of unnecessary effort or waste

Timmy liked to eat his corn on the cob in an efficient manner by neatly chomping off one row at a time.

Synonyms: resourceful, proficient

• • •

EFFIGY

noun (<u>eh</u> fuh jee)

stuffed doll, likeness of a person

The anti-American militants burned Uncle Sam in effigy during their demonstration.

Synonyms: dummy, figure, image

EFFLUVIA

noun (ih <u>floo</u> vee uh)

waste, odorous fumes given off by waste

He took out the garbage at 3 AM because the effluvia had begun wafting into the bedroom.

Synonyms: odor, stench

• • •

EFFRONTERY

noun (ih <u>fruhnt</u> uhr ee) (eh <u>fruhnt</u> uhr ee)

impudent boldness, audacity

The receptionist had the effrontery to laugh out loud when the CEO tripped over a computer wire and fell flat on his face.

Synonyms: brashness, gall, nerve, presumption, temerity

• • •

EFFUSIVE

adjective (ih <u>fyoo</u> sihv) (eh <u>fyoo</u> sihv) (eh <u>fyoo</u> zihv)

expressing emotion without restraint

The teacher's praise for Brian's brilliant essays was effusive.

Synonyms: gushy, overflowing, profuse

EGOTIST
noun (<u>ee</u> go tist)

self-entered person

*Everybody knew that Chantalle was an **egotist**, but nobody could believe it when she spent three hours talking about getting her legs waxed.*

Synonyms: **boaster, braggart**

• • •

EGREGIOUS
adjective (ih <u>gree</u> juhs)

conspicuously bad

*The English textbook contained several **egregious** errors, for example, "grammar" was misspelled as "gramer" throughout.*

Synonyms: **blatant, flagrant, glaring, gross, rank**

• • •

EGRESS
noun (<u>ee</u> grehs)

exit

*Commuter trains should have points of convenient **egress** so that during rush hour, passengers can leave the train easily.*

Synonym: **outlet**

ELATE
verb (ee <u>layt</u>)

to make joyful

*Timmy was **elated** when he found out he got into every Ivy League school he applied to.*

Synonyms: **excite, thrill**

• • •

ELEGY
noun (<u>eh</u> luh jee)

a mournful poem, usually about the dead

*A memorable **elegy** was read aloud for the spiritual leader.*

Synonyms: **memorial, lament**

• • •

ELEVATED
adjective (<u>el</u> uh vay tid)

raised, increased

*Ashley felt an **elevated** sense of nervousness when she picked up the phone to call her crush.*

Synonyms: **prominent, high**

ELIMINATE
verb (ee <u>lim</u> uh)

get rid of, remove

*Paul **eliminated** all the wrong answers to the test question before he chose the correct one.*

• • •

ELOCUTIONIST
noun (el oh <u>q</u> shun ist)

trained public speaker

*It was evident that Shanna was the real **elocutionist** in the class-presidential race and that her opponent was a sputtering mess.*

• • •

ELOQUENT
adjective (<u>el</u> uh kwent)

strongly expressing emotion

*Paul gave an **eloquent** speech in his English class about his grandmother and how she led him to volunteer in a senior citizens' center.*

Synonyms: feeling, passion

ELUCIDATE
verb (ih <u>loo</u> suh dayt)

to explain, clarify

*The teacher **elucidated** the reasons why she had failed the student to his upset parents.*

Synonyms: define, explicate, illuminate, interpret

• • •

ELUDE
verb (ih <u>lood</u>)

to avoid cleverly, to escape the perception of

*Somehow, the runaway **eluded** detection for weeks.*

Synonyms: evade, dodge

• • •

ELUSIVE
adjective (ee <u>loo</u> siv)

tending to evade

*Timmy gripped his camera as he hid in the woods, determined to prove that the **elusive** Big Foot was not a myth.*

Synonyms: indefinable, hard to pin down

EMBELLISH
verb (em <u>bell</u> ish)

to ornament, make attractive with decorations or details, add details to a statement

*Marisol **embellished** the walls of her room with a string of lights shaped like hot chili peppers.*

Synonyms: over-stated, larger-than-life

• • •

EMBEZZLE
verb (em <u>bez</u> ul)

to steal money in violation of a trust

*Shanna was surprised to uncover that the school board had **embezzled** thousands of dollars from the library fund and used it for a "business trip" to the Bahamas.*

Synonyms: filch, misappropriate

• • •

EMBITTERED
adjective (em <u>bit</u> urd)

resentful, cynical

*Willow found herself **embittered** after she put so much work into her "leather shoes stink" rally at school, and no one showed up.*

Synonyms: bitter, sour

EMEND
verb (ee <u>mend</u>)

to correct a text

*George had to **emend** the incorrect price tags he stamped on the canned peas because the cost was $.50, not $.05.*

Synonyms: alter, revise

• • •

EMIGRATE
verb (<u>em</u> ih grayt)

to leave one country to live in another

*As soon as she graduates college, Marisol plans to **emigrate** from America to live in Italy.*

Synonyms: move abroad, live elsewhere

• • •

EMISSARY
noun (<u>em</u> ih ser ee)

an agent sent as a representative

*Chantalle sent her **emissary**, Shanna, to tell the cute guy at the other end of the food court that Chantalle wanted his phone number.*

Synonyms: envoy, messenger

E

EMOLLIENT
adjective (ih <u>mohl</u> yuhnt)

soothing, especially to the skin

*After being out in the sun for so long, the **emollient** cream was a welcome relief on my skin.*

Synonyms: softening, mollifying

. . .

EMPATHY
noun (<u>em</u> puh thee)

identification with the feelings of others

*Having been bullied himself, Timmy felt a strong **empathy** for the little kid who was being pushed around on the playground.*

Synonyms: sympathy, compassion

. . .

EMPHATIC
adjective (em <u>fat</u> ik)

forceful and definite

*When Josh was asked if he wanted to meet his favorite professional basketball player, he answered with an **emphatic** "Yes!"*

Synonyms: vigorous, absolute

EMULATE
verb (<u>ehm</u> yuh layt)

to strive to equal or excel, to imitate

*Children often **emulate** their parents.*

Synonyms: follow, mimic

. . .

ENCHANT
verb (en <u>chant</u>)

attract and delight

*Paul was **enchanted** by the total hotness of the new girl who had entered his chemistry class, and quickly made room for her to sit next to him.*

Synonyms: charm, captivate

. . .

ENCOMIUM
noun (ehn <u>koh</u> me uhm)

warm praise

*Georgias's **"Encomium** to Helen" was written as a tribute to Helen of Troy.*

Synonyms: citation, eulogy, panegyric, salutation, tribute

ENCOMPASS

verb (en com pass)

to constitute, include

*Ashley taught the new cheerleaders the Flip-Flop cheer, which **encompassed** everything from basic back flips to a perfect "perma-grin."*

Synonym: encircle

. . .

ENCROACH

verb (en kroch)

to infringe, intrude upon

*George and Paul went to the movies together, but sat a few seats apart to avoid **encroaching** on each other's snack space.*

Synonyms: creep, inch, worm

. . .

ENCUMBER

verb (ehn kuhm buhr)

to weigh down, to burden

*She brought only her laptop to the cabin, where she wrote **unencumbered** by the distractions of the city.*

Synonym: hamper

ENDEMIC

adjective (ehn deh mihk)

belonging to a particular area, inherent

*The health department determined that the outbreak was **endemic** to the small village, so they quarantined the inhabitants before the virus could spread.*

Synonyms: indigenous, local, native

. . .

ENDORSE

verb (en dorss)

to give approval to, sanction

*Remarkably, the principal **endorsed** Shanna's idea for Senior Cut Day.*

Synonyms: support, back

. . .

ENDURANCE

noun (en door)

ability to withstand hardships

*It's tough being on the bottom of the cheerleader pyramid, so Ashley builds her **endurance** by balancing a sack of potatoes on her back for one hour each day.*

Synonyms: survival, stamina

ENDURE
verb (en <u>door</u>)

carry on despite hardships

*Derek could not **endure** for one more second the boring chamber music concert his parents dragged him to, so he left.*

Synonyms: bear, tolerate

• • •

ENDURING
adjective (en <u>door</u> ing)

lasting, continuing

*The enormous statue standing in the courtyard is an **enduring** reminder of the school's founder ... as well as a popular resting spot for pigeons.*

Synonyms: stable, long-term

• • •

ENERVATE
verb (<u>en</u> er vayt)

to weaken, drain strength from

*George told his mom that he was too tired to take out the garbage because playing video games for three hours had **enervated** him.*

Synonyms: lethargic, lacking energy

ENFORCE
verb (en <u>fors</u>)

to compel others to adhere or observe

*Chantalle **enforced** her authority as "Queen Bee" by having the girls in her clique hang out at the mall with her every Tuesday.*

Synonyms: implement, put in force

• • •

ENFRANCHISE
verb (en <u>fran</u> chiz)

set free

*Willow couldn't wait to become **enfranchised** so she could vote in the next election for the politicians who supported environmental issues.*

Synonyms: emancipate, empower

• • •

ENGENDER
verb (ehn <u>gehn</u> duhr)

to produce, cause, or bring about

*His fear and hatred of clowns was **engendered** when he witnessed a bank robbery carried out by five men wearing clown suits and make up.*

Synonyms: beget, generate, proliferate

ENHANCE
verb (in hanss)

to improve, bring to a greater level of intensity

*Chantalle **enhanced** her almond-shaped eyes with two coats of mascara.*

Synonyms: augment, add to

. . .

ENIGMA
noun (ih nig muh)

a puzzle, a mystery

*Speaking in riddles and dressed in old robes, the artist gained a reputation as something of an **enigma**.*

Synonyms: conundrum, perplexity

. . .

ENIGMATIC
adjective (en ig mat ik)

puzzling

*Paul asked out the cute blonde, but her response was so **enigmatic**, he wasn't sure if they had a date or not.*

Synonyms: mysterious, unknowable

ENJOIN
verb (ehn joyn)

to direct or impose with urgent appeal, to order with emphasis, to forbid

*Patel is **enjoined** by his culture from eating the flesh of a cow, which is sacred in India.*

Synonyms: instruct, charge

. . .

ENMITY
noun (EN mi tee)

hostility, antagonism, ill will

*Chantalle couldn't believe the **enmity** she felt toward her best friend, Shanna, when Shanna asked out a guy that Chantalle liked.*

Synonyms: hate, bad feeling

. . .

ENNUI
noun (ahn wee) (ahn wee)

boredom, lack of interest and energy

*Joe tried to alleviate the **ennui** he felt while doing his tedious job by shopping online.*

Synonyms: listlessness, tedium, world-weariness

ENSCONCE
verb (ehn <u>skahns</u>)

to settle comfortably into a place

*Wayne sold the big, old family house and **ensconced** his aged mother in a cozy little cottage.*

Synonym: settle

• • •

ENSEMBLE
noun (on <u>som</u> bul)

group of parts that contribute to a whole single effect

*Marisol put together an **ensemble** to wear to her school's art show that was part disco fabulous and part hippie chic.*

Synonyms: collection, as one

• • •

ENTANGLE
verb (en <u>tang</u> ul)

to complicate, entwine into a confusing mass, involve in

*Derek **entangled** himself in a lunchroom argument to try to break it up, but in the end, everyone thought that he was the one who started it.*

Synonyms: snare, entrap

ENTREAT
verb (ehn <u>treet</u>)

to plead, beg

*I **entreated** him to just tell me what the problem was instead of bottling it up inside, but he refused.*

Synonyms: beseech, implore, importune, petition, request

• • •

ENUMERATE
verb (ih <u>noo</u> muhr ayt)

to count, list, itemize

*Before making his decision, Jacob asked the waiter to **enumerate** the different varieties of ice cream that the restaurant carried.*

Synonyms: catalog, index, tabulate

• • •

EPHEMERAL
adjective (ih <u>fehm</u> uhr uhl)

momentary, transient, fleeting

*The lives of mayflies seem **ephemeral** to us, because the flies' average life span is a matter of hours.*

Synonyms: evanescent, fugitive, momentary, transitory

EPICURE
noun (<u>eh</u> pih kyoor) (<u>eh</u> pih kyuhr)

a person with refined taste in cuisine

*Restaurant critics should be **epicures**, as people rely on their judgments in choosing where to eat.*

Synonyms: connoisseur, gastronome, gourmand, gourmet

• • •

EPIGRAM
noun (<u>eh</u> puh graam)

short, witty saying or poem

*The poet was renowned for his skill in making up amusing **epigrams**.*

Synonyms: adage, aphorism, maxim, saw

• • •

EPILOGUE
noun (<u>ep</u> uh log)

concluding section of a literary work

*Paul couldn't wait to find out what happened to the characters in the book, so he skipped to the end, read the **epilogue**, and spoiled the surprise.*

Synonyms: conclusion, ending

EPISTOLARY
noun (eh <u>pis</u> tuh ler ee)

associated with letter writing

*Even though **epistolary** discourses are a thing of the past, Marisol thinks it's romantic to correspond with boyfriends through letters.*

• • •

EPITAPH
noun (<u>eh</u> pih taf)

engraving on a tombstone, literary piece for a dead person

*Although she didn't know him well, Willow wrote an extensive **epitaph** for the caterpillar she accidentally squashed on the way to school.*

• • •

EPOCHAL
adjective (<u>ehp</u> uh kuhl) (ehp <u>ahk</u> uhl)

momentous, highly significant

*The Supreme Court's **epochal** decision will no doubt affect generations to come.*

Synonyms: unparalleled, notable

EPONYMOUS
adjective (ih pahn uh muhs)

giving one's name to a place, book, restaurant

*Macbeth was the **eponymous** protagonist of Shakespeare's play.*

Synonyms: named after

• • •

EQUANIMITY
noun (ee kwuh nihm ih tee) (ehk wuh nihm ih tee)

calmness, composure

*Kelly took the news that she had been fired with outward **equanimity**, though she was crying inside.*

Synonyms: aplomb, coolness, poise

• • •

EQUITABLE
adjective (eh kwi tuh bul)

fair, just and impartial

*Ashley could come up with only one **equitable** solution for the two football players who were fighting over her. She would date them both.*

Synonyms: reasonable, unbiased

EQUIVOCATE
verb (ih kwihv uh kayt)

to avoid committing oneself in what one says, to be deliberately unclear

*Not wanting to implicate himself in the crime, the suspect **equivocated** for hours.*

Synonyms: lie, mislead

• • •

ERADICATE
verb (ee rad ih kayt)

to erase or wipe out

*Paul wished trigonometry could be **eradicated**, so he would never have to study for another test.*

Synonyms: annihilate, demolish

• • •

ERASURE
noun (ee ray shur)

the act or instance of erasing

*Timmy swore his name wasn't on the guest list due to an accidental **erasure**, but that still didn't get him into the party.*

Synonyms: removal, crossing out

EROSION
noun (ee <u>row</u> zhin)

the process or condition of wearing away

*Shanna joined Willow in the fight to save the beaches from **erosion** because if she didn't, she might not have a place to wear her bikini in a few years.*

Synonyms: corrosion, wearing down

. . .

ERRATIC
adjective (ee <u>rat</u> ik)

unpredictable, inconsistent

*Paul made his friends laugh with his **erratic** movements on the dance floor.*

Synonyms: unreliable, irregular

. . .

ERRONEOUSLY
adverb (ee <u>rown</u> ee us lee)

mistakenly, inaccurately

*Shanna apologized when she **erroneously** accused her little sister of taking her favorite Diggity Dawgz CD.*

Synonyms: incorrectly, wrongly

ERSATZ
adjective (uhr <u>sahtz</u>)

being an artificial and inferior substitute or imitation

*The **ersatz** strawberry shortcake tasted more like plastic than like real cake.*

Synonyms: fake, counterfeit

. . .

ERUDITE
adjective (<u>ehr</u> yuh diet) (ehr uh diet)

learned, scholarly

*The annual meeting of professors brought together the most **erudite** individuals in the field.*

Synonyms: cultured, educated, knowledgeable, literate, well-read

. . .

ESCHEW
verb (ehs <u>choo</u>)

to shun, to avoid (as something wrong or distasteful)

*The filmmaker **eschewed** artifical light for her actors, resulting in a stark movie style.*

Synonyms: evade, escape

ESOTERIC

adjective (eh suh <u>tehr</u> ihk)

understood by only a learned few

*Only a handful of experts are knowledgeable about the **esoteric** world of particle physics.*

Synonyms: arcane, mysterious, occult, recondite, secret

. . .

ESPOUSE

verb (ih <u>spowz</u>)

to take up and support as a cause, to marry

*Because of his religious beliefs, the preacher could not **espouse** the use of capital punishment.*

Synonyms: champion, adopt

. . .

ESPY

verb (ehs <u>peye</u>)

to catch sight of, glimpse

*Amidst a crowd in black clothing, she **espied** the colorful dress that her friend was wearing.*

Synonym: discern

ESSENTIAL

noun (<u>e</u> sen shul)

something fundamental or indispensable

*Josh is a little embarrassed that he still needs his teddy bear, but it's **essential** for a good night's sleep.*

Synonyms: necessary, vital

. . .

ESTIMABLE

adjective (<u>eh</u> stuh muh buhl)

admirable

*Most people consider it **estimable** that Mother Teresa spent her life helping the poor of India.*

Synonyms: admirable, commendable

. . .

ETHEREAL

adjective (ih <u>theer</u> ee uhl)

not earthly, spiritual, delicate

*Her delicate, **ethereal** beauty made her a popular model for pre-Raphaelite artists.*

Synonyms: airy, diaphanous, gossamer, intangible, sheer

ETHICAL

adjective (<u>eth</u> ih kul)

moral, right-minded

*George knew it wasn't **ethical** to peek at the test answers on the teacher's desk ... so he looked at only one answer.*

Synonyms: principled, decent

. . .

ETHOS

noun (<u>ee</u> thohs)

beliefs or character of a group

*In accordance with the **ethos** of his people, the man completed the tasks that would allow him to become the new chief.*

Synonym: sentiment

. . .

EULOGY

noun (<u>yoo</u> luh jee)

high praise for a person who has died

*Timmy wrote a **eulogy** for his dog, Marbles, who had been with the family for fourteen years.*

Synonyms: tribute, acclamation

EUPHEMISM

noun (<u>yoo</u> fuh mihz uhm)

an inoffensive expression that is substituted for one that is considered offensive

*The funeral director preferred to use the **euphemism** "passed away" instead of the word "dead."*

Synonyms: delicacy, floridness

. . .

EUPHONY

noun (<u>yoo</u> fuh nee)

pleasant, harmonious sound

*To their loving parents, the children's orchestra performance sounded like **euphony**, although an outside observer probably would have called it a cacophony of hideous sounds.*

Synonyms: harmony, melody, music, sweetness

. . .

EUPHORIA

noun (yoo <u>for</u> ee uh)

a great feeling of happiness or well-being

*Derek was overcome with **euphoria** when an agent saw his band's show and told them that he'd make them stars.*

Synonyms: jubilation, rapture

EUTHANASIA
noun (yoo thun <u>nay</u> zhuh)

the practice of ending the life of hope-lessly ill individuals, assisted suicide

Euthanasia has always been the topic of much moral debate.

Synonym: mercy-killing

. . .

EVADE
verb (ee <u>vayd</u>)

to avoid, dodge

*When George's parents asked him how he did on his science test, he **evaded** the question as best he could before admitting that he had gotten a C-.*

Synonym: escape

. . .

EVALUATE
verb (ee <u>val</u> yoo ayt)

to examine or judge carefully

*The English teacher told the class that she would **evaluate** the students' essays based on tone, grammar, and content.*

Synonyms: assess, appraise

EVANESCENT
adjective (eh vuh <u>nehs</u> uhnt)

momentary, transitory, short-lived

*It is lucky that solar eclipses are **evanescent**, or the world would never see sunlight.*

Synonyms: ephemeral, fleeting, fugitive, transient

. . .

EVAPORATE
verb (ee <u>vap</u> uh rayt)

to vanish quickly

*Timmy's smile **evaporated** when he realized that the crowd was not laughing with him, but at him.*

Synonyms: fade away, disperse

. . .

EVENHANDED
adjective (ee ven <u>hand</u> id)

fair, impartial

*Ashley thought she could be **evenhanded** when picking girls for the cheerleading team, but she wound up choosing all of her friends instead.*

Synonyms: unbiased, neutral

EVINCE

verb (ih vihns)

to show clearly, display, signify

*The new secretary **evinced** impressive typing and filing skills.*

Synonym: demonstrate

• • •

EXACERBATE

verb (ihg zaas uhr bayt)

to aggravate, intensify the bad qualities of

*It is unwise to take aspirin to relieve heartburn, instead of providing relief, the drug will only **exacerbate** the problem.*

Synonyms: deepen, escalate, worsen

• • •

EXACTING

adjective (eg zak ting)

requiring a lot of care or attention

*Dating Chantalle is an **exacting** task because if you give her too much or too little attention, she'll drop you like a hot potato.*

Synonyms: demanding, challenging

EXAGGERATE

verb (eg zaj uh rayt)

to represent something as greater than it actually is

*George stubbed his toe and **exaggerated** the pain he was feeling so that his girlfriend would rub his feet.*

Synonyms: overstated, embellished

• • •

EXALT

verb (eg zalt)

to glorify or honor

*"We're the best!" Ashley cheered, **exalting** the soccer team who, until their last game, hadn't won all year.*

Synonyms: praise, applaud

• • •

EXASPERATION

noun (eg zas pe ray shun)

irritation

*Josh, unable to hide his **exasperation** at his team's fumbling the football, yelled at the coach to put him in the game.*

Synonyms: frustration, annoyance

EXCEPTION
noun (ek <u>sep</u> shun)

a case that doesn't conform to a generalization

*With the **exception** of I Love My Puppy, all of the band Snakebite's alternative rock songs are about overcoming the many injustices in the world.*

Synonyms: exemption, omission

. . .

EXCLUDE
verb (ek <u>sklood</u>)

to prevent from being accepted or included

*Timmy knew he was a bit nerdy at times, but that was no reason to **exclude** him from the cool group ... was it?*

Synonyms: keep out, prohibit

. . .

EXCORIATE
verb (ehk <u>skohr</u> ee ayt)

to censure scathingly, to express strong disapproval of

*The three-page letter to the editor **excoriated** the publication for printing the rumor without verifying the source.*

Synonym: denounce

EXCULPATE
verb (<u>ehk</u> skuhl payt) (ihk <u>skuhl</u> payt)

to clear of blame or fault, vindicate

*The legal system is intended to convict those who are guilty and to **exculpate** those who are innocent.*

Synonyms: acquit, exonerate

. . .

EXCURSION
noun (ek <u>skuhr</u> zhen)

short journey, usually for pleasure

*Shanna accompanied Chantalle on her **excursion** to the mall even though Shanna had already spent her allowance for that week.*

Synonyms: outing, jaunt

. . .

EXECRABLE
adjective (<u>ehk</u> sih kruh buhl)

utterly detestable, abhorrent

*The stew tasted **execrable** after the cook accidentally dumped a pound of salt into it.*

Synonyms: awful, hateful, horrible, inferior, terrible

EXEMPLARY
adjective (egg <u>zem</u> pluh ree)

outstanding, an example to others

*The teacher told the unruly students that Paul's **exemplary** behavior was something to learn from. Of course, she hadn't seen Paul throw the paper airplane across the room five minutes earlier.*

Synonyms: excellent, commendable

• • •

EXEMPLIFY
verb (eg <u>zemp</u> lih fi)

to show by example

*Josh used Timmy's boxer shorts to **exemplify** the precise way of stringing underwear up a flagpole.*

Synonyms: demonstrate, illustrate

• • •

EXHORT
verb (ihg <u>zohrt</u>)

to urge or incite by strong appeals

*Rob's friends **exhorted** him to beware of ice on the roads when he insisted on driving home in the middle of a snowstorm.*

Synonyms: convince, inspire, press, prod, provoke

EXHORTATION
noun (eg zor <u>tay</u> shun)

speech that advises or pleads

*Willow's **exhortation** did not get the kids to help the plight of the dung beetle, but it did result in students putting beetles in her locker.*

Synonyms: catchphrase, refrain

• • •

EXHUME
verb (ihg <u>zoom</u>) (ihg <u>zyoom</u>) (ihk <u>syoom</u>) (ehks <u>hyoom</u>)

to remove from a grave, uncover a secret

*The archaeologist **exhumed** the scrolls from the ancient tomb.*

Synonyms: disinter, unearth

• • •

EXIGENT
adjective (<u>ehk</u> suh juhnt)

urgent, excessively demanding

*The tank was losing gasoline so rapidly that it was **exigent** to stop the source of the leak.*

Synonyms: compelling, critical, crucial, imperative, pressing

EXONERATE
verb (ihg <u>zahn</u> uh rayt)

to clear of blame, absolve

*The fugitive was **exonerated** when another criminal confessed to committing the crime.*

Synonyms: acquit, exculpate, vindicate

• • •

EXORBITANT
adjective (eg <u>zorb</u> ih tant)

extravagant, greater than reasonable

*Because of the **exorbitant** prices of oil-based paints, Marisol decided to switch to watercolors.*

Synonyms: excessive, very expensive

• • •

EXPEDIENT
adjective (ihk <u>spee</u> dee uhnt)

convenient, efficient, practical

*It was considered more **expedient** to send the fruit directly to the retailer instead of through a middleman.*

Synonyms: appropriate, sensible, useful

EXPEDITE
verb (<u>ek</u> spe diyt)

to speed up the progress of

*Derek would not sacrifice the quality of his band's music just to **expedite** the release of their first single.*

Synonyms: accelerate, advance

• • •

EXPERTISE
adjective (ek spur <u>teez</u>)

skill or knowledge in a particular area

*Timmy called the talk-radio show to show off his **expertise** on that morning's topic: extraterrestrials.*

Synonyms: capability, proficiency

• • •

EXPIATE
verb (<u>ehk</u> spee ayt)

to atone for, make amends for

*The nun **expiated** her sins by scrubbing the floor of the convent on her hands and knees.*

Synonyms: answer, compensate, pay

EXPLANATORY
adjective (ek splan uh tor ee)

serving to make clear

*George's parents sent his school an **explanatory** note about his absence.*

Synonyms: elucidative, expository, illuminative

• • •

EXPLICIT
adjective (ehk splih siht)

clearly stated or shown, forthright in expression

*In Reading Comprehension, questions that ask directly about a detail in the passage are sometimes called **Explicit** Text questions.*

Synonyms: candid, clear-cut, definite, definitive, express

• • •

EXPLOIT
verb (ek sployt)

take advantage of

*Chantalle **exploited** her friendship with Paul by getting him to do her math homework for her.*

Synonyms: abuse, use

EXPONENT
noun (ehk spoh nuhnt)

one who champions or advocates

*The vice president was an enthusiastic **exponent** of computer technology.*

Synonyms: supporter, representative

• • •

EXPOUND
verb (ihk spownd)

to explain or describe in detail

*The teacher **expounded** on the theory of relativity for hours.*

Synonyms: elucidate, elaborate

• • •

EXPROPRIATE
verb (ek spro pree ayt)

forcibly take one's property

*Josh **expropriated** Timmy's seat in the lunchroom by sitting in his chair.*

Synonym: confiscate

EXPUNGE
verb (ihk <u>spuhnj</u>)

to erase, eliminate completely

*The parents' association **expunged** the questionable texts from the children's reading list.*

Synonyms: delete, obliterate

. . .

EXPURGATE
verb (<u>ehk</u> spuhr gayt)

to censor

*Government propagandists **expurgated** all negative references to the dictator from the film.*

Synonyms: bowdlerize, cut, sanitize

. . .

EXTANT
adjective (<u>ek</u> stant)

still in existence

*Chantalle was horrified when she discovered that pictures of her with braces were **extant**.*

Synonyms: existent, existing, living

EXTEMPORANEOUS
adjective (ihk stehm puh <u>ray</u> nee uhs)

unrehearsed, on the spur of the moment

*Jan gave an **extemporaneous** performance of a Monty Python skit at her surprise birthday party.*

Synonyms: impromptu, spontaneous, unprepared

. . .

EXTENSIVE
adjective (ek <u>sten</u> siv)

large in range, comprehensive

*Chantalle yawned when her mom gave her a long and **extensive** lecture.*

Synonyms: broad, expansive

. . .

EXTENUATING
adjective (ek <u>sten</u> yoo ayt ing)

partially excusing

*Despite **extenuating** circumstances, Shanna was grounded for missing curfew.*

Synonym: palliate

EXTERMINATE
verb (ek <u>stur</u> mu nayt)

destroy completely

*The hero single-handedly **exterminated** the bad guys in the movie.*

Synonym: annihilate

· · ·

EXTERNAL
adjective (ek <u>stur</u> nel)

exterior, outer part

*Paul liked Marisol not only because of her **external** beauty, but because she was beautiful inside as well.*

Synonym: outer

· · ·

EXTIRPATE
verb (<u>ehk</u> stuhr payt)

to root out, eradicate, literally or figuratively, to destroy wholly

*The terrorist cells were **extirpated** after many years of investigation.*

Synonym: wipe out

EXTOL
verb (ek <u>stol</u>)

to praise

*The art teacher **extolled** Marisol's brilliant painting.*

Synonyms: glorify, laud

· · ·

EXTRAPOLATION
verb (ihk <u>strap</u> uh lay shuhn)

using known data and information to determine what will happen in the future, prediction

*Through the process of **extrapolation**, we were able to determine which mutual funds to invest in.*

Synonyms: projection, forecast

· · ·

EXTRAVAGANT
adjective (ek <u>strav</u> uh gent)

unreasonably high, exorbitant

*Josh preferred a nice juicy burger to the **extravagant** meals his parents enjoyed.*

Synonym: excessive

EXTREME
adjective (ek <u>streem</u>)

very intense, of the greatest severity

*Paul wondered if offering the principal some trick gum was a little **extreme**, but he did it anyway.*

Synonyms: furthest, outermost

• • •

EXTRICATE
verb (<u>ehk</u> strih kayt)

to free from, disentangle

*The fly was unable to **extricate** itself from the flypaper.*

Synonyms: disencumber, disengage, release, untangle

• • •

EXTRINSIC
adjective (ihk <u>strihn</u> sihk)
(ihk <u>strihn</u> zihk)

external, unessential, originating from the outside

"Though they are interesting to note," the meeting manager claimed, *"those facts are **extrinsic** to the matter under discussion."*

Synonyms: extraneous, foreign

EXTROVERTED
adjective (<u>ek</u> stro ver tid)

outgoing, easily talks to others

*Shanna was elected class president because she was the most **extroverted** candidate.*

Synonym: convivial

• • •

EXTRUDE
verb (ihk <u>strood</u>)

to form or shape something by pushing it out, to force out, especially through a small opening

*We watched in awe as the volcano **extruded** molten lava.*

Synonyms: squeeze out

• • •

EXULTANT
adjective (eg <u>zul</u> tent)

triumphant

*Timmy cheered, **exultant**, after finally getting the bully to leave him alone.*

Synonyms: jubilant, rejoicing

FABRICATED
adjective (fab rih <u>kay</u> tid)

constructed, invented

*George **fabricated** an excuse for missing choir practice.*

Synonyms: faked, falsified

• • •

FAÇADE
noun (fuh <u>sod</u>)

front, superficial appearance

*Timmy put on a **facade** of not caring if the popular crowd liked him.*

Synonyms: face, mask

• • •

FACETIOUS
adjective (fuh <u>see</u> shuhs)

witty, humorous

*Her **facetious** remarks made the uninteresting meeting more lively.*

Synonyms: amusing, comical

FACILE
adjective (<u>faa</u> suhl)

easily accomplished, seeming to lack sincerity or depth, arrived at without due effort

*Given the complexity of the problem, it seemed a rather **facile** solution.*

Synonyms: effortless, superficial

• • •

FACTUAL
adjective (fak choo ul)

real

*The teacher had a hunch that Timmy had cheated, but she did not have any **factual** evidence.*

Synonyms: objective, true

FALLACIOUS
adjective (fuh <u>lay</u> shuhs)

tending to deceive or mislead, based on a fallacy

*The **fallacious** statement "the Earth is flat" misled people for many years.*

Synonyms: false, erroneous

· · ·

FALLOW
adjective (<u>faa</u> loh)

uncultivated, unused

*This field should lie **fallow** for a year so that the soil does not become completely depleted.*

Synonyms: idle, inactive, unseeded

· · ·

FALSIFY
verb (<u>fal</u> sih fiy)

misrepresent, state untruthfully

*George considered **falsifying** the D on his report card by changing it to a B.*

Synonyms: distort, misinterpret, misrepresent

FANATICAL
adjective (fuh <u>nah</u> tih kuhl)

acting excessively enthusiastic, filled with extreme, unquestioned devotion

*The stormtroopers were **fanatical** in their devotion to the Emperor, readily sacrificing their lives for him.*

Synonyms: extremist, fiery, frenzied, zealous

· · ·

FANFARE
noun (<u>fan</u> fayr)

a showy public display

*Josh enjoyed the **fanfare** the football team received at the start of every game.*

· · ·

FASTIDIOUS
adjective (faa <u>stihd</u> ee uhs) (fuh <u>stihd</u> ee uhs)

careful with details

*Brett was normally so **fastidious** that Rachel was astonished to find his desk littered with clutter.*

Synonyms: meticulous, painstaking, precise, punctilious, scrupulous

FATHOM
verb (<u>fah</u> thom)

penetrate the meaning of

*Chantalle could not **fathom** why her mom wore her hair in a beehive.*

Synonym: comprehend

. . .

FATUOUS
adjective (<u>faach</u> oo uhs)

stupid, foolishly self-satisfied

*Ted's **fatuous** comments always embarrassed his keen-witted wife.*

Synonyms: absurd, ludicrous, preposterous, ridiculous, silly

. . .

FAVORITISM
noun (fav uh rih tizm)

partiality to one side

*The teacher clearly showed **favoritism** for the girls in the class.*

Synonym: one-sidedness

FAWN
verb (fahn)

to grovel

*The understudy **fawned** over the director in hopes of being cast in the part on a permanent basis.*

Synonyms: bootlick, grovel, pander, toady

. . .

FEBRILE
adjective (<u>fehb</u> ruhl) (<u>fee</u> bruhl)

feverish, marked by intense emotion or activity

*Awaiting the mysterious announcement, there was a **febrile** excitement in the crowd.*

Synonyms: agitated, flushed

. . .

FECKLESS
adjective (<u>fehk</u> lihs)

ineffective, worthless

*Anja took on the responsibility of caring for her aged mother, realizing that her **feckless** sister was not up to the task.*

Synonym: incompetent

FECUND

adjective (<u>fee</u> kuhn) (<u>fehk</u> uhnd)

fertile, fruitful, productive

*The **fecund** woman gave birth to a total of twenty children.*

Synonyms: flourishing, prolific

. . .

FEIGN

verb (fayn)

to pretend, to give a false appearance of

*Though she had discovered they were planning a party, she **feigned** surprise so as not to spoil the festivities.*

Synonym: fake

. . .

FELICITOUS

adjective (fih <u>lihs</u> ih tuhs)

suitable, appropriate, well spoken

*The father of bride made a **felicitous** speech at the wedding, contributing to the success of the event.*

Synonym: fitting

FERAL

adjective (<u>fehr</u> uhl)

suggestive of a wild beast, not domesticated

*Though the animal-rights activists did not want to see the **feral** dogs harmed, they offered no solution to the problem.*

Synonyms: wild, savage

. . .

FERTILE

adjective (<u>fir</u> tul)

highly productive, prolific

*Willow's whimsical art is a direct result of her **fertile** imagination.*

Synonyms: fruitful, luxuriant, productive

. . .

FERVID

adjective (<u>fuhr</u> vihd

passionate, intense, zealous

*The fans of Maria Callas were particularly **fervid**, doing anything to catch a glimpse of the great singer.*

Synonyms: ardent, avid, eager, enthusiastic, vehement

FETID
adjective (<u>feh</u> tihd)

foul-smelling, putrid

*The **fetid** stench from the outhouse caused Laura to wrinkle her nose in disgust.*

Synonyms: funky, malodorous, noisome, rank, stinky

• • •

FETTER
verb (<u>feh</u> tuhr)

to bind, chain, confine

*Lorna **fettered** the bikes together so that it was less likely that they would be stolen.*

Synonyms: curb, handcuff, manacle, shackle, tether

• • •

FICKLE
adjective (<u>fik</u> ul)

erratically unstable about affections

*Chantalle is **fickle** when it comes to choosing just the right clothing.*

Synonyms: capricious, inconstant

FICTIVE
adjective (<u>fihk</u> tihv)

fictional, relating to imaginative creation

*She found she was more productive when writing **fictive** stories rather than autobiography.*

Synonyms: not genuine

• • •

FIDELITY
noun (fih <u>del</u> ih tee)

loyalty, faithfulness

*Shanna relied on her little sister's **fidelity** to back her excuses for being late.*

Synonyms: allegiance, constancy, dedication

• • •

FIGURATIVE
adjective (<u>fig</u> ur uh tiv)

symbolic

*Shanna told Timmy that she'd date him "when pigs fly," which is a **figurative** way of saying "never."*

Synonym: metaphorical

FILIBUSTER
verb (<u>fihl</u> ih buhs tuhr)

to use obstructionist tactics, especially prolonged speech making, in order to delay something

*The congressman read names from the phonebook in an attempt to **filibuster** a pending bill.*

Synonym: stall

• • •

FINITE
adjective (<u>fi</u> niyt)

having bounds

*Timmy learned that six was the **finite** number of days he could eat chicken in a row before getting sick of it.*

Synonym: limited

• • •

FIREBRAND
noun (<u>fiyr</u> brand)

one who stirs up trouble

*Derek is considered a **firebrand** because of his blue mohawk.*

Synonym: agitator

FISSION
noun (<u>fish</u> in)

process of splitting into two parts

*Timmy stared at the amoeba, going through the process of **fission**, through his microscope.*

Synonyms: dividing, parting

• • •

FITFUL
adjective (<u>fiht</u> fuhl)

intermittent, lacking steadiness, characterized by irregular bursts of activity

*Her **fitful** breathing became cause for concern, and eventually, she phoned the doctor.*

Synonyms: sporadic, periodic

• • •

FLABBERGAST
verb (<u>flab</u> ur gast)

astound

*Shanna was **flabbergasted** when her parents gave her a car for her birthday.*

Synonym: surprise

FLACCID
adjective (<u>flaa</u> sihd)

limp, flabby, weak

*The woman jiggled her **flaccid** arms in disgust, resolving to begin lifting weights as soon as possible.*

Synonyms: floppy, soft

• • •

FLAG
verb (flaag)

to decline in vigor, strength, or interest

*The marathon runner slowed down as his strength **flagged**.*

Synonyms: dwindle, ebb, slacken, subside, wane

• • •

FLAGRANT
adjective (<u>flay</u> grent)

outrageous, shameless

*The couple's **flagrant** display of affection in the hallway led to a trip to detention.*

Synonym: egregious

FLANK
verb (<u>flank</u>)

to put on the sides of

*Ashley smiled to her friends who were **flanking** the school hallway as she walked past.*

Synonym: adjoin

• • •

FLAUNT
verb (<u>flawnt</u>)

to show off

*Timmy **flaunted** the gold medal that he won in the Academic Olympics.*

Synonyms: display, disport, exhibit

• • •

FLAW
noun (<u>flaw</u>)

imperfection, defect

*John thought the birthmark on his cheek was a **flaw**, but Marisol saw it as a work of art on a blank canvas.*

Synonym: blemish

FLEE
verb (flee)

run away from

*The kids **fled** the house party when the police arrived at the door.*

Synonym: escape

. . .

FLIPPANCY
adjective (flip an see)

casualness, inappropriate pertness

*Ashley couldn't stand the **flippancy** of the other cheerleaders.*

Synonym: frivolity

. . .

FLIPPANT
adjective (flihp uhnt)

marked by disrespectful lighthearted-ness or casualness

*Her **flippant** response was unacceptable and she was asked again to explain herself.*

Synonyms: pert, disrespectful

FLORID
adjective (flohr ihd) (flahr ihd)

gaudy, extremely ornate, ruddy, flushed

*The palace had been decorated in an excessively **florid** style, every surface had been carved and gilded.*

Synonyms: flamboyant, garish, loud, ornate, ostentatious

. . .

FLOURISH
verb (flur ish)

prosper, thrive

*Shanna's academic career was **flourishing** and she hoped to do well in college.*

Synonym: succeed

. . .

FLOUT
verb (flowt)

to scorn, to disregard with contempt

*The protestors **flouted** the committee's decision and hoped to sway public opinion.*

Synonyms: mock, sneer, spurn

FODDER
noun (<u>fohd</u> uhr)

raw material, as for artistic creation, readily abundant ideas or images

*The governor's hilarious blunder was good **fodder** for the comedian.*

Synonym: resources

• • •

FOIBLE
noun (<u>foy</u> buhl)

minor weakness or character flaw

*Her habit of always arriving late is just a **foible**, although it is somewhat rude.*

Synonyms: blemish, failing, fault, frailty, vice

• • •

FOIL
noun (<u>foyl</u>)

something used to contrast with something else

*George's stomach churned when his boss said that his **foil** was the new employee of the month.*

Synonym: opposite

FOMENT
verb (foh <u>mehnt</u>)

*The protesters tried to **foment** feeling against the war through their speeches and demonstrations.*

Synonyms: abet, instigate, promote

• • •

FORBEARANCE
noun (fohr <u>baar</u> uhns)

patience, restraint, leniency

*Collette decided to exercise **forbearance** with her assistant's numerous errors in light of the fact that he was new on the job.*

Synonyms: long-suffering, resignation, tolerance

• • •

FORD
verb (fohrd)

to cross a body of water by wading

*Because of the recent torrential rains, the cowboys were unable to **ford** the swollen river.*

Synonyms: traverse, wade

FOREGO
verb (fohr <u>goh</u>)

to precede, to go ahead of

*Because of the risks of the expedition, the team leader made sure to **forego** the climbers.*

Synonyms: antedate, predate

. . .

FORESHADOW
verb (<u>for</u> shah dow)

to indicate beforehand

*Shanna hoped her landslide election as senior class president **foreshadowed** her future political career.*

Synonym: prefigure

. . .

FORESTALL
verb (fohr <u>stahl</u>)

to prevent, delay, anticipate

*The landlord **forestalled** T.J.'s attempt to avoid paying the rent by waiting for him outside his door.*

Synonyms: avert, deter, hinder, obviate, preclude

FORGE
verb (forj)

to advance gradually but steadily

*Although she was tired, Willow **forged** through the rest of her workout.*

Synonym: proceed

. . .

FORGERY
noun (<u>forj</u> uh ree)

something counterfeit or fraudulent, pertaining to a document

*Chantalle refused to commit **forgery** by signing her mother's name on her report card.*

Synonym: fake

. . .

FORGO
verb (fohr <u>goh</u>)

to do without, to abstain from

*As much as I wanted to **forgo** statistics, I knew it would serve me well in my field of study.*

Synonym: pass on

FORLORN

adjective (for lorn)

dreary, deserted, unhappy

*Derek felt **forlorn** at the prospect of telling his band that his agent wanted him to go solo.*

Synonyms: hopeless, depressing

. . .

FORMIDABLE

adjective (fohr mih duh buhl) (fohr mih duh buhl)

fearsome, daunting, tending to inspire awe or wonder

*The wrestler was not very big, but his skill and speed made him a **formidable** opponent.*

Synonym: overpowering

. . .

FORSWEAR

verb (fohr swayr)

to repudiate, renounce, disclaim, reject

*I was forced to **forswear** french fries after the doctor told me that my cholesterol was too high.*

Synonym: abjure

FORTE

noun (fohr tay)

strong point, something a person does well

*Because math was Dan's **forte**, his friends always asked him to calculate the bill whenever they went out to dinner together.*

Synonyms: métier, specialty

. . .

FORTITUDE

noun (fohr tih tood)

strength of mind that allows one to encounter adversity with courage

*Months in the trenches exacted great **fortitude** of the soldiers.*

Synonyms: endurance, courage

. . .

FORTUITOUS

adjective (fohr too ih tuhs)

by chance, especially by favorable chance

*After a **fortuitous** run-in with an agent, Roxy was offered a recording contract.*

Synonym: accidental

FORUM
noun (<u>for</u> um)

public place for discussion, a public discussion

*Shanna, the class president, held an open **forum** in the auditorium to discuss student issues.*

Synonyms: assembly, conclave, congregation

• • •

FOUNDER
verb (<u>fown</u> duhr)

to fall helplessly, to sink

*After colliding with the jagged rock, the ship **foundered**, forcing the crew to abandon it.*

Synonyms: immerse, miscarry, plunge

• • •

FRACAS
noun (<u>fraak</u> uhs) (<u>fray</u> kuhs)

noisy dispute

*When the players discovered that the other team was cheating, a violent **fracas** ensued.*

Synonyms: brawl, broil, donnybrook, fray, melee

FRACTIOUS
adjective (<u>fraak</u> shuhs)

unruly, rebellious

*The general had a hard time maintaining discipline among his **fractious** troops.*

Synonyms: contentious, cranky, peevish, quarrelsome

• • •

FRAUD
noun (<u>frawd</u>)

deception, hoax

*Ashley felt like a total **fraud** in chorus class when she couldn't remember the words to the song.*

Synonyms: imposter, phony

• • •

FRENETIC
adjective (freh <u>neht</u> ihk)

frantic, frenzied

*The employee's **frenetic** schedule left him little time to socialize.*

Synonym: feverish

FRIVOLOUS
adjective (friv uh luss)

petty, trivial

*Willow's parents think that her new hairstyle and clothes are part of a **frivolous** phase.*

Synonyms: flippant, silly

. . .

FROLICSOME
adjective (frol ik sum)

frisky, playful

*The first snowfall of the season put George in a **frolicsome** mood.*

Synonym: exuberant

. . .

FRUGAL
adjective (froo gul)

thrifty, cheap

*Ashley is **frugal** when it comes to lip gloss and buys the cheapest brand on the market.*

Synonyms: economical, sparing

FRUGALITY
noun (fru gaa luh tee)

tending to be thrifty or cheap

*Scrooge McDuck's **frugality** was so great that he accumulated enough wealth to fill a giant storehouse with money.*

Synonyms: economical, parsimony

. . .

FULSOME
adjective (fool suhm)

abundant, flattering in an insincere way

*The king's servant showered him with **fulsome** compliments in hopes of currying favor.*

Synonyms: overdone, extravagant

. . .

FUNDAMENTAL
adjective (fun da men tul)

basic, essential

*Marisol learned that one of the **fundamental** rules of art is that there are no rules.*

Synonym: elementary

FURLOUGH
noun (<u>fuhr</u> loh)

a leave of absence, especially granted to soldier or a prisoner

After seeing months of combat, the soldier received a much-deserved furlough.

Synonym: time off

• • •

FURTIVE
adjective (<u>fuhr</u> tihv)

sly, with hidden motives

The furtive glances they exchanged made me suspect they were up to something.

Synonyms: secret, surreptitious

FUTILE
adjective (<u>fyoo</u> tiyl)

useless, hopeless

George realized that studying further for his Spanish test was futile, so he decided to play video games instead.

Synonyms: fruitless, ineffectual

GALVANIZE

verb (<u>gaal</u> vuh niez)

to shock, to arouse awareness

*The closing down of another homeless shelter **galvanized** the activist group into taking political action.*

Synonyms: vitalize, energize

• • •

GAMBOL

verb (<u>gaam</u> buhl)

to arouse or incite

to dance or skip around playfully

*The parents gathered to watch the children **gambol** about the yard.*

Synonym: frolic

GAMELY

adjective (<u>gaym</u> lee)

spiritedly, bravely

*The park ranger **gamely** navigated the trail up the steepest face of the mountain.*

Synonym: excitedly

• • •

GARGANTUAN

adjective (gar <u>gan</u> shoo in)

giant, enormous

*Chantalle needs a **gargantuan** closet to store all of her shoes in.*

Synonym: tremendous

• • •

GARISH

adjective (<u>gah</u> rish)

gaudy, glaring

*Marisol loved the **garish** candelabra that she bought at the flea market.*

Synonyms: flamboyant, flashy

149

GARNER
verb (<u>gahr</u> nuhr)

to gather and store

*The director managed to **garner** financial backing from several different sources for her next project.*

Synonyms: amass, acquire, glean, harvest, reap

• • •

GARRULOUS
adjective (<u>gaar</u> uh luhs) (<u>gaar</u> yuh luhs)

very talkative

*The **garrulous** parakeet distracted its owner with its continuous talking.*

Synonyms: chatty, loquacious, prolix, verbose, voluble

• • •

GAUCHE
adjective (gohsh)

lacking social refinement

*Snapping one's fingers to get the waiter's attention is considered **gauche**.*

Synonyms: tactless, simple

GENERALIZE
verb (<u>jen</u> er uh liyz)

reduce to a general form

*Chantalle is clearly **generalizing** when she says that all jocks are stupid.*

• • •

GENIAL
adjective (<u>jeen</u> yul)

pleasant, friendly

*Ashley's **genial** manner often rubs off on the people around her.*

Synonym: gracious

• • •

GESTATION
noun (jeh <u>stay</u> shuhn)

growth process from conception to birth

*The longer the **gestation** period of an organism, the more developed the baby is at birth.*

Synonyms: development, gravidity, pregnancy

GIBBER

verb (ji buhr)

prattle unintelligibly

*Ashley's baby cousin **gibbered** happily whenever Ashley picked him up.*

Synonym: babble

• • •

GIBE

verb (jieb)

to make heckling, taunting remarks

*Tina **gibed** at her brothers mercilessly as they clumsily attempted to pitch the tent.*

Synonyms: deride, jeer, mock, ridicule, twit

• • •

GLACIER

noun (glay sher)

slow-moving, large mass of ice

*Willow's family went to Alaska to get a close-up look at the enormous **glaciers**.*

Synonym: iceberg

GLIB

adjective (glihb)

fluent in an insincere manner, offhand, casual

*The slimy politician managed to continue gaining supporters because he was a **glib** speaker.*

Synonyms: easy, superficial

• • •

GLOSSY

adjective (glaw see)

shiny, showy

*Josh was psyched when his dad tossed him the keys to his **glossy** red sports car.*

Synonym: sleek

• • •

GLOWER

verb (glow uhr)

to glare, stare angrily and intensely

*The cranky waitress **glowered** at the indecisive customer.*

Synonyms: frown, scowl

G

GLUTTON
noun (glut in)

person who eats and drinks excessively

It was well known that George was a **glutton,** *but thirteen cupcakes was a lot of food even for him to eat.*

Synonyms: gorger, overeater

. . .

GOAD
verb (gohd)

to prod or urge

Denise **goaded** *her sister Leigh into running the marathon with her.*

Synonyms: impel, incite, provoke, rouse, stimulate

. . .

GOURMAND
noun (goor mond)

lover of fine food

Marisol thought her date was a **gourmand** *when he took her to a fancy French restaurant.*

Synonyms: glutton, epicure

GRACIOUS
adjective (gray shus)

kind, compassionate, warm-hearted, courteous

Ashley was quite **gracious** *when the huge football player accidentally stepped on her foot.*

Synonyms: affable, cordial, genial

. . .

GRADATION
noun (gray day shuhn)

process occurring by regular degrees or stages, variation in color

The paint store offers so many different **gradations** *of red that it's impossible to choose among them.*

Synonyms: nuance, shade, step, subtlety

. . .

GRANDILOQUENCE
noun (graan dihl uh kwuhns)

pompous talk, fancy but meaningless language

The headmistress was notorious for her **grandiloquence** *at the lectern and her ostentatious clothes.*

Synonyms: bravado, pretension

GRANDIOSE
adjective (<u>gran</u> dee ohss)

magnificent and imposing, exaggerated

*Paul made a **grandiose** gesture of pulling out Marisol's chair for her when she came into the classroom.*

Synonyms: pretentious, grand

. . .

GRATIS
adjective (<u>grah</u> tihs) (<u>gray</u> tihs)

free, costing nothing

*The college students swarmed around the **gratis** buffet in the lobby.*

Synonyms: complimentary, costless

. . .

GRATUITY
noun (<u>gruh</u> too ih tee)

something given voluntarily

*The bellboy expected a **gratuity** for dragging Derek's luggage up six flights of stairs.*

Synonyms: bonus, tip

GRAVITY
adjective (<u>grah</u> vih tee)

importance, seriousness

*It took only one stern look from the state trooper for Josh to realize the **gravity** of his situation.*

Synonym: earnestness

. . .

GREGARIOUS
adjective (greh <u>gaar</u> ee uhs)

outgoing, sociable

*Unlike her introverted friends, Susan was very **gregarious**.*

Synonyms: convivial, friendly

. . .

GRIEVOUS
adjective (<u>gree</u> vuhs)

causing grief or sorrow, serious and distressing

*Maude and Bertha sobbed loudly throughout the **grievous** event.*

Synonyms: dire, dolorous, grave, mournful

G

GROTTO
noun (grah toh)

a small cave

*Alone on the island, Philoctetes sought shelter in a **grotto**.*

Synonyms: cavern, recess, burrow

• • •

GROVE
noun (grohv)

a group of trees

*Willow loves to lie under the trees in the apple **grove** and contemplate life.*

• • •

GROVEL
verb (grah vuhl)

to humble oneself in a demeaning way

*Thor **groveled** to his ex-girlfriend, hoping she would take him back.*

Synonyms: bootlick, cringe, fawn, kowtow, toady

GRUDGINGLY
adverb (grudj ing lee)

reluctantly

*Marisol **grudgingly** agreed to be in the school fashion show.*

Synonym: resentfully

• • •

GRUFF
adjective (gruff)

brusque, stern, harsh

*Josh was terrified of his father's **gruff** voice.*

Synonym: grim

• • •

GUILE
noun (gie uhl)

trickery, deception

*Greg used considerable **guile** to acquire his rent-controlled apartment, even claiming to be a Vietnam Vet.*

Synonyms: artifice, cunning, duplicity, wiliness

GULLIBLE

adjective (<u>guh</u> luh buhl)

easily deceived

*The con man pretended to be a bank officer so as to fool **gullible** bank customers into giving him their account information.*

Synonyms: credulous, exploitable, naïve

GUSTATORY

adjective (<u>goos</u> tuh tohr ee)

relating to sense of taste

*Murdock claimed that he loved cooking because he enjoyed the **gustatory** pleasures in life.*

Synonym: culinary

HACKNEYED
adjective (<u>haak</u> need)

worn out by overuse

We always mock my father for his **hackneyed** *expressions and dated hairstyle.*

Synonyms: banal, shopworn, stale, trite

• • •

HALLMARK
noun (<u>haul</u> mark)

specific feature, characteristc

A cheery disposition and gymnastic ability are two **hallmarks** *of a great cheerleader.*

Synonym: emblem

HAPLESS
adjective (<u>haap</u> luhs)

unfortunate, having bad luck

I wish someone would give that poor, **hapless** *soul some food and shelter.*

Synonyms: ill-fated, ill-starred, luck-less, jinxed, unlucky

• • •

HARANGUE
verb (huh <u>raang</u>)

to give a long speech

Maria's parents **harangued** *her when she told them she'd spent her money on magic beans.*

Synonyms: lecture, reprimand

HARASS
verb (hu <u>rass</u>)

to irritate

*Timmy **harassed** his parents until they finally agreed to buy him a microscope.*

Synonym: torment

. . .

HARBINGER
noun (<u>haar</u> buhn juhr)

precursor, sign of something to come

*The groundhog's appearance on February 2 is a **harbinger** of spring.*

Synonyms: forerunner, herald, omen, presage

. . .

HARROWING
adjective (<u>haa</u> roh ng)

extremely distressing, terrifying

*We stayed up all night listening to Dave and Will talk about their **harrowing** adventures at sea.*

Synonyms: tormenting, vexing

HAUGHTY
adjective (<u>haw</u> tee)

arrogant and condescending

*George did not like the **haughty** attitude that Chantalle was giving him.*

Synonyms: lofty, pompous

. . .

HAZARDOUS
adjective (<u>ha</u> zer duss)

risky, perilous

*Willow panicked when she spotted **hazardous** waste materials in the school stairwell.*

Synonym: dangerous

. . .

HECKLER
noun (hek ler)

someone who tries to embarrass and annoy others

*During her speech to the students, Shanna silenced a **heckler** in the audience.*

Synonym: tormenter

HEDONISM
noun (<u>hee</u> doh nizm)

pursuit of pleasure as a goal

*Chantalle spent six hours getting pampered at a spa, calling it her day of **hedonism**.*

Synonym: debauchery

• • •

HEDONIST
noun (<u>hee</u> duhn ihst)

one who pursues pleasure as a goal

*Michelle, an admitted **hedonist**, lays on the couch eating cookies every Saturday.*

Synonyms: pleasure-seeker, glutton

• • •

HEED
verb (<u>heed</u>)

pay attention to

*Paul chose to **heed** the officer's advice and drive at the speed limit.*

Synonyms: mind, note, observe

HEGEMONY
noun (hih <u>jeh</u> muh nee)

the domination of one state or group over its allies

*When Germany claimed **hegemony** over Russia, Stalin was outraged.*

Synonyms: power, authority

• • •

HEINOUS
adjective (<u>hay</u> nes)

shocking, wicked

*Everyone thought Josh's constant teasing of Timmy was completely **heinous**.*

Synonym: terrible

• • •

HERETICAL
adjective (huh <u>reh</u> tih kuhl)

departing from accepted beliefs or standards, oppositional

*At the onset of the Inquisition, the **heretical** priest was forced to flee the country.*

Synonym: unorthodox

HERMETIC
adjective (huhr meh tihk)

tightly sealed

The hermetic seal of the jar proved impossible to break.

Synonyms: airtight, impervious, watertight

. . .

HESITANT
adjective (he zih tent)

doubtful, reluctant

Marisol was hesitant to discuss the details of her next big art project.

Synonyms: afraid, disinclined, dubious

. . .

HETEROGENEOUS
adjective (heh tuh ruh jee nee uhs) (he truh jee nyuhs)

composed of unlike parts, different, diverse

The United Nations is by nature a heterogeneous body.

Synonyms: assorted, miscellaneous, mixed, motley, varied

HIATUS
noun (hie ay tuhs)

a gap or interruption in space, time, or continuity

After a long hiatus in Greece, the philosophy professor returned to the university.

Synonym: break

. . .

HIDEBOUND
adjective (hied bownd)

excessively rigid, dry and stiff

The hidebound old patriarch would not tolerate any opposition to his orders.

Synonyms: conservative, inflexible

. . .

HIERARCHY
noun (hiyr ar kee)

ranking system of authority groups

As senior class president, Shanna is at the top of the student government hierarchy.

Synonyms: echelons, position

HINDRANCE
noun (<u>hin</u> drins)

impediment, clog, stumbling block

*Timmy faints at the sight of blood, which could be a **hindrance** if he wants to become a doctor someday.*

Synonyms: obstacle, encumbrance

. . .

HINDSIGHT
noun (<u>hiynd</u> siyt)

perception of events after they happen

*In **hindsight**, Paul realized that you should never talk about people behind their backs.*

Synonym: recollection

. . .

HINTERLAND
noun (<u>hihn</u> tuhr laand)

wilderness

The anthropologists noticed that the people had moved out of the cities and into the ***hinterland***.

Synonyms: backcountry, frontier

HISTRIONICS
noun (hihs tree <u>ahn</u> ihks)

deliberate display of emotion for effect, exaggerated behavior calculated for effect

*With such **histrionics**, she should really consider becoming an actress.*

Synonyms: melodrama, theatrics

. . .

HOARY
adjective (<u>hohr</u> ee) (<u>haw</u> ree)

very old, whitish or gray from age

*The old man's **hoary** beard contrasted starkly to the new stubble of his teenage grandson.*

Synonyms: ancient, antediluvian, antique, vernerable, vintage

. . .

HODGEPODGE
noun (<u>hoj</u> poj)

jumble, mixture of assorted objects

*Marisol pasted a **hodgepodge** of momentos onto her collage.*

Synonyms: assortment, medley

HOIST
verb (<u>hoyst</u>)

lift, raise

*Josh was **hoisted** into the air by his teammates after hitting the winning home run.*

Synonyms: boost, elevate

• • •

HOMOGENOUS
adjective (huh mah juhn uhs)

of a similar kind

*The class was fairly **homogenous** because almost all of the students were journalism majors.*

Synonyms: consistent, standardized, uniform, unvarying

• • •

HUBRIS
noun (<u>hyoo</u> brihs)

excessive pride or self-confidence

*Nathan's **hubris** spurred him to do things that many considered insensitive.*

Synonyms: presumption, arrogance

HUMANE
adjective (hyoo <u>mayn</u>)

merciful, kind

*When Willow found a puppy at her doorstep, she did the **humane** thing and found its owner.*

Synonyms: compassionate, benevolent

• • •

HUSBAND
verb (<u>huhz</u> buhnd)

to manage economically, to use sparingly

*The cyclist paced herself at the start of the race, knowing that if she **husbanded** her resources she'd have the strength to break out of the pack later on.*

Synonym: conserve

• • •

HYPERBOLE
noun (hie <u>puhr</u> boh lee)

purposeful exaggeration for effect

*When the mayor claimed his town was one of the seven wonders of the world, outsiders classified his statement as **hyperbole**.*

Synonyms: embellishment, inflation, magnification

HYPOCRISY

noun (hih <u>pok</u> rih see)

claiming of beliefs that one doesn't really possess

*Willow considered it **hypocrisy** when students said they cared about animals, but continued to eat meat.*

Synonyms: insincerity, sanctimoniousness

. . .

HYPOCRITE

noun (<u>hih</u> puh kriht)

one who puts on a false appearance of virtue, one who criticizes a flaw he in fact possesses

*What a **hypocrite**: He criticizes those who wear fur but then he buys for himself a leather shearling coat.*

Synonyms: pretender, deceiver

HYPOTHESIS

noun (hi <u>poth</u> a siss)

an assumption requiring proof

*Timmy's **hypothesis** about bullies is that they need to put people down to feel good about themselves.*

Synonym: theory

ICONOCLAST
noun (ie <u>kahn</u> uh klaast)

one who attacks traditional beliefs

*His lack of regard for traditional beliefs soon established him as an **iconoclast**.*

Synonyms: dissident, nonconformist, rebel

• • •

IDEALIST
noun (iy <u>deel</u> ist)

someone that is unrealistic and impractical in their beliefs

*The reason that Willow pursues so many causes is that she is an **idealist**.*

Synonyms: dreamer, visionary

IDIOSYNCRASY
noun (ih dee uh <u>sihn</u> kruh see)

peculiarity of temperament, eccentricity

*His numerous **idiosyncrasies** included a fondness for wearing bright green shoes with mauve socks.*

Synonyms: humor, oddity, quirk

• • •

IGNOBLE
adjective (ihg <u>noh</u> buhl)

having low moral standards, not noble in character, mean

*The photographer was paid a princely sum for the picture of the self-proclaimed ethicist in the **ignoble** act of pick-pocketing.*

Synonyms: lowly, vulgar

IGNOMINIOUS
adjective (ihg nuh <u>mih</u> nee uhs)

disgraceful and dishonorable

*He was humiliated by his **ignominious** dismissal.*

Synonyms: debasing, degrading, despicable

• • •

ILK
noun (ihlk)

type or kind

*"I try not to associate with men of his **ilk**," sniffed the respectable old lady.*

Synonyms: character, class, nature, sort, variety

• • •

ILLEGIBLE
adjective (ih <u>lej</u> ih bul)

unreadable

*Ashley appreciated George lending her his notes, but unfortunately his handwriting was **illegible** and she couldn't figure out what he had written.*

Synonym: undecipherable

ILLUMINATE
verb (il <u>loom</u> ih nayt)

fill with light

*Timmy's imitation Star Wars light saber **illuminated** his room when he switched it on.*

Synonym: irradiate

• • •

ILLUSORY
adjective (ih <u>loo</u> suhr ee) (ih <u>loos</u> ree)

producing illusion, deceptive

*The desert explorer was devastated to discover that the lake he thought he had seen was in fact **illusory**.*

Synonyms: false, imaginary

• • •

ILLUSTRATE
verb (<u>il</u> uh strayt)

provide an example, explain

*George's mom used the videotape of her son watching television to **illustrate** the point that he was a couch potato.*

Synonyms: demonstrate, exemplify, instance

IMBIBE
verb (ihm <u>bieb</u>)

to receive into the mind and take in, absorb

*If I always attend class, I can **imbibe** as much knowledge as possible.*

Synonym: absorb

. . .

IMBUE
verb (ihm <u>byoo</u>)

to infuse, to dye, wet, moisten

*Marcia struggled to **imbue** her children with decent values, a difficult task in this day and age.*

Synonyms: charge, freight, impregnate, permeate, pervade

. . .

IMITATE
verb (im ih <u>tayt</u>)

copy, impersonate

*Knock-off designers often **imitate** the popular designs of expensive brands.*

Synonyms: ape, emulate, mime

IMMODERATE
adjective (im <u>mod</u> ih rit)

excessive

*Ashley's mother did not approve of the **immoderate** amount of soda her daughter drank.*

Synonyms: inordinate, exorbitant

. . .

IMMUNITY
noun (im <u>myoo</u> ni tee)

invulnerability, exemption

*The principal had offered Toby **immunity** from punishment if he told him who helped him trash the boy's bathroom.*

Synonym: impunity

. . .

IMMUTABLE
adjective (ihm <u>myoot</u> uh buhl)

unchangeable, invariable

*Poverty was an **immutable** fact of life for the unfortunate Wood family, every moneymaking scheme they tried failed.*

Synonyms: fixed, permanent, stationary, steady

I

IMPASSE

noun (ihm <u>paas</u>) (ihm <u>pass</u>)

blocked path, dilemma with no solution

*The rock slide produced an **impasse**, so no one could proceed further on the road.*

Synonyms: cul-de-sac, deadlock, stalemate

. . .

IMPASSIONED

adjective (im <u>pash</u> ind)

with great feeling

*Shanna made an **impassioned** plea to the principal to use school funds to fix the bleachers.*

Synonym: fervent

. . .

IMPASSIVE

adjective (ihm <u>pahs</u> sihv)

absent of any external sign of emotion, expressionless

*Given his **impassive** expression, it was hard to tell whether he approved of my plan.*

Synonyms: apathetic, unemotional

IMPECUNIOUS

adjective (ihm pih <u>kyoo</u> nyuhs) (ihm pih <u>kyoo</u> nee uhs)

poor, having no money

*After the crash of thousands of tech startups, many Internet millionaires found themselves **impecunious**.*

Synonyms: destitute, impoverished, indigent, needy, penniless

. . .

IMPENITENT

adjective (im <u>pen</u> ih tent)

not remorseful

*Shanna's **impenitent** behavior for missing curfew, yet again, outraged her parents and she was grounded for three weeks.*

Synonym: unrepentant

. . .

IMPERCEPTIBLE

adjective (im per <u>sep</u> ti buhl)

subtle, difficult to perceive

*Even though her burp was almost **imperceptible**, Ashley felt mortified for doing it in front of her friends.*

Synonyms: impalpable, inappreciable

IMPERIOUS
adjective (ihm <u>pihr</u> ee uhs)

commanding, domineering, urgent

*Though the king had been a kind leader, his daughter was **imperious** and demanding during her rule.*

Synonym: authoritarian

. . .

IMPERTURBABLE
adjective (<u>ihm</u> puhr <u>tuhr</u> buh buhl)

unshakably calm and steady

*No matter how disruptive the children became, the babysitter remained **imperturbable**.*

Synonyms: cool, unflappable

. . .

IMPERVIOUS
adjective (ihm <u>puhr</u> vee uhs)

impossible to penetrate, incapable of being affected

*A good raincoat should be **impervious** to moisture.*

Synonyms: callous, immune

IMPETUOUS
adjective (ihm <u>peh</u> choo uhs) (ihm <u>pehch</u> wuhs)

quick to act without thinking

*The **impetuous** day trader rushed to sell his stocks at the first hint of trouble, and lost $300,000.*

Synonyms: impulsive, passionate

. . .

IMPIOUS
adjective (<u>ihm</u> pee uhs)(ihm <u>pie</u> uhs)

not devout in religion

*The nun cut herself off from her **impious** family after she entered the convent.*

Synonyms: immoral, irreverent, profane

. . .

IMPLACABLE
adjective (ihm <u>play</u> kuh buhl) (ihm <u>plaa</u> kuh buhl)

inflexible, not capable of being changed or pacified

*The **implacable** teasing was hard for the child to take.*

Synonyms: merciless, relentless

IMPLAUSIBLE
adjective (im <u>plaw</u> zuh bul)

improbable, inconceivable

*Although Timmy tried to prove he was abducted by aliens, his friends found the story highly **implausible**.*

Synonym: incredible

• • •

IMPLEMENT
verb (<u>imp</u> luh ment)

carry out, put into effect

*Chantalle was thrilled when her parents decided to **implement** a higher allowance for her.*

Synonym: enforce

• • •

IMPORTUNATE
adjective (ihm <u>pohr</u> chuh niht)

troublesomely urgent, extremely persistent in request or demand

*Her **importunate** appeal for a job caused me to grant her an interview.*

Synonyms: insistent, obstinate

IMPORTUNE
verb (ihm pohr <u>toon</u>) (ihm <u>pohr</u> chuhn)

to ask repeatedly, beg

*The assistant **importuned** her boss with constant requests for a raise and promotion.*

Synonyms: annoy, trouble

• • •

IMPOTENT
adjective (<u>im</u> puh tent)

ineffective, lacking strength

*The local swim team was **impotent** against the reigning state champs.*

Synonym: **powerless**

• • •

IMPRECATION
noun (ihm prih <u>kay</u> shuhn)

a curse

*Spouting violent **imprecations**, Hank searched for the person who had vandalized his truck.*

Synonym: damnation

IMPRESSIONABLE

adjective (im <u>presh</u> in uh bul)

easily influenced or affected

*The freshmen were highly **impressionable** and believed everything the upperclassmen told them.*

Synonym: believing

. . .

IMPROVIDENT

adjective (ihm <u>prahv</u> ih duhnt)

without planning or foresight, negligent

*The **improvident** woman spent all the money she received in her court settlement within two weeks.*

Synonym: unprepared

. . .

IMPUDENT

adjective (<u>ihm</u> pyuh duhnt)

marked by cocky boldness or disregard for others

*Considering the judge had been lenient in her sentence, it was **impudent** of the defendant to refer to her by her first name.*

Synonyms: arrogant, insolent

IMPUGN

verb (ihm <u>pyoon</u>)

to call into question, attack verbally

*"How dare you **impugn** my honorable motives?" protested the lawyer on being accused of ambulance chasing.*

Synonyms: challenge, dispute

. . .

IMPUTE

verb (ihm <u>pyoot</u>)

to lay the responsibility or blame for, often unjustly

*It seemed unfair to **impute** the accident on me, especially because they were the ones who ran the red light.*

Synonyms: ascribe, attribute, pin on

. . .

INACCESSIBLE

adjective (in ak <u>ses</u> uh bul)

unreachable, unapproachable

*Most kids thought the principal's office was **inaccessible**, but Paul found a way in through an air vent in the library.*

Synonyms: inconvenient, unattainable

INARTICULATE
adjective (in ar <u>tik</u> yoo lit)

unable to speak clearly

*As he stared at the confused faces of his classmates, Josh had a feeling that his oral report was completely **inarticulate**.*

Synonym: incomprehensible

. . .

INAUSPICIOUS
adjective (in aw <u>spish</u> is)

unfavorable

*Chantalle's cell phone always rings at the most **inauspicious** times.*

Synonyms: baleful, dire, foreboding

. . .

INCANDESCENT
adjective (ihn kahn <u>dehs</u> uhnt)

shining brightly

*The **incandescent** glow of the moon made it a night I'll never forget.*

Synonyms: brilliant, radiant

INCANTATION
noun (in kan <u>tay</u> shun)

a verbal spell

*Willow burned a bundle of sage, waved it around, and said a quiet **incantation** for good luck.*

Synonyms: bewitchment, enchantment

. . .

INCARNADINE
adjective (ihn <u>kaar</u> nuh dien) (ihn <u>kaar</u> nuh dihn)

red, especially blood red

*The **incarnadine** lipstick she wore made her look much older than she was.*

. . .

INCENDIARY
adjective (ihn <u>sehn</u> dee ehr ee)

combustible, flammable, burning easily

*Gasoline is so **incendiary** that cigarette smoking is forbidden at gas stations.*

Synonyms: explosive, inflammable

. . .

INCHOATE
adjective (ihn <u>koh</u> iht)

imperfectly formed or formulated

*As her thoughts on the subject were still **inchoate**, Amalia could not explain what she meant.*

Synonyms: formless, undefined

INCIDENTAL
adjective (in sih <u>den</u> tul)

minor, casual

Derek did not take into account the incidental necessities of a road trip, and had to call his mom for money.

Synonyms: casual, unplanned

• • •

INCIPIENT
adjective (ihn <u>sihp</u> ee uhnt)

beginning to exist or appear, in an initial stage

At that point, her financial problems were only incipient and she could still pay her bills.

Synonyms: basic, developing

• • •

INCISIVE
adjective (in <u>sy</u> siv)

perceptive

The teacher was surprised when the normally silent George raised his hand and gave an incisive comment on the American Revolution.

Synonym: penetrating

INCOMPETENT
adjective (in <u>kom</u> puh tent)

unqualified, inept

Marisol thought her art teacher was totally incompetent because he didn't even know who Picasso was.

Synonyms: incapable, inexpert, unfit

• • •

INCONGRUOUS
adjective (in <u>kong</u> roo us)

inappropriate, incompatible

Willow's letter to the editor, which demanded that all tests be abolished, was deemed incongruous with the newspaper's focus.

Synonyms: improper, mismatched

• • •

INCONSEQUENTIAL
adjective (in con se <u>kwen</u> shul)

unimportant, trivial

Willow's parents considered Willow's grades inconsequential, as long as they knew she's trying her best.

Synonym: negligible

INCONSISTENT

adjective (in kon <u>sis</u> tent)

contradictory

*George told his gym teacher that he exercised every day, but his statement was **inconsistent** with the size of his stomach.*

Synonyms: conflicting, disagreeing, discordant

• • •

INCONSPICUOUS

adjective (in con <u>spik</u> yoo us)

not easily noticeable

*Shanna hid her diary in a safe and **inconspicuous** spot in her closet.*

Synonym: unobtrusive

• • •

INCORRIGIBLE

adjective (ihn <u>kohr</u> ih juh buhl)

incapable of being corrected or amended, difficult to control or manage

*"You're **incorrigible**," yelled the frustrated mother to her son, in the middle of his third tantrum of the day.*

Synonyms: delinquent, unfixable

INCREDULOUS

adjective (ihn <u>krehj</u> uh luhs)

unwilling to accept what is true, skeptical

*The Lasky children were **incredulous** when their parents sat them down and told them the facts of life.*

Synonyms: doubtful, disbelieving

• • •

INCRIMINATE

verb (in <u>krim</u> uh nayt)

to accuse of a crime

*Willow swore that she didn't eat meat, but the half-eaten burger in her hand was **incriminating**.*

Synonym: implicate

• • •

INCULCATE

verb (ihn <u>kuhl</u> kayt) (<u>ihn</u> kuhl kayt)

to teach, impress in the mind

*Most parents blithely **inculcate** their children with their political views instead of allowing their children to select their own.*

Synonyms: implant, indoctrinate, instill, preach

INCULPATE
verb (ihn <u>kuhl</u> payt) (ihn kuhl payt)

to blame, charge with a crime

*His suspicious behavior after the break-in led authorities to **inculpate** him.*

Synonym: incriminate

• • •

INCUMBENT
adjective (in <u>kum</u> bent)

holding a specified office, often political

*Shanna isn't the only **incumbent** officer in the school, there are also the vice president, secretary, and treasurer.*

Synonym: occupant

• • •

INCURSION
noun (ihn <u>kuhr</u> zhuhn) (ihn <u>kuhr</u> shuhn)

sudden invasion

*The army was unable to resist the **incursion** of the rebel forces into their territory.*

Synonym: raid

INDEBTED
adjective (in <u>det</u> id)

obligated to someone else

*Shanna is **indebted** to Chantalle for getting her a date with the cute foreign-exchange student.*

Synonym: beholden

• • •

INDECOROUS
adjective (in <u>dek</u> uh rus)

improper, lacking good taste

*George's girlfriend was embarrassed by his **indecorous** behavior in front of her parents.*

Synonym: inappropriate

• • •

INDEFATIGABLE
adjective (ihn dih <u>faat</u> ih guh buhl)

never tired

*Theresa seemed **indefatigable**, barely sweating after a ten-mile run.*

Synonyms: inexhaustible, unflagging, weariless

INDEFINITE
adjective (in <u>def</u> in it)

vague, undecided, unclear

*George swore he was going to join a gym, though the start date was **indefinite**.*

Synonyms: fuzzy, hazy

• • •

INDETERMINATE
adjective (in de <u>ter</u> mi nit)

unknown, imprecise

*Willow marveled at the **indeterminate** number of causes she could support at one time.*

Synonym: vague

• • •

INDIGENT
adjective (<u>ihn</u> dih juhnt)

very poor

*Because the suspect was **indigent**, the state paid for his legal representation.*

Synonyms: destitute, impecunious, impoverished, needy, penniless

INDIGNANT
adjective (ihn <u>dihg</u> nuhnt)

angry, incensed, offended

*The innocent passerby was **indignant** when the police treated him as a suspect in the crime.*

Synonyms: furious, irate, ireful, mad, wrathful

• • •

INDISCERNIBLE
adjective (in di <u>ser</u> nu bul)

difficult to detect

*Ashley's new black pants are **indiscernible** from her old pair.*

Synonym: indistinct

• • •

INDISCRETION
noun (in dis <u>kresh</u> un)

lack of prudence, mistake

*Josh's **indiscretion** on the football field cost his team the play-offs.*

Synonym: impropriety

INDISCRIMINATE
adjective (in dis <u>krim</u> uh nit)

not based on careful distinctions

*Because Derek lost his **indiscriminate** bet, he was forced to baby-sit his four-year-old brother.*

Synonym: chaotic

• • •

INDISTINCT
adjective (in di <u>stinkt</u>)

vague, unclear

*After years of being a bully, Josh's nerdy middle school days became **indistinct** in his mind.*

Synonyms: dim, indefinite

• • •

INDOLENT
adjective (<u>ihn</u> duh luhnt)

habitually lazy, idle

*Her **indolent** ways got her fired from many jobs.*

Synonyms: fainéant, languid, lethargic, slothful, sluggish

INDOMITABLE
adjective (ihn <u>dahm</u> ih tuuh buhl)

incapable of being conquered

*Climbing Mount Everest would seem an **indomitable** task, but it has been done many times.*

Synonym: insurmountable

• • •

INDUBITABLE
adjective (ihn <u>doo</u> bih tuh buhl) (ihn <u>dyoo</u> bih tuh buhl)

unquestionable

*His **indubitable** cooking skills made it all the more astonishing when the Thanksgiving dinner he prepared tasted awful.*

Synonyms: apparent, certain, unassailable

• • •

INDUCE
verb (in <u>doos</u>)

to persuade, bring about

*Paul **induced** laughter from his friends with his classroom antics.*

Synonym: convince

INDUSTRIOUS
adjective (in dus tree us)

hardworking, diligent

*Willow, an **industrious** tree hugger, devoted herself to preserving the forest.*

Synonyms: assiduous, busy

• • •

INEFFABLE
adjective (in ef uh bul)

indescribable, inexpressible

*Chantalle found Marisol's outrageous style **ineffable,** so she took a picture and sent it to her friends.*

Synonyms: incommunicable, indefinable

• • •

INEFFICACIOUS
adjective (in ef ih kay shus)

ineffective, incompetent

*No matter how hard he tried, George's effort to get to work on time was **inefficacious.***

Synonym: incapable

INEFFICIENT
adjective (in ih fish ent)

inadequate use of resources, time, or energy

*Willow wrote her report on the **inefficient** use of toilet water in the United States.*

Synonym: wasteful

• • •

INEPT
adjective (in ept)

clumsy, awkward, foolish, nonsensical

*Although Marisol was terrific at producing abstract paintings, she was completely **inept** at sculpting.*

Synonyms: bungling, unfit

• • •

INERT
adjective (ihn uhrt)

unable to move, tending to inactivity

*In the heat of the desert afternoon, lizards lie **inert.***

Synonyms: dormant, idle, inactive, lethargic, sluggish

INEVITABLE
adjective (in <u>ev</u> ih tu bul)

unavoidable

*Marisol's passion for art was so strong, it was **inevitable** that she would go to art school.*

Synonyms: certain, definite

. . .

INEXORABLE
adjective (ihn <u>ehk</u> suhr uh buhl)

inflexible, unyielding

*The **inexorable** force of the tornado swept away their house.*

Synonyms: adamant, obdurate, relentless

. . .

INFINITE
adjective (<u>in</u> fu nit)

unlimited, boundless

*Shanna did not have the **infinite** patience required for baby-sitting her noisy sister.*

Synonyms: endless, inexhaustable

INFLAMMATORY
adjective (in <u>flam</u> uh tor ee)

arousing passion, usually anger

*Willow's **inflammatory** remarks about the girl wearing fur-lined gloves in the schoolyard embarrassed her.*

Synonym: seditious

. . .

INFLATION
noun (in <u>flay</u> shun)

undue amplification

*The students knew that the gossip flying through the halls was an **inflation** of the truth, and ignored it.*

Synonym: exaggeration

. . .

INFLEXIBLE
adjective (in <u>flek</u> su bul)

rigid, unbending

*Despite his parents' objections, George remained **inflexible** in his decision not to clean his room.*

Synonyms: unalterable, unchangeable

INFUSION
noun (in <u>fyoo</u> zhin)

the introduction of, the addition of

*Josh told the coach he got an **infusion** of energy from eating candy bars.*

Synonym: immersion

. . .

INGENIOUS
adjective (ih <u>jeen</u> yuhs)

original, clever, inventive

*Luther found an **ingenious** way to solve the complex math problem.*

Synonyms: cunning, imaginative, shrewd

. . .

INGENUOUS
adjective (ihn <u>jehn</u> yoo uhs)

straightforward, open, naïve and unsophisticated

*She was so **ingenuous** that her friends feared her innocence would be exploited when she visited the big city.*

Synonyms: artless, candid, natural, simple, unaffected

INGRATE
noun (<u>ihn</u> grayt)

ungrateful person

*When none of her relatives thanked her for the fruitcakes she had sent them, Audrey condemned them all as **ingrates**.*

Synonyms: cad, churl

. . .

INGRATIATE
verb (ihn <u>gray</u> shee ayt)

to gain favor with another by deliberate effort, to seek to please somebody so as to gain an advantage

*The new intern tried to **ingratiate** herself with the managers so that they might consider her for a future job.*

Synonyms: flatter, curry favor

. . .

INGRESS
noun (<u>ihn</u> grehs)

entrance

*Ed hoped that the mailroom job would provide him with an **ingress** into the company.*

Synonym: entry

INHERENT

adjective (ihn <u>hehr</u> ehnt)

involved essential character of something, built-in, inborn

*The class was dazzled by the experiment and as a result more likely to remember the **inherent** scientific principle.*

Synonym: intrinsic

. . .

INHIBIT

verb (in <u>hib</u> it)

to hold back, prevent, restrain

*Marisol was a bit **inhibited** at the start of the party but was soon dancing.*

Synonym: hamper

. . .

INIMICAL

adjective (ih <u>nihm</u> ih kuhl)

hostile, unfriendly

*Even though a cease-fire had been in place for months, the two sides were still **inimical** to each other.*

Synonyms: adverse, antagonistic, harmful, injurious

INIQUITY

noun (ih <u>nihk</u> wih tee)

sin, evil act

*The principal believed that the **iniquity** the student committed was grounds for expulsion.*

Synonyms: enormity, immorality, injustice, vice, wickedness

. . .

INNOCUOUS

adjective (ih <u>nahk</u> yoo uhs)

harmless

*Some snakes are poisonous, but most species are **innocuous** and pose no danger to humans.*

Synonyms: benign, harmless, inoffensive, insipid

. . .

INNUMERABLE

adjective (ih <u>noom</u> ur uh bul)

too many to be counted

*Willow's mom sighed as she picked up another of her daughter's **innumerable** shoes scattered around the house.*

Synonym: countless

INORDINATE
adjective (in <u>or</u> di net)

excessive

*Shanna was a sloppy painter, and always wound up with an **inordinate** amount of stains on her pants.*

Synonym: immoderate

• • •

INQUEST
noun (<u>ihn</u> kwehst)

an investigation, an inquiry

*The police chief ordered an **inquest** to determine what went wrong.*

Synonyms: inquiry, investigation

• • •

INSCRIPTION
noun (in <u>skrip</u> shun)

engraving

*George laughed at the **inscription** on the watch he found; it said, "To Hunny, Luv Bunny."*

Synonym: etching

INSENSATE
adjective (ihn <u>sehn</u> sayt) (ihn <u>sehn</u> siht)

lacking sensibility and understanding, foolish

*The shock of the accident left him **insensate**, but after some time, the numbness subsided and he was able to tell the officer what had happened.*

Synonyms: unfeeling, callous

• • •

INSIDIOUS
adjective (ihn <u>sihd</u> ee uhs)

sly, treacherous, devious

*Iago's **insidious** comments about Desdemona fueled Othello's feelings of jealousy regarding his wife.*

Synonyms: alluring, deceitful, perfidious

• • •

INSIGHTFUL
adjective (in <u>siyt</u> ful)

clever, perceptive

*Ashley was hoping to get some **insightful** feedback on her report from her teacher.*

Synonym: intuitive

INSINUATE
verb (in <u>sin</u> yoo ayt)

to suggest, say indirectly

*Timmy hurtfully **insinuated** that Josh wouldn't be smart enough to get a job after college.*

Synonym: imply

. . .

INSIPID
adjective (in <u>sih</u> pid)

lacking interest or flavor

*The critic claimed that the painting was **insipid**, containing no interesting qualities at all.*

Synonyms: banal, bland, dull, stale, vapid

. . .

INSOLENCE
noun (<u>in</u> su luns)

rudeness, impertinence

*Chantalle was angered by the **insolence** of the sales clerk and made a complaint.*

Synonyms: disrespect, impoliteness, impudence

INSOLENT
adjective (<u>ihn</u> suh luhnt)

insultingly arrogant, overbearing

*After having spoken with three **insolent** customer service representatives, Shelly was relieved when the fourth one sympathized with her complaint.*

Synonyms: offensive, rude

. . .

INSTANTANEOUS
adjective (in sten <u>tay</u> nee us)

immediate, without delay

*Timmy always gets an **instantaneous** response when he emails his friends, who are always online.*

Synonyms: instant, straightaway

. . .

INSULAR
adjective (<u>ihn</u> suh luhr) (<u>ihn</u> syuh luhr)

characteristic of an isolated people, especially having a narrow viewpoint

*It was a shock for Kendra to go from her small high school, with her **insular** group of friends, to a huge college with students from all over the country.*

Synonyms: provincial, narrow-minded

INSUPERABLE
adjective (ihn <u>soo</u> puhr uh buhl)

incapable of being surmounted or overcome

Insuperable as though our problems may seem, I'm confident we'll come out ahead.

Synonym: unconquerable

. . .

INSURRECTION
noun (ihn suh <u>rehk</u> shuhn)

rebellion

*After the Emperor's troops crushed the **insurrection,** its leaders fled the country.*

Synonyms: mutiny, revolt, revolution, uprising

. . .

INTEGRATE
verb (<u>in</u> tih grayt)

to incorporate, unite

*Willow tried to **integrate** tofu into her parents' diet, but her father resisted.*

Synonyms: embody, blend

INTEGRITY
noun (in <u>teg</u> rih tee)

decency, honesty

*Josh showed a shred of **integrity** when he gave Timmy a ride home during the rainstorm.*

Synonyms: honor, wholeness

. . .

INTELLECTUAL
noun (in te <u>lek</u> shoo ul)

intelligent, scholarly

*Shanna thought George was surprisingly **intellectual** for a guy who watches cartoons every day.*

Synonyms: cerebral, highbrow

. . .

INTEMPERATE
adjective (in <u>tem</u> per ut)

not moderate

*Although Willow and her father's political views are both **intemperate,** they are on opposite sides of the spectrum.*

Synonyms: uncurbed, unhampered

INTER

verb (ihn tuhr)

to bury

*After giving the masses one last chance to pay their respects, the leader's body was **interred**.*

Synonym: entomb

. . .

INTERDICT

verb (ihn tuhr dihkt)

to forbid, prohibit

*The matron **interdicted** male visits to the girls' dorm rooms after midnight.*

Synonyms: ban, outlaw

. . .

INTERLOCUTOR

noun (ihn tuhr lahk yuh tuhr)

one who takes part in conversation

*Though always the **interlocutor**, the professor actually preferred that his students guide the class discussion.*

Synonym: speaker

INTERLOPER

noun (ihn tuhr loh puhr)

trespasser, meddler in others' affairs

*The wolf pack rejected the lone pup as an **interloper**.*

Synonym: intruder

. . .

INTERLUDE

noun (in ter lood)

an intervening period of time

*Paul was glad for the **interlude** between the first and second acts of the boring play.*

Synonyms: break, intermission

. . .

INTERMINABLE

adjective (in ter mi nu bul)

endless

*The dull topic of the history class made it seem **interminable**.*

Synonym: everlasting

INTERNECINE
adjective (ihn tuhr _nehs_ een)

mutually destructive, equally devastating to both sides

Though it looked as though there was a victor, the **internecine** _battle benefited no one._

Synonyms: exterminatory, deadly

• • •

INTERPOLATE
verb (ihn _tuhr_ puh layt)

to insert, to change by adding new words or material

The editor **interpolated** _a few new sentences into the manuscript, and the new edition was ready to print._

Synonym: intercalate

• • •

INTERPOSE
verb (ihn tuhr _pohz_)

to insert, to intervene

The policeman **interposed** _himself between the two men who were about to start fighting._

Synonym: interfere

INTERREGNUM
noun (ihn tuhr _rehg_ nuhm)

a temporary halting of the usual operations of government or control

The new king began his reign by restoring order that the lawless **interregnum** _had destroyed._

Synonyms: hiatus, interruption

• • •

INTIMATION
noun (ihn tuh _may_ shuhn)

a subtle and indirect hint

Abby chose to ignore Babu's **intimation** _that she wasn't as good a swimmer as she claimed._

Synonyms: suggestion, insinuation

• • •

INTRACTABLE
adjective (ihn _traak_ tuh buhl)

not easily managed or manipulated

Intractable _for hours, the wild horse eventually allowed the rider to mount._

Synonyms: stubborn, unruly

INTRANSIGENT

adjective (ihn <u>traan</u> suh juhnt) (ihn <u>traan</u> zuh juhnt)

uncompromising, refusing to abandon an extreme position

*His **intransigent** positions on social issues cost him the election.*

Synonyms: obstinate, unyielding

• • •

INTREPID

adjective (ihn <u>trehp</u> ihd)

fearless, resolutely courageous

*Despite freezing winds, the **intrepid** hiker completed his ascent.*

Synonym: brave

• • •

INTRICATE

adjective (<u>in</u> tri kit)

elaborate, complex

*Willow was mesmerized as she watched the spider spin an **intricate** web to catch its prey.*

Synonyms: detailed, ornate

INTRUSION

noun (in <u>troo</u> zhin)

invasion of another's privacy

*Shanna complained about her little sister's constant **intrusion** into her room.*

Synonyms: interruption, incursion

• • •

INUNDATE

verb (ihn uhn dayt)

to cover with a flood, to overwhelm as if with a flood

*The box office was **inundated** with requests for tickets to the award-winning play.*

Synonyms: swamp, drown

• • •

INURE

verb (ihn <u>yoor</u>)

to harden, to accustom, to become used to

*Eventually, Hassad became **inured** to the sirens that went off every night and could sleep through them.*

Synonyms: condition, familiarize, habituate

INVARIABLE
adjective (in var ee uh bul)

constant, unchanging

*When his science teacher asked for an **invariable** law of nature, Timmy mentioned gravity.*

Synonym: inflexible

• • •

INVECTIVE
noun (ihn vehk tihv)

verbal abuse

*A stream of **invective** poured from Mrs. Pratt's mouth as she watched the vandals smash her ceramic frog.*

Synonyms: denunciation, revilement, vituperation

• • •

INVENTORY
noun (in vin tohr ee)

the quantity of goods on hand

*Chantalle checked the **inventory** of purses in her closet and realized that she was missing her pink one.*

Synonym: list

INVESTIGATE
verb (in ves tih gayt)

examine, look into

*Shanna **investigated** the top twenty colleges in the country and applied to the ones that were closest to home.*

Synonym: explore

• • •

INVESTITURE
noun (in ves tuh chur)

ceremony conferring authority

*At Napoleon's **investiture**, he grabbed the crown from the Pope's hands and placed it on his head himself.*

Synonyms: inaugural, inauguration

• • •

INVESTMENT
noun (in vest mint)

a commitment of time, support, or money

*Timmy's **investment** in Spanish lessons paid off when he was able to speak with the exchange student from Spain.*

Synonym: contribution

INVETERATE
adjective (ihn <u>veht</u> uhr iht)

firmly established, especially with respect to a habit or attitude

*An **inveterate** risk-taker, Lori tried her luck at bungee-jumping.*

Synonyms: habitual, chronic

• • •

INVIDIOUS
adjective (ihn <u>vihd</u> ee uhs)

envious, obnoxious

*It is cruel and **invidious** for parents to play favorites with their children.*

Synonyms: discriminatory, insulting, jaundiced, resentful

• • •

INVIOLABLE
adjective (in <u>vy</u> uh lu bul)

safe from violation or assault

*After a tough day of protesting, Willow retreats to her house where she feels **inviolable**.*

Synonym: sacred

IRASCIBLE
adjective (ih <u>raas</u> uh buhl)

easily angered, hot-tempered

*One of the most **irascible** barbarians of all time, Attila the Hun, ravaged much of Europe during his time.*

Synonyms: irritable, crabby

• • •

IRIDESCENT
adjective (ih ri <u>des</u> ent)

showing many colors

*George spotted an **iridescent** rainbow and wondered if there was a pot of gold at the end of it.*

Synonyms: polychromatic, prismatic

• • •

IRONIC
adjective (ie <u>rahn</u> ihk)

poignantly contrary or incongruous to what was expected

*It was **ironic** to learn that shy Wendy from high school grew up to be the loud-mouthed host of the daily talk show.*

Synonym: satirical

IRONY
noun (i ur nee)

incogruity between expectations and actualities

*Derek seethed at the **irony** of leaving his band for a solo record deal.*

Synonym: sarcasm

. . .

IRRATIONAL
adjective (ih rash ih null)

illogical, nonsensical

*Even though Timmy is very allergic to strawberries, he has an **irrational** desire to eat them.*

Synonym: unreasonable

. . .

IRRESOLUTE
adjective (ih rez uh loot)

undecided, indecisive

*Chantalle was so **irresolute** about the outfit she wanted to wear that by the time she picked one out, she was late.*

Synonym: fickle

IRREVERENT
adjective (ih rehv uhr uhnt)

disrespectful in a gentle or humorous way

*Kevin's **irreverent** attitude toward the principal annoyed the teacher but amused the other children.*

Synonyms: cheeky, satiric

. . .

ISOLATED
adjective (i suh lay tid)

solitary, singular

*Shanna realized that her decision to wear knickers to school was an **isolated** case of bad judgment.*

Synonym: unique

. . .

ITINERANT
adjective (ie tihn uhr uhnt)

wandering from place to place, unsettled

*The **itinerant** tomcat came back to the Johansson homestead every two months.*

Synonyms: nomadic, vagrant

JADED
adjective (<u>jay</u> ded)

tired by excess or overuse, slightly cynical

*Ashley told anyone she met who had a **jaded** attitude to lighten up.*

Synonym: weary

. . .

JARGON
noun (<u>jahr</u> guhn)

nonsensical talk, specialized language

*You need to master technical **jargon** in order to communicate successfully with engineers.*

Synonyms: argot, cant, dialect, idiom

JEOPADIZE
verb (<u>jep</u> er diyz)

expose to injury

*Shanna hoped her late-breaking case of chicken pox wasn't going to **jeopardize** her perfect attendance.*

Synonym: endanger

. . .

JEST
verb (<u>jest</u>)

to act playfully

*"Surely you **jest**," Chantalle said, when her mother asked her to accompany her to the thrift store.*

Synonyms: joke, ridicule

JETTISON
verb (<u>jeht</u> ih zuhn) (<u>jeht</u> ih suhn)

to discard, to get rid of as unnecessary or encumbering

*The sinking ship **jettisoned** its cargo in a desperate attempt to reduce its weight.*

Synonyms: eject, dump

. . .

JINGOISM
noun (<u>jing</u> goh ihz uhm)

belligerent support of one's country

*The president's **jingoism** made him declare war on other countries at the slightest provocation.*

Synonyms: chauvinism, nationalism

. . .

JOCULAR
adjective (<u>jahk</u> yuh luhr)

playful, humorous

*The **jocular** old man entertained his grandchildren for hours.*

Synonyms: comical, amusing

JOLLITY
noun (<u>jol</u> ih tee)

cheerfulness, liveliness, celebration

*Ashley's **jollity** seemed insincere to some students because there was no way someone could smile 24/7.*

Synonym: merrymaking

. . .

JUBILATION
noun (<u>joo</u> bi lay shin)

joy, celebration

*Derek's **jubilation** over having his band beg him to come back was strong.*

Synonym: exultation

. . .

JUDICIOUS
adjective (joo <u>dih</u> shuhs)

sensible, showing good judgment

*The wise and distinguished judge was well known for having a **judicious** temperament.*

Synonyms: circumspect, prudent, sagacious, sapient

JUGGERNAUT
noun (juhg uhr naht)

huge force destroying everything in its path

*The **juggernaut** of the army surged ahead until it was halted in its tracks by the brutal winter.*

Synonym: overwhelming force

. . .

JUNCTURE
noun (juhnk chuhr)

point of time, especially where two things are joined

*At this **juncture**, I think it would be a good idea for us to take a coffee break.*

Synonyms: confluence, convergence, crossroads, moment

. . .

JUNTA
noun (hoon tuh) (juhn tuh)

a small governing body, especially after a revolutionary seizure of power

*Only one member of the **junta** was satisfactory enough to be elected once the new government was established.*

Synonym: council

JURISPRUDENCE
noun (joor his prood ns)

philosophy of law

*An expert in **jurisprudence**, the esteemed lawyer was often consulted by his colleagues.*

Synonym: legal matters

. . .

JUSTIFY
verb (jus tih fi)

to prove valid

*Paul **justified** not helping his father clean out the garage by saying he had to volunteer at the Senior Center that afternoon.*

Synonyms: excuse, defend

. . .

JUXTAPOSITION
noun (juk stuh puh zihsh uhn)

side-by-side placement

*The porcelain dog was placed in **juxtaposition** with the straw doghouse on the mantelpiece.*

Synonyms: comparison, contrast

J

KEEN
adjective (keen)

having a sharp edge, intellectually sharp, perceptive

*With her **keen** intelligence, she figured out the puzzle in seconds flat.*

Synonyms: acute, canny, quick

• • •

KIN
noun (kin)

family, relatives

*George had to admit that he loved the holidays; it was the only time he and his widespread **kin** got together.*

Synonyms: relations, family connections

KINDLE
verb (kihn duhl)

to set fire to or ignite, excite or inspire

*With only damp wood to work with, Tilda had great difficulty trying to **kindle** the camp fire.*

Synonyms: arouse, awaken, light, spark

• • •

KINETIC
adjective (kih neh tihk)

relating to motion, characterized by movement

*The **kinetic** sculpture moved back and forth, startling the museum visitors.*

Synonyms: active, dynamic, mobile

KISMET

noun (kihz meht) (kihz miht)

destiny

*When Eve found out that Garret also played the harmonica, she knew their meeting was **kismet**.*

Synonym: fate

. . .

KNELL

noun (nehl)

sound of a funeral bell, omen of death or failure

*When the townspeople heard the **knell** from the church belfry, they knew that their mayor had died.*

Synonyms: chime, peal, toll

KUDOS

noun (koo dohz)

fame, glory, honor

*The actress happily accepted **kudos** from the press for her stunning performance in the film.*

Synonyms: acclaim, accolade, encomium, homage, praise

K

LACHRYMOSE
adjective (<u>laak</u> ruh mohs)

tearful

*Heather always became **lachrymose** when it was time to bid her daughter good-bye.*

Synonyms: teary, weepy

• • •

LACONIC
adjective (luh <u>kah</u> nihk)

using few words

*She was a **laconic** poet who built her reputation on using words as sparingly as possible.*

Synonyms: concise, pithy, succinct, terse

LAGGARD
noun (<u>laag</u> uhrd)

dawdler, loafer, lazy person

*The manager hesitated to fire Biff, his incompetent **laggard** of an assistant, because Biff was the CEO's son.*

Synonym: slowpoke

• • •

LAMENT
verb (luh <u>mehnt</u>)

to express sorrow, to grieve

*The children continued to **lament** the death of the goldfish weeks after its demise.*

Synonyms: bewail, deplore, grieve, mourn

LAMPOON
verb (lam <u>poon</u>)

to ridicule with satire

*The mayor hated being **lampooned** by the press for his efforts to improve people's politeness.*

Synonym: tease

. . .

LANGUID
adjective (<u>laang</u> gwihd)

lacking energy, indifferent, slow

*The **languid** cat cleaned its fur, ignoring the vicious, snarling dog chained a few feet away from it.*

Synonyms: fainéant, lackadaisical, listless, sluggish, weak

. . .

LAPIDARY
adjective (<u>laa</u> puh der ee)

relating to precious stones or the art of cutting them

*Most **lapidary** work today is done with the use of motorized equipment.*

Synonym: jeweler

LARCENY
noun (<u>lar</u> suh nee)

theft of property

*Paul quickly dialed the police when he witnessed a man committing **larceny** by stealing a car.*

Synonyms: breaking and entering, robbery

. . .

LARGESS
adjective (laar <u>jehs</u>)

generosity

*She'd always relied on her parent's **largess**, but after graduation, she had to get a job.*

Synonym: philanthropy

. . .

LASSITUDE
noun (<u>laas</u> ih tood)

lethargy, sluggishness

*The defeated French army plunged into a state of depressed **lassitude** as they trudged home from Russia.*

Synonyms: listlessness, stupor, torpor, weariness

LATENT

adjective (<u>lay</u> tent)

present but hidden, potential

*Ashley's **latent** aggravation began to emerge when she yelled at the other cheerleaders to stop socializing and start practicing.*

Synonyms: concealed, underlying

. . .

LAUD

verb (lawd)

to give praise, to glorify

*Parades and fireworks were staged to **laud** the success of the rebels.*

Synonyms: acclaim, applaud, commend, compliment

. . .

LAUDABLE

adjective (<u>law</u> duh buhl)

deserving of praise

*Kristin's dedication is **laudable**, but she doesn't have the necessary skills to be a good paralegal.*

Synonyms: commendable, admirable

LAVISH

adjective (<u>la</u> vish)

extravagant, profuse

*Josh felt as if he was going to burst after eating one portion of everything at the **lavish** dinner party his aunt was hosting.*

Synonyms: plentiful, abundant

. . .

LAX

adjective (laaks)

not rigid, loose, negligent

*Because our delivery boy is **lax**, the newspaper often arrives late and sopping wet.*

Synonyms: careless, imprecise

. . .

LECHEROUS

adjective (<u>lehch</u> uh ruhs)

lewd, lustful

*The school board censored the movie because of its portrayal of the **lecherous** criminal.*

Synonyms: lascivious, promiscuous

LEDGER
noun (lej er)

a book that tracks finances

Shanna noticed in the student council ledger that some funds seemed to be missing and vowed to locate them by the end of the day.

Synonym: register

• • •

LEERY
adjective (lihr ree)

suspicious

After being swindled once, Ruth became leery of strangers trying to sell things to her.

Synonyms: distrustful, guarded, wary

• • •

LEGERDEMAIN
noun (lehj uhr duh mayn)

trickery

The little boy thought his legerdemain was working on his mother, but she knew about every hidden toy and stolen cookie.

Synonyms: chicanery, conjuring

LEGION
noun (lee jun)

a great number, a multitude

On Valentine's Day morning, there was a legion of boys waiting to give Chantalle flowers when she arrived in homeroom.

Synoyms: crowd, mass

• • •

LENIENT
adjective (leen yent)

easygoing, permissive

George felt the principal was too lenient when he gave Willow a warning for cutting class because he always gave George detention for the same offense.

Synonyms: merciful, soft

• • •

LETHARGIC
adjective (luh thar jik)

acting in an indifferent or slow, sluggish manner

The clerk was so lethargic that, even when business was slow, he always had a long line in front of him.

Synonyms: apathetic, lackadaisical, languid, listless, torpid

LEVITY
noun (<u>leh</u> vih tee)

an inappropriate lack of seriousness, overly casual

The joke added needed levity to the otherwise serious meeting.

Synonyms: amusement, humor

• • •

LEXICON
noun (<u>lehk</u> sih kahn)

a dictionary, a stock of terms pertaining to a particular subject or vocabulary

The author coined the term Gen-X, which has since entered the lexicon.

Synonyms: dictionary, vocabulary

• • •

LIABILITY
noun (li uh <u>bil</u> uh tee)

handicap, something holding one back

Chantalle sometimes felt that being beautiful was a liability because it made guys feel intimidated around her.

Synonyms: accountability, burden

LIBERAL
adjective (<u>lihb</u> uh ruhl) (<u>lihb</u> ruhl)

tolerant, broad-minded, generous, lavish

Cali's liberal parents trusted her and allowed her to manage her own affairs to a large extent.

Synonyms: bounteous, latitudinarian, munificent, permissive, progressive

• • •

LIBERATE
verb (<u>lib</u> uh rayt)

emancipate, set free

On Friday afternoon, the students were liberated for the weekend by the sound of the final bell.

Synonyms: release, unshackle

• • •

LIBERTARIAN
noun (lih buhr <u>tehr</u> ee uhn)

one who advocates individual rights and free will

The libertarian was always at odds with the conservatives.

LIBERTINE
noun (<u>lihb</u> uhr teen)

a free thinker, usually used disparagingly, one without moral restraint

*The **libertine** took pleasure in gambling away his family's money.*

Synonyms: hedonist

• • •

LICENTIOUS
adjective (lih <u>sehn</u> shuhs)

immoral, unrestrained by society

*Religious citizens were outraged by the **licentious** exploits of the free-spirited artists living in town.*

Synonyms: wanton, lewd

• • •

LILLIPUTIAN
noun (lihl ee <u>pyoo</u> shun)

a very small person or thing

*Next to her Amazonian roommate, the girl appeared to be **lilliputian**.*

Synonyms: diminutive, small

LIMBER
adjective (<u>lihm</u> buhr)

flexible, capable of being shaped

*After years of doing so much yoga, the elderly man was remarkably **limber**.*

Synonyms: agile, nimble

• • •

LIMPID
adjective (<u>lim</u> pihd)

clear, transparent

*Shelley could see all the way to the bottom through the pond's **limpid** water.*

Synonyms: lucid, pellucid, serene

• • •

LINCHPIN
noun (<u>linch</u> pin)

central cohesive element

*Paul's grandmother is the **linchpin** of the family.*

Synonyms: key player, top dog

• • •

LIONIZE
verb (<u>lie</u> uhn iez)

to treat as a celebrity

*After the success of his novel, the author was **lionized** by the press.*

Synonyms: feast, honor, ply, regale

LISSOME
adjective (<u>lihs</u> uhm)

The **lissome** yoga instructor twisted herself into shapes that her students could only dream of.

Synonyms: graceful, lithe, supple

• • •

LISTLESS
adjective (<u>lihst</u> lihs)

lacking energy and enthusiasm

Listless and depressed after breaking up with his girlfriend, Raj spent his days moping on the couch.

Synonyms: fainéant, indolent, languid, lethargic, sluggish

• • •

LITHE
adjective (lieth)

moving and bending with ease, marked by effortless grace

The dancer's **lithe** movements proved her to be a rising star in the ballet corps.

Synonyms: flexible, limber

LITIGANT
noun (<u>lit</u> ih gant)

one involved in a lawsuit

George watched the **litigants** enter the courtroom on his favorite television show, The People's Courtroom.

• • •

LIVID
adjective (<u>lih</u> vihd)

discolored from a bruise, pale, reddened with anger

André was **livid** when he discovered that someone had spilled grape juice all over his cashmere coat.

Synonyms: ashen, black-and-blue, furious, pallid

• • •

LOATH
adjective (<u>lowth</u>)

reluctant, unwilling

Josh was **loath** to enter the coach's office because he knew he was in trouble for missing practice.

Synonyms: not keen, wary

LOBBY
verb (lob bee)

to petition

*Willow **lobbied** her congressman to stop the cigarette companies from advertising to teens.*

Synonyms: campaign, persuade

. . .

LONGEVITY
noun (lon jev ih tee)

long life

*Timmy's ninety-eight-year-old grand-father says he owes his **longevity** to eating yogurt every day.*

Synonyms: prolonged existence, durability

. . .

LOQUACIOUS
adjective (loh kway shuhs)

talkative

*She was naturally **loquacious**, which was always a challenge when she was in a library or movie theater.*

Synonym: chatty

LUBRICATE
verb (loob rih kayt)

To grease up, make slippery

*Timmy **lubricated** the joints on his robot so that they would not squeak during the science demonstration.*

Synonym: oil

. . .

LUCID
adjective (loo sihd)

clear and easily understood

*The explanations were written in a simple and **lucid** manner so that students were immediately able to apply what they learned.*

Synonyms: clear, coherent, explicit, intelligible, limpid

. . .

LUGUBRIOUS
adjective (loo goo bree uhs)

sorrowful, mournful, dismal

*Irish wakes are a rousing departure from the **lugubrious** funeral services most people are accustomed to.*

Synonyms: funereal, gloomy, melancholy, somber, woeful

L

LULL
verb (<u>lul</u>)

to calm

*George used white noise to **lull** himself to sleep at night.*

Synonyms: stillness, silence

. . .

LUMBER
verb (<u>luhm</u> buhr)

to move slowly and awkwardly

*The bear **lumbered** towards the garbage, drooling at the prospect of the Big Mac leftovers he smelled.*

Synonyms: galumph, hulk, lurch, stumble

. . .

LUMINOUS
adjective (<u>loo</u> muhn uhs)

bright, brilliant, glowing

*The park was bathed in **luminous** sunshine that warmed the bodies and the souls of the visitors.*

Synonyms: incandescent, lucent, lustrous, radiant, resplendent

LUMMOX
noun (<u>lum</u> iks)

clumsy or stupid oaf

*A bit of a **lummox,** Shanna avoids going into stores displaying breakables because she knows she's liable to knock something over.*

Synonyms: blunder, brute

. . .

LURID
adjective (<u>loo</u> rid)

harshly shocking, sensational, glowing

*Intrigued by the **lurid** headline in the tabloid, Ashley quickly moved on to read the juicy celebrity gossip.*

Synonyms: striking, gaudy

. . .

LYRICIST
noun (<u>lir</u> ih sist)

person who writes words for a song

*Timmy approached Derek about being a **lyricist** for Derek's band by suggesting they put Timmy's poetry to music.*

Synonyms: rhymester, versifier

MACABRE

adjective (muh <u>kaa</u> bruh) (muh <u>kaa</u> buhr)

having death as a subject, dwelling on the gruesome

*Martin enjoyed **macabre** tales about werewolves and vampires.*

Synonyms: ghastly, grim

· · ·

MACHINATION

noun (mahk uh <u>nay</u> shuhn)

plot or scheme

*Tired of his employees' endless **machinations** to destroy the company, the boss had them fired.*

Synonyms: cabal, conspiracy, design, intrigue

MACROCOSM

noun (<u>maak</u> roh cahz uhm)

the whole universe, a large-scale reflection of a part of the great world

*Some scientists focus on a particular aspect of space, while others study the entire **macrocosm** and how its parts relate to one another.*

Synonym: cosmos

· · ·

MAELSTROM

noun (<u>mayl</u> struhm)

whirlpool, turmoil, agitated state of mind

*The transportation system of the city had collapsed in the **maelstrom** of war.*

Synonyms: eddy, turbulence

MAGNANIMOUS
adjective (maag naan uh muhs)

generous, noble in spirit

Although at first he seemed mean, Uncle Frank turned out to be a very magnanimous fellow.

Synonyms: forgiving, unselfish

. . .

MAGNATE
noun (maag nayt) (maag niht)

powerful or influential person

The entertainment magnate bought two cable TV stations to add to his collection of magazines and publishing houses.

Synonyms: dignitary, luminary, nabob, potentate, tycoon

. . .

MAGNIFY
verb (mag nih fiy)

make greater in size, enlarge

Timmy really wanted to pop the zit on his chin, but he resisted, knowing it would only magnify the problem.

Synonyms: expand, amplify

MALADROIT
adjective (maal uh droyt)

clumsy, tactless

His maladroit comments about the host's poor cooking skills were viewed as inexcusable by the other guests.

Synonyms: awkward, gauche, inept, ungainly

. . .

MALAISE
noun (maa layz)

a sense of mental or moral ill-being

During his presidency, Jimmy Carter spoke of a "national malaise" and was subsequently criticized for being too negative.

Synonyms: discomfort, unhappiness

. . .

MALAPROPISM
noun (maal uh prahp ihz uhm)

the accidental, often comical, use of a word which resembles the one intended, but has a different, often contradictory meaning

She meant to say "public broadcasting" but instead it came out a malapropism: "public boredcasting."

Synonym: misstatement

MALEDICTION
noun (maal ih <u>dihk</u> shun)

a curse, a wish of evil upon another

*The frog prince looked for a princess
to kiss him and put an end to the
witch's **malediction**.*

Synonyms: damn, denunciation

. . .

MALEVOLENT
adjective (muh <u>lehv</u> uh luhnt)

exhibiting ill will, wishing harm to
others

*The **malevolent** gossiper spread false
rumors with frequency.*

Synonyms: malicious, hateful

. . .

MALFEASANCE
noun (maal <u>fee</u> zuhns)

wrongdoing or misconduct, especially
by a public official

*Not only was the deputy's **malfeasance**
humiliating, it also spelled the end of
his career.*

Synonyms: corruption, fraud

MALICIOUS
adjective (ma <u>li</u> cious)

showing malice

*Patrick exhibited **malicious** behavior,
and soon no one trusted him.*

Synonym: malevolent

. . .

MALIGN
noun (ma <u>lign</u>)

to speak about in an evil manner

*The candidate **maligned** her opponent
in an effort to ruin his campaign.*

Synonym: defame, vilify

. . .

MALINGER
verb (muh <u>ling</u> guhr)

to evade responsibility by pretending
to be ill

*A common way to dodge the draft was
by **malingering**—faking an illness so as
to avoid having to serve in the Army.*

Synonyms: fake, shirk

MALLEABLE
adjective (<u>maal</u> ee uh buhl)

easily influenced or shaped, capable of being altered by outside forces

The welder heated the metal before shaping it because the heat made it ***malleable***.

Synonyms: adaptable, pliable

• • •

MALLET
noun (<u>mal</u> it)

short-handled hammer

A ***mallet***, *which is a short-handed hammer, should not be confused with a mullet, which is an unfashionable haircut.*

Synonyms: tack hammer, sledge hammer

• • •

MANDATE
noun (<u>man</u> dayt)

a command or instruction

As the leader of the popular group, Chantalle felt she had a ***mandate*** *to make fun of those whom she considered uncool.*

Synonyms: permission, authorization

MANIFEST
adjective (<u>man</u> ih fest)

obvious

Shanna's mom thought their shopping trip was successful, but Shanna's disagreement became ***manifest*** *when she never once wore the outfit they bought.*

Synonyms: apparent, evident

• • •

MANNERED
adjective (<u>maan</u> uhrd)

a feeling of unease or depression

artificial or stilted in character

The portrait is an example of the ***mannered*** *style that was favored in that era.*

Synonyms: affected, unnatural

• • •

MAR
verb (mahr)

to damage, deface, spoil

Telephone poles ***mar*** *the natural beauty of the countryside.*

Synonyms: blemish, disfigure

MARTINET
noun (mahr tihn <u>eht</u>)

strict disciplinarian, one who rigidly follows rules

*A complete **martinet**, the official insisted that Pete fill out all the forms again even though he was already familiar with his case.*

Synonyms: dictator, stickler, tyrant

• • •

MASOCHIST
noun (<u>maas</u> uhk ihst)

one who enjoys being subjected to pain or humiliation

*Only a **masochist** would volunteer to take on this nightmarish project.*

• • •

MATERIALISM
noun (mu <u>teer</u> ee uh lizm)

preoccupation with worldly goods

*As Chantalle sat in front of her plasma screen television talking on her new pda/cell phone, she couldn't understand why some people thought **materialism** was a bad thing.*

Synonyms: greed, greediness

MATRIARCH
noun (<u>may</u> tree ark)

woman who rules family or clan

*As the **matriarch**, Timmy's mom often makes decisions for the entire family.*

Synonym: matron

• • •

MATRICULATE
verb (muh <u>trihk</u> yuh layt)

to enroll as a member of a college or university

*When Suda-May **matriculates** at Yale University this coming fall, she will move to New Haven.*

Synonyms: enlist, join

• • •

MAUDLIN
adjective (<u>mawd</u> lihn)

overly sentimental

*The mother's death should have been a touching scene, but the movie's treatment of it was so **maudlin** that, instead of making the audience cry, it made them cringe.*

Synonyms: mawkish, saccharine, weepy

MAVERICK
noun (<u>maav</u> rihk) (<u>maav</u> uh rihk)

an independent individual who does not go along with a group

*The senator was a **maverick** who was willing to vote against his own party's position.*

Synonym: nonconformist

• • •

MAWKISH
adjective (<u>maw</u> kihsh)

sickeningly sentimental

*The poet hoped to charm his girlfriend with his flowery poem, but its **mawkish** tone sickened her instead.*

Synonym: maudlin

• • •

MAXIM
noun (<u>mak</u> sim)

fundamental principle

*Chantalle lives under the **maxim** "Do unto others before they do it to you."*

Synonyms: saying, proverb

MEAGER
adjective (<u>mee</u> grr)

minimal, scanty, deficient

*George told the lunch lady to pile it on because there was no way he could get through the day on a **meager** portion of sloppy joe.*

Synonyms: too little, inadequate

• • •

MEASURED
adjective (<u>me</u> zherd)

calculated, deliberate

*The student took **measured** steps to improve his score on the SAT by studying vocabulary, grammar, and math.*

Synonyms: precise, exact

• • •

MECHANISM
noun (<u>mehk</u> uh nizm)

a machine or machine part

*The "send" **mechanism** on Chantalle's two-way pager broke, leaving her unable to tell Shanna, who was in the next classroom, about her new pair of shoes.*

Synonyms: device, instrument

MEDDLER
noun (<u>med</u> ler)

person interfering in others' affairs

*Some people think that Willow is a **meddler** and should just mind her own business instead of trying to fix the world.*

Synonyms: nuisance, pest

• • •

MEDIATE
verb (<u>mee</u> dee ayt)

to resolve a dispute between two other parties

*The referee **mediated** the disagreement on the soccer field.*

Synonyms: arbitrate, referee

• • •

MEDITATE
verb (<u>med</u> ih tayt)

reflect on, contemplate

*Sometimes Marisol **meditates** for weeks about her vision of a painting before she ever puts a brush to canvas.*

Synonyms: ponder, consider

MEDIUM
noun (<u>mee</u> dee um)

psychic

*After breaking up with her boyfriend, Willow decided to visit her favorite **medium** to find out if she would ever date again.*

Synonyms: clairvoyant, seer

• • •

MEGALOMANIA
noun (<u>mehg</u> uh loh <u>may</u> nee uh)

obsession with great or grandiose performance

*Many of the Roman emperors suffered from severe **megalomania**.*

Synonyms: egoism, self-centeredness

• • •

MELEE
noun (<u>may</u> <u>lay</u>)

tumultuous free-for-all

*Josh got suspended from school after starting a **melee** with the other team on the basketball court.*

Synonyms: encounter, scuffle

MELLIFLUOUS
adjective (muh <u>lihf</u> loo uhs)

having a smooth, rich flow

She was so talented that her **mellifluous** *flute playing transported me to another world.*

Synonym: melodious

• • •

MELODIUS
adjective (meh <u>low</u> dee us)

musical, pleasant to hear

Derek does his homework to the **melodious** *sounds of the band Burns Like Rubber.*

Synonyms: harmonious, tuneful

• • •

MENDACIOUS
adjective (mehn <u>day</u> shuhs)

dishonest

So many of her stories were **mendacious** *that I decided she must be a pathological liar.*

Synonyms: deceitful, false, lying, untruthful

MENDICANT
noun (<u>mehn</u> dih kuhnt)

beggar

"Please, sir, can you spare a dime?" *begged the* **mendicant** *as the business-man walked past.*

Synonyms: panhandler, pauper

• • •

MERCILESS
adjective (<u>mer</u> sih less)

without pity

The Spanish teacher was notorious for his **merciless** *pop quizzes, so his students were always prepared.*

Synonyms: harsh, heartless

• • •

MERCURIAL
adjective (muhr <u>kyoor</u> ee uhl)

quick, shrewd, and unpredictable

Her **mercurial** *personality made it difficult to guess how she would react to the bad news.*

Synonyms: clever, crafty, volatile, whimsical

MERETRICIOUS
adjective (mehr ih <u>trihsh</u> uhs)

gaudy, falsely attractive

*The casino's **meretricious** decor horrified the cultivated interior designer.*

Synonyms: flashy, insincere, loud, specious, tawdry

• • •

MERRIMENT
noun (<u>mer</u> ree ment)

high-spirited fun

*The senior ski trip was full of **merriment** until Shanna sprained her ankle.*

Synonyms: jollity, gaiety

• • •

METAMORPHOSIS
noun (meta <u>mor</u> pho sis)

a physical or structural change, sometimes occurring quickly and by supernatural means

*Mrs. Weintraub used live frogs and butterflies to teach her fifth-graders about **metamorphosis**.*

Synonym: transformation

METAPHOR
noun (<u>meht</u> uh fohr) (<u>meht</u> uh fuhr)

figure of speech comparing two different things

*The **metaphor** "a sea of troubles" suggests a lot of troubles by comparing their number to the vastness of the sea.*

Synonyms: allegory, analogy, simile, symbol

• • •

METHODICAL
adjective (me <u>thod</u> ih kul)

systematic, orderly

*The **methodical** way Timmy lined up his sixteen No. 2 pencils as he got ready to take his exam—one up, one down—was a little weird.*

Synonyms: disciplined, meticulous

• • •

METICULOUS
adjective (mih <u>tihk</u> yuh luhs)

extremely careful, fastidious, painstaking

*To clean every square inch of the huge mural, the restorers had to be **meticulous**.*

Synonyms: finicky, fussy, precise, punctilious, scrupulous

METTLE
noun (<u>meht</u> l)

courageousness, endurance

*The helicopter pilot showed her **mettle** as she landed in the battlefield to rescue the wounded soldiers.*

Synonyms: character, fortitude, spirit

• • •

MICROCOSM
noun (<u>mie</u> kruh kahz uhm)

a small scale representation of a larger system

*This department is in fact a **microcosm** of the entire corporation.*

• • •

MIFFED
adjective (<u>mift</u>)

offended, annoyed

*Ashley was **miffed** when her boyfriend dumped her two days after she'd given him a birthday present.*

Synonyms: peeved, displeased

MILESTONE
noun (<u>miyl</u> stohn)

important event in something or someone's history

*Graduating high school is an important **milestone** in any student's life.*

Synonyms: highlight, high point

• • •

MILIEU
noun (mihl <u>yoo</u>)

the physical or social setting in which something occurs or develops, environment

*The **milieu** at the club wasn't one I was comfortable with, so I left right away.*

Synonym: background

• • •

MILITATE
verb (<u>mihl</u> ih tayt)

to operate against, work against

*The unprofessional employee **militated** against his supervisor, without realizing the ramifications of his actions.*

Synonyms: affect, change, influence

MIMIC
verb (<u>mim</u> ik)

copy, imitate

*Shanna complained to her mother because her little sister was **mimicking** everything she said.*

Synonyms: impersonate, impressionist

. . .

MIRAGE
noun (mih <u>razh</u>)

optical illusion, apparition

*Timmy thought the pretty girl waving at him was a **mirage**, but she really did want to talk to him!*

Synonyms: hallucination, delusion

. . .

MIRTH
noun (muhrth)

frivolity, gaiety, laughter

*Vera's hilarious jokes contributed to the general **mirth** at the dinner party.*

Synonyms: glee, hilarity, jollity, merriment

MISANTHROPE
noun (<u>mihs</u> ahn throhp)

a person who hates or distrusts mankind

*Scrooge was such a **misanthrope** that even the sight of children singing made him angry.*

Synonym: curmudgeon

. . .

MISCONCEPTION
noun (mis kon <u>sep</u> shun)

wrong understanding

*It is a common **misconception** that all blondes are stupid.*

Synonyms: mistaken belief, misunderstanding

. . .

MISNOMER
noun (mihs <u>noh</u> muhr)

an error in naming a person or place

*Iceland is a **misnomer** because it isn't really icy, the name means "island."*

Synonyms: error, misapplication

MISSIVE
noun (<u>mihs</u> ihv)

a written note or letter

*Priscilla spent hours composing a romantic **missive** for Elvis.*

Synonym: message

• • •

MITIGATE
verb (<u>miht</u> ih gayt)

to make less severe, make milder

*A judge may **mitigate** a sentence if it's decided that the crime was committed out of necessity.*

Synonyms: relieve, alleviate

• • •

MOCK
verb (mok)

to deride, ridicule

*The basketball team **mocked** Josh for forgetting his sneakers and having to practice in shorts, socks, and leather shoes.*

Synonyms: tease, scorn

MODERATE
adjective (<u>mod</u> uh rit)

reasonable, not extreme

*Chantalle might have fibbed a little when she told her mom that her new handbag was **moderately** priced.*

Synonyms: sensible, fair

• • •

MODEST
adjective (<u>mod</u> est)

shy, plain, unassuming, moderate in size

*Although she wished she could give more, Willow made a **modest** donation to the Save the Seals organization.*

Synonyms: humble, meek

• • •

MODICUM
noun (<u>mahd</u> ih kuhm)

a small portion, limited quantity

*I expect at least a **modicum** of assistance from you on the day of the party.*

Synonyms: crumb, iota

MODULATE
verb (<u>moj</u> uh layt)

to change pitch, intensity, or tone, to regulate

*Derek **modulated** the tone of his guitar with a special effects pedal that was plugged into his speakers.*

Synonyms: adjust, alter

• • •

MOLLIFY
verb (<u>mahl</u> uh fie)

to soothe in temper or disposition

*A small raise and increased break time **mollified** the unhappy staff, at least for the moment.*

Synonyms: pacify, appease

• • •

MOLT
verb (muhlt)

to shed hair, skin, or an outer layer periodically

*The snake **molted** its skin and left it behind in a crumpled mass.*

Synonyms: cast, defoliate, desquamate

MOMENTARY
adjective (<u>moh</u> men <u>te</u> ree)

short-lived, lasting only for a short time

*The **momentary** connection Willow and Derek felt in English class when they called out the same answer at the same time quickly passed, and by the end of the period they were back to disliking each other.*

Synonyms: brief, temporary

• • •

MOMENTOUS
adjective (moh <u>men</u> tuss)

very important or significant

*According to his mom, George choosing to clean his room rather than watch television was a **momentous** occasion—she never thought it would happen.*

Synonyms: historic, meaningful

• • •

MONASTIC
adjective (muh <u>naas</u> tihk)

extremely plain or secluded, as in a monastery

*The philosopher retired to his **monastic** lodgings to contemplate life free from any worldly distraction.*

Synonyms: austere, contemplative

MONOTONY
noun (muh naht nee)

no variation, tediously the same

The **monotony** of the sound of the dripping faucet almost drove the research assistant crazy.

Synonyms: drone, tedium

• • •

MORALITY
noun (mo ra li tee)

concern for right and wrong

Willow's **morality** required her to always stand up for the underdog.

Synonyms: ethics, principles

• • •

MORASS
noun (mu rass)

marsh, an area of soggy ground

On a class trip, Chantalle lost a heel from her favorite pair of shoes in a grassy **morass**.

Synonyms: tangle, jungle

MORDANT
adjective (mohr dnt)

biting and caustic in manner and style

Roald Dahl's stories are **mordant** alternatives to bland kids' stories.

Synonyms: scathing, hurtful

• • •

MORES
noun (mawr ayz)

fixed customs or manners, moral attitudes

In keeping with the **mores** of ancient Roman society, Nero held a celebration every weekend.

Synonyms: conventions, practices

• • •

MORIBUND
adjective (mohr uh buhnd)

dying, decaying

Thanks to the feminist movement, many sexist customs are now **moribund** in this society.

Synonyms: deceasing, succumbing

MOROSE
adjective (muh <u>rohs</u>) (maw <u>rohs</u>)

gloomy, sullen

*After hearing that the internship had been given to someone else, Lenny was **morose** for days.*

Synonyms: pessimistic, dour

• • •

MOTE
noun (moht)

a small particle, speck

*Monica's eye watered, irritated by a **mote** of dust.*

Synonyms: bit, shred

• • •

MOTTLE
verb (<u>maht</u> l)

to mark with spots

*Food stains **mottled** the tablecloth.*

Synonym: spotted

MUDDLE
verb (<u>mud</u> il)

to jumble, to confuse, to bungle

*Timmy tried to explain to the science fair judges how he had built his robot, but he was so nervous that he **muddled** the whole presentation.*

Synonyms: disorder, mix-up

• • •

MULTIFARIOUS
adjective (muhl tuh <u>faar</u> ee uhs)

diverse

*Ken opened the hotel room window, letting in the **multifarious** noises of the great city.*

Synonym: various

• • •

MUNDANE
adjective (mun <u>dayn</u>)

ordinary, commonplace

*The **mundane** lunchroom menu was spiced up one day by a visit from the chefs of a neighboring restaurant.*

Synonyms: routine, humdrum

MUNIFICENT
adjective (myoo <u>nihf</u> ih suhnt)

generous

*The **munificent** millionaire donated ten million dollars to the hospital.*

Synonyms: bountiful, liberal

• • •

MUTABILITY
noun (myoo tuh <u>bihl</u> uh tee)

the quality of being capable of change, in form or character, susceptibility of change

*The actress lacked the **mutability** needed to perform in the improvisational play.*

Synonyms: inconstancy, variation

• • •

MUTTER
verb (<u>mut</u> er)

to grumble or complain

*The class **muttered** and groaned when they were given a ton of physics homework.*

Synonyms: grunt, murmur

MYOPIC
adjective (mie <u>ahp</u> ihk) (mie <u>oh</u> pihk)

lacking foresight, having a narrow view or long-range perspective

*Not wanting to spend a lot of money up front, the **myopic** business owner would likely suffer the consequences later.*

Synonyms: short-sighted, unthinking

• • •

MYSTIFY
verb (<u>mist</u> ih fiy)

to confuse or puzzle, to make obscure

*George's parents were **mystified** when they heard him explaining calculus to a friend over the phone.*

Synonyms: stun, baffle

• • •

MYTHICAL
adjective (<u>mith</u> ih kul)

fictitious element belonging to ancient stories

*Most people believe that the unicorn is a **mythical** creature, but Willow suspects that they really do exist.*

Synonym: fabled

MYTHOLOGICAL

adjective (myth o log i cal)

imaginary

*Ever since Mark read about unicorns, he had been fascinated by **mythological** stories.*

Synonym: fictitious

NADIR

noun (<u>nay</u> dihr)

lowest point

*As Lou waited in line to audition for the diaper commercial, he realized he had reached the **nadir** of his acting career.*

Synonyms: bottom, depth, pit

• • •

NAÏVE

adjective (niy <u>eev</u>)

lacking experience and understanding

*Ashley had no idea how **naïve** she would feel once she left her small town to attend college in a big city.*

Synonyms: simple, innocent

NARCISSISM

noun (<u>nar</u> sih sizm)

excessive love or admiration of oneself

*Chantalle, the poster girl for **narcissism**, would not admit that she did, in fact, have a pimple.*

Synonym: vain

• • •

NASCENT

adjective (<u>nay</u> sehnt)

starting to develop, coming into existence

*The advertising campaign was still in a **nascent** stage, and nothing had been finalized yet.*

Synonyms: embryonic, emerging, inchoate, incipient

NAVIGABLE

adjective (<u>nav</u> ih guh bul)

sufficient for vessels to pass through

*Although **navigable** for some, the choppy waters on the lake were too rough for Josh to sail safely.*

Synonym: passable

. . .

NEBULOUS

adjective (<u>neh</u> <u>byoo</u> luhs)

vague, undefined

*The candidate's **nebulous** plans to fight crime made many voters skeptical.*

Synonyms: hazy, unclear

. . .

NECROMANCY

noun (<u>nehk</u> ruh maan see)

the practice of communicating with the dead in order to predict the future

*The practice of **necromancy** supposes belief in survival of the soul after death.*

Synonyms: sorcery, black magic

NEFARIOUS

adjective (nih <u>fahr</u> ee uhs)

intensely wicked or vicous

***Nefarious** deeds are never far from an evil-doer's mind.*

Synonyms: malevolent, sinister

. . .

NEGATE

verb (neh <u>gayt</u>)

nullify, deny

*Chantalle **negated** the rumor that she said Shanna looked like a stuffed sausage in her jeans.*

Synonym: contradict

. . .

NEGLIGENT

adjective (<u>neg</u> lih jent)

careless, inattentive

*Ashley was **negligent** in her duties as pep squad captain when she forgot to order uniforms for the three new members.*

Synonyms: derelict, lax

NEGLIGIBLE

adjective (<u>nehg</u> lih jih buhl)

not worth considering

*It's obvious from our **negligible** dropout rate that our students love our program.*

Synonyms: insignificant, nugatory, trifling, trivial

• • •

NEOLOGISM

noun (nee <u>ah</u> luh ji zuhm)

new word or expression

*Aunt Mable simply does not understand today's youth, she is perplexed by their clothing, music, and **neologisms**.*

Synonyms: slang, slip-of-the-tongue

• • •

NEONATE

noun (<u>nee</u> uh nayt)

a newborn child

*The **neonate** was born prematurely so she's still in the hospital.*

Synonyms: baby, infant

NEOPHYTE

noun (<u>nee</u> oh fiet)

novice, beginner

*A relative **neophyte** at bowling, Seth rolled all of his balls into the gutter.*

Synonyms: apprentice, greenhorn, tyro

• • •

NETTLE

verb (<u>neh</u> tuhl)

to irritate

*I don't particularly like having blue hair—I just do it to **nettle** my parents.*

Synonyms: annoy, vex

• • •

NEUTRALITY

noun (noo <u>tral</u> ih tee)

disinterest, impartiality

*Derek tried to emit a vibe of **neutrality** when, in fact, he was psyched that his old girlfriend wanted him back.*

Synonym: detachment

NEUTRALIZE
verb (<u>noo</u> truh liyz)

to balance

*When Timmy cleaned his fish tank, he added chemicals to **neutralize** the chlorine in the new water.*

Synonym: offset

• • •

NIHILISM
noun (<u>nie</u> hihl iz uhm)

belief that traditional values and beliefs are unfounded and that existence is useless, belief that conditions in the social organization are so bad as to make destruction desirable

*Robert's **nihilism** expressed itself in his lack of concern with the norms of moral society.*

Synonyms: skepticism, terrorism

• • •

NOISOME
adjective (<u>noy</u> suhm)

stinking, putrid

*A dead mouse trapped in your walls produces a **noisome** odor.*

Synonyms: disgusting, foul, malodorous

NOMENCLATURE
noun (<u>noh</u> muhn klay chuhr)

a system of scientific names

*In botany class, we learned the **nomenclature** used to identify different species of roses.*

Synonyms: classification, codification

• • •

NOMINAL
adjective (nah mihn uhl)

existing in name only, negligible

*A **nominal** but far from devoted member of the high school yearbook committee, she rarely attends meetings.*

Synonyms: minimal, titular

• • •

NONCHALANT
adjective (non shuh <u>lahnt</u>)

calm, casual, seemingly unexcited

*Paul acted **nonchalant** when he heard Marisol had broken up with her boyfriend, but inside he was totally excited.*

Synonym: indifferent

NONDESCRIPT
adjective (non des <u>kript</u>)

lacking interesting or distinctive qualities

*Marisol liked the fact that her dress made a statement, unlike the **nondescript** black evening gowns everyone else was wearing.*

Synonym: unremarkable

. . .

NON SEQUITUR
noun (nahn <u>sehk</u> wih tuhr)

a statement that does not follow logically from anything previously said

*After the heated political debate, her comment about cake was a real **non sequitur.***

Synonyms: illogical argument, off-topic comment

. . .

NOSTALGIC
adjective (nah <u>stahl</u> jik)

longing for things of the past

*After listening to his father's CD, Paul began to feel **nostalgic** for the times he used to attend concerts with his dad.*

Synonym: homesick

NOTABLE
adjective (<u>no</u> tu bul)

remarkable, worthy of notice

*Josh's performance on the baseball field was so **notable** that scouts from colleges came to watch him play.*

Synonyms: prominent, memorable

. . .

NOTION
noun (<u>no</u> shin)

idea or conception

*The **notion** that Willow would become a public advocate after college was within the realm of possibility.*

Synonym: opinion

. . .

NOTORIETY
noun (noh tohr <u>ie eh</u> tee)

unfavorable fame

*Wayne realized from the silence that greeted him as he entered the office that his **notoriety** preceded him.*

Synonyms: disgrace, dishonor, disrepute, infamy, opprobrium

NOVEL
adjective (<u>nah</u> vuhl)

new and not resembling anything formerly known

*Piercing any part of the body other than the earlobes was **novel** in the 1950s, but now it is quite common.*

Synonyms: original, innovative

. . .

NOVELTY
noun (<u>nov</u> ul tee)

something new and unusual

*At first George loved playing with his new video game unit, but soon the **novelty** wore off and he tossed it aside for something else.*

Synonym: originality

. . .

NOVICE
noun (<u>nahv</u> is)

beginner

*Although Ashley is a **novice** bowler, she scored 102 when she went bowling with her friends.*

Synonym: apprentice

NOXIOUS
adjective (nahk shuhs)

harmful, unwholesome

*The people on the sidewalk covered their noses and mouths as the bus passed to avoid breathing in the **noxious** exhaust fumes.*

Synonyms: corrupting, poisonous, toxic, unhealthy

. . .

NUANCE
noun (<u>noo</u> ahns)

shade of meaning

*The scholars argued for hours over tiny **nuances** in the interpretation of the last line of the poem.*

Synonyms: gradation, subtlety, tone

. . .

NUDGE
noun (<u>nuj</u>)

gentle push

*When his friend didn't laugh at his joke, Timmy **nudged** him in the ribs.*

Synonym: brush

NULLIFY
verb (<u>nuh</u> lih fie)

to make legally invalid, to counteract the effect of

*Crystal **nullified** her contract with her publisher when she received a better offer from another company.*

Synonyms: cancel, negate, neutralize, undo

• • •

NUMISMATICS
noun (nu miz <u>maa</u> tiks)

coin collecting

*Tomas's passion for **numismatics** has resulted in an impressive collection of coins from all over the world.*

NURTURE
verb (<u>nur</u> chur)

to help develop, cultivate

*Timmy dedicated his science fair win to all the teachers who **nurtured** his curiosity for knowledge.*

Synonym: foster

OBDURATE
adjective (<u>ahb</u> duhr uht)

stubbornly persistent, resistant to persuasion

*The president was **obdurate** on the matter, and no amount of public protest could change his mind.*

Synonyms: inflexible, inexorable, adamant

• • •

OBFUSCATE
verb (<u>ahb</u> fyoo skayt)

to confuse, make obscure

*Benny always **obfuscates** the discussion by bringing in irrelevant facts.*

Synonyms: shadow, complicate

OBJECTIVE
adjective (ob jek <u>tiv</u>)

impartial, uninfluenced by emotion

*It was tough for Shanna to remain calm and **objective** when her best friend was always criticizing her.*

Synonym: fair

• • •

OBLIQUE
adjective (oh <u>bleek</u>)

indirect, evasive, misleading, devious

*Usually open and friendly, Veronica has been behaving in a curiously **oblique** manner lately.*

Synonyms: glancing, slanted, tangential

OBLIVIOUS
adjective (ahb <u>liv</u> ee us)

unaware, inattentive

*Ashley walked around in a happy daze, totally **oblivious** that she had toilet paper on her sneaker.*

Synonym: ignorant

. . .

OBNOXIOUS
adjective (ob <u>nok</u> shiss)

objectionable

*George's **obnoxious** belch at lunch confirmed to his girlfriend that he would never change.*

Synonym: offensive

. . .

OBSCURE
adjective (ahb <u>skyoor</u>)

not easily seen, inconspicuous

*Timmy liked to study the life cycles of **obscure** insects for fun.*

Synonym: ambiguous

OBSEQUIOUS
adjective (uhb <u>see kwee</u> uhs)

overly submissive, brownnosing

*The **obsequious** new employee complimented her supervisor's tie and agreed with him on every issue.*

Synonyms: compliant, fawning, groveling, servile, unctuous

. . .

OBSOLETE
adjective (ahb so <u>leet</u>)

no longer in use

*The invention of email has made the concept of a handwritten letter almost **obsolete**.*

Synonym: outdated

. . .

OBSTACLE
noun (<u>ahb</u> stukl)

impediment

*Shanna never let her dyslexia become an **obstacle** to getting top grades.*

Synonym: encumbrance

OBSTINATE
adjective (<u>ahb</u> stih nuht)

unreasonably persistent

*The **obstinate** journalist would not reveal his source, and thus, was jailed for thirty days.*

Synonyms: **stubborn, headstrong**

. . .

OBSTREPEROUS
adjective (<u>ahb</u> strehp uhr uhs) (<u>uhb</u> strehp uhr uhs)

troublesome, boisterous, unruly

*The **obstreperous** toddler, who was always breaking things, was the terror of his nursery school.*

Synonym: **vociferous**

. . .

OBTRUSIVE
adjective (ahb <u>troo</u> siv)

pushy, too conspicuous

*Although it was a bit **obtrusive**, Shanna interrupted the teacher's conversation to ask him why she received a C on her paper.*

Synonym: **intrusive**

OBTUSE
adjective (uhb <u>toos</u>)

insensitive, stupid, dull, unclear

*The directions were so **obtuse** that Alfred did not understand what was expected of him.*

Synonyms: **blunt, dense, slow**

. . .

OBVIATE
verb (<u>ahb</u> vee ayt)

to make unnecessary, to anticipate and prevent

*The river was shallow enough for the riders to wade across, which **obviated** the need for a bridge.*

Synonyms: **avert, deter, forestall, preclude**

. . .

OCCLUDE
verb (uh k<u>lood</u>)

to shut, block

*A shadow is thrown across the Earth's surface during a solar eclipse, when the light from the sun is **occluded** by the moon.*

Synonyms: **close, obstruct**

ODOMETER

noun (oh <u>dom</u> ih ter)

instrument in vehicles that indicates distance traveled

*Josh accidentally cracked the **odometer** in his father's new car.*

• • •

OFFICIOUS

adjective (uh <u>fihsh</u> uhs)

too helpful, meddlesome

*The **officious** waiter butted into the couple's conversation, advising them on how to take out a mortgage.*

Synonyms: eager, intrusive, unwanted

• • •

OLFACTORY

adjective (ohl <u>faak</u> tuh ree)

relating to the sense of smell

*Whenever she entered a candle store, her **olfactory** sense was awakened.*

Synonyms: fragrant, odorous

OLIGARCHY

noun (<u>oh</u> lih gaar kee)

a government in which a small group exercises supreme control

*In an **oligarchy**, the few who rule are generally wealthier and have more status than the others.*

Synonym: small government

• • •

OMNISCIENT

adjective (ahm <u>nih</u> shehnt)

having infinite knowledge, all-seeing

*Fiction writers have the ability to be **omniscient** about the characters they create.*

Synonyms: all-knowing, divine

• • •

ONEROUS

adjective (<u>oh</u> neh ruhs)

burdensome

*The assignment was so difficult to manage that it proved **onerous** to the team in charge of it.*

Synonyms: arduous, demanding, exacting, oppressive, rigorous

ONSET
noun (<u>on</u> set)

start

*Ashley had lots of energy at the **onset** of the dance, but by the end she was totally exhausted.*

Synonyms: commencement, beginning

. . .

ONUS
noun (<u>oh</u> nuhs)

a burden, an obligation

*Antonia was beginning to feel the **onus** of having to feed her friend's cat for the month.*

Synonyms: responsibility, hardship

. . .

OPAQUE
adjective (oh <u>payk</u>)

impossible to see through, preventing the passage of light

*The heavy build-up of dirt and grime on the windows made them almost **opaque**.*

Synonym: obscure

OPINE
verb (oh <u>pien</u>)

to express an opinion

*At the "Let's Chat Talk Show," the audience member **opined** that the guest was in the wrong.*

Synonym: point out

. . .

OPPORTUNE
adjective (ahp pur toon)

appropriate, fitting

*Paul finds that the **opportune** time to call his girlfriend is right after her favorite TV show.*

Synonym: timely

. . .

OPPORTUNIST
noun (aap ore <u>too</u> nist)

one who takes advantage of any opportunity to achieve an end, with little regard for principles

*The **opportunist** wasted no time in stealing the idea and presenting it as his own.*

Synonyms: user, self-seeker

OPPROBRIOUS
adjective (uh proh bree uhs)

disgraceful, shameful

*She wrote an **opprobrious** editorial in the newspaper about the critic who tore her new play to shreds.*

Synonym: scornful

. . .

OPPROBIRUM
noun (uh pro bree uhm)

public disgrace

*After the scheme to embezzle the elderly was made public, the treasurer resigned in utter **opprobrium**.*

Synonyms: discredit, disgrace, dishonor, disrepute

. . .

OPTIMISTIC
adjective (op tuh mis tik)

expecting things to turn out well

*George was **optimistic** about getting into Yale, but was still nervous until he heard their decision.*

Synonym: hopeful

OPULENCE
noun (ah pyoo lehns)

wealth

*Livingston considered his expensive car to be a symbol of both **opulence** and style.*

Synonyms: affluence, luxury, prosperity

. . .

ORATION
noun (aw ray shun)

formal speech

*Shanna made sure her voice was loud and clear during her **oration** in front of the PTA.*

Synonym: lecture

. . .

ORDERLY
adjective (or der lee)

neat, systematic

*Josh had arranged his collection of college brochures into a neat and **orderly** stack on his desk.*

Synonyms: methodical, organized

ORIGINALITY
noun (uh rij uh <u>nal</u> ih tee)

the ability to think independently

*In an effort to prove her **originality**, Marisol shaved her head.*

Synonym: creativity

• • •

ORNATE
adjective (ohr <u>nayt</u>)

elaborately ornamented

*The **ornate** design on Chantalle's fingernails seemed a little too much to Ashley.*

Synonyms: florid, overwrought

• • •

ORNERY
adjective (<u>ohr</u> nuh ree)

having an irritable disposition, cantankerous

*My first impression of the taxi driver was that he was **ornery**, but then he explained that he'd just had a bad day.*

Synonyms: disagreeable, unfriendly

OROTUND
adjective (<u>or</u> uh tuhnd) (<u>ah</u> ruh tuhnd)

pompous

*Roberto soon grew tired of his date's **orotund** babble about her new job, and decided their first date would probably be their last.*

Synonyms: aureate, bombastic, declamatory, euphuistic

• • •

ORTHODOX
adjective (<u>or</u> thu doks)

adhering to what is customary or traditional

*Derek's parents asked him to dress in an **orthodox** fashion for his college interview.*

Synonyms: conservative, formal

• • •

OSCILLATE
verb (<u>ah</u> sihl ayt)

to swing back and forth like a pendulum, to vary between opposing beliefs or feelings

*The move meant a new house in a lovely neighborhood, but she missed her friends, so she **oscillated** between joy and sadness.*

Synonyms: fluctuate, vary

OSSIFY
verb (<u>ah</u> sih fie)

to change into bone, to become hardened or set in a rigidly conventional pattern

*The forensics expert ascertained the body's age based on the degree to which the facial structure had **ossified**.*

Synonyms: fossilize, petrify

• • •

OSTENSIBLE
adjective (ah <u>stehn</u> sih buhl)

apparent

*The **ostensible** reason for his visit was to borrow a book, but secretly he wanted to chat with Wanda.*

Synonyms: represented, supposed, surface

• • •

OSTENTATION
noun (ah stehn <u>tay</u> shuhn)

excessive showiness

*The **ostentation** of The Sun King's court is evident in the lavish decoration and luxuriousness of his palace at Versailles.*

Synonyms: conspicuousness, flashiness, pretentiousness, showiness

OSTENTATIOUS
adjective (ah stehn <u>tay</u> shuhs)

showy

*The billionaire's 200-room palace was considered by many to be an overly **ostentatious** display of wealth.*

Synonyms: flamboyant, fulsome, gaudy, ornate, pretentious

• • •

OSTRACISM
noun (<u>ahs</u> tra sizm)

temporary banishment

*Derek's **ostracism** from the dinner table was rescinded when he apologized for talking rudely to his parents.*

Synonym: exclusion

• • •

OSTRACIZE
verb (<u>ahs</u> truh size)

to exclude from a group by common consent

*Feeling **ostracized** from her friends, Tabitha couldn't figure out what she had done.*

Synonyms: isolate, excommunicate

OUST

verb (owst)

to remove from position by force, eject

*After President Nixon so offensively lied to the country during Watergate, he was **ousted** from office.*

Synonyms: dismiss, evict

. . .

OUTCAST

noun (owt kast)

someone rejected from a society

*Timmy was tired of feeling like an **outcast**, so he introduced himself to some new kids at his lunch table.*

Synonyms: castoff, pariah, reject

. . .

OUTDATED

adjective (owt day tid)

old-fashioned, out of style

*Although it was an **outdated** gesture, Ashley placed an apple on her favorite teacher's desk.*

Synonym: obsolete

OVERCOME

verb (oh ver kum)

defeat, conquer

*Willow **overcame** her fear of snakes by touching one at the zoo.*

Synonym: beat

. . .

OVERPOWERING

adjective (oh ver pow er ing)

overwhelming

*After watching a musical on TV, Josh had to fight the **overpowering** urge to burst into song.*

Synonym: powerful

. . .

OVERSHADOW

verb (oh ver sha dow)

to obscure, to dominate

*Although Paul was an excellent student, his troublemaking **overshadowed** his grades.*

Synonyms: outweigh, cloud

O

OVERWROUGHT
adjective (oh vuhr <u>rawt</u>)

agitated, overdone

*The lawyer's **overwrought** voice on the phone made her clients worry about the outcome of their case.*

Synonyms: elaborate, excited, nervous, ornate

PAEAN
noun (<u>pee</u> uhn)

a tribute, a song or expression of praise

He considered his newest painting a
***paean** to his late wife.*

Synonyms: laudation, ode

. . .

PALATABLE
adjective (<u>pa</u> le te bel)

having a good taste

Josh found his mother's new chicken
*dish extremely **palatable** and had*
seconds.

Synonyms: agreeable, appetizing

PALATIAL
adjective (puh <u>lay</u> shuhl)

relating to a palace, magnificent

After living in a cramped studio apart-
ment for years, Alicia thought the modest
*one-bedroom looked downright **palatial**.*

Synonyms: grand, stately

. . .

PALAVER
noun (puh <u>laav</u> uhr) (puh <u>lah</u> vuhr)

idle talk

The journalist eagerly recorded the
***palaver** among the football players in*
the locker room.

Synonym: chit-chat

PALIMPSEST
noun (<u>pahl</u> ihmp sehst)

an object or place having diverse layers or aspects beneath the surface

*Paper was very expensive, so the practice was to write over previous words, creating a **palimpsest** of writing.*

. . .

PALL
noun (pawl)

covering that darkens or obscures, coffin

*A **pall** fell over the landscape as the clouds obscured the moon in the night sky.*

Synonym: obscurity

. . .

PALL
verb (pawl)

to lose strength or interest

*Over time, the model's beauty **palled**, though her haughty attitude remained intact.*

Synonyms: tire, weary

PALLIATE
verb (<u>paa</u> lee ayt)

to make less serious, ease

*The accused's crime was so vicious that the defense lawyer could not **palliate** it for the jury.*

Synonyms: alleviate, assuage, extenuate, mitigate

. . .

PALLID
adjective (<u>pal</u> id)

lacking color or liveliness

*George's **pallid** complexion was due to the fact that he spent most of his free time in front of the TV.*

Synonym: pale

. . .

PALPABLE
adjective (<u>pahlp</u> uh buhl)

capable of being touched or felt, easily perceived

*The tension was **palpable** as I walked into the room.*

Synonyms: readily detected, tangible

PALTRY
adjective (pawl tree)

pitifully small or worthless

Bernardo paid the ragged boy the **paltry** *sum of 25 cents to carry his luggage all the way to the hotel.*

Synonyms: trifling, petty

. . .

PANACEA
noun (paan uh see uh)

cure-all

Some claim that vitamin C is a **panacea** *for all sorts of illnesses, but I have my doubts.*

Synonyms: elixir, miracle drug, sovereign remedy

. . .

PANACHE
noun (puh nahsh)

flamboyance or dash in style and action

Leah has such **panache** *when planning parties, even when they're last-minute affairs.*

Synonym: flair

PANDEMIC
adjective (paan deh mihk)

occurring over a wide geographic area and affecting a large portion of the population

Pandemic *alarm spread throughout Colombia after the devastating earthquake.*

Synonyms: general, extensive

. . .

PANEGYRIC
noun (paan uh geer ihk)

elaborate praise, formal hymn of praise

The director's **panegyric** *for the donor who kept his charity going was heartwarming.*

Synonyms: compliment, homage

. . .

PANGLOSSIAN
adjective (pan gloss ian)

excessively hopeful, marked by the thought that all is for the best

Jesse was so **Panglossian** *about their finances that Nicole often had to leave the room to keep from screaming.*

Synonym: optimistic

PANOPLY
noun (<u>paan</u> uh plee)

impressive array

*Corrina casually sifted through a **panoply** of job offers before finally deciding on one.*

Synonym: large variety

• • •

PANTOMIME
noun (pan toh <u>miym</u>)

communication through gestures

*Marisol thought it would be fun to spend a day communicating through **pantomime** rather than talking to people.*

Synonym: gesture

• • •

PARADIGM
noun (<u>paar</u> uh diem)

an outstandingly clear or typical example

*The new restaurant owner used the fast-food giant as a **paradigm** for expansion into new locales.*

Synonym: model

PARADOX
noun (<u>par</u> uh doks)

incongruity, dilemma, puzzle

*It's a sad **paradox** that so many girls assume they need to diet to be beautiful when lots of guys are attracted to girls with curves.*

Synonym: contradiction

• • •

PARAGON
noun (<u>paar</u> uh gon)

a model of excellence or perfection

*She's the **paragon** of what a judge should be: honest, intelligent, and just.*

Synonyms: ideal, paradigm

• • •

PARAMOUNT
adjective (<u>paar</u> uh mownt)

supreme, of chief importance

*It's of **paramount** importance that we make it back to camp before the storm hits.*

Synonyms: primary, dominant

PARANOID
adjective (par uh noyd)

exhibiting extreme mistrust

*After walking underneath a ladder, Paul became **paranoid** that something awful was going to happen to him.*

Synonyms: nervous, wary

• • •

PARAPHRASE
verb (par uh frayz)

to reword, usually in simpler terms

*Some students believe that it's not plagiarism if you **paraphrase** a section from a book to use in a school paper, but technically, it is.*

Synonyms: restate, rephrase

• • •

PARASITE
noun (par uh siyt)

person or animal that lives at another's expense

*Chantalle was disgusted as she watched her **parasite** of a date shove large handfuls of her popcorn into his mouth.*

Synonym: leech

PARCHED
adjective (parch t)

shriveled

*Chantalle's date was **parched** after eating all of her popcorn during the movie, so he took a big swig of her soda.*

Synonym: dry

• • •

PARE
verb (payr)

to trim off excess, reduce

*The cook's hands were sore after she **pared** hundreds of potatoes for the banquet.*

Synonyms: peel, clip

• • •

PARIAH
noun (puh rie uh)

an outcast

*Once he betrayed those in his community, he was banished and lived the life of a **pariah**.*

Synonyms: castaway, derelict, leper, offscouring, untouchable

PARITY
noun (<u>paa</u> ruh tee)

equality

*Mrs. Lutskaya tried to maintain **parity** between her children, although each claimed she gave the other preferential treatment.*

Synonyms: equivalence, evenness, par

• • •

PARLEY
noun (<u>pahr</u> lee)

discussion, usually between enemies

*The peace organization tried in vain to schedule a **parley** between the warring countries.*

Synonyms: confabulation, conference

• • •

PAROCHIAL
adjective (puh <u>ro</u> kee uhl)

of limited scope or outlook, provincial

*It was obvious that Victor's **parochial** mentality would clash with Ivonne's liberal open-mindedness.*

Synonyms: insular, narrow, restricted

PARRY
verb (<u>paa</u> ree)

To ward off or deflect

*Kari **parried** every question the interviewer fired at her, much to his frustration.*

Synonyms: avoid, evade, repel

• • •

PARSIMONY
noun (<u>pahr</u> sih moh nee)

stinginess

*Ethel gained a reputation for **parsimony** when she refused to pay for her daughter's college education.*

Synonyms: economy, frugality, meanness, miserliness

• • •

PARTISAN
noun (<u>par</u> ti zun)

strong supporter

*Willow is known as a **partisan** of almost every cause that protects the environment.*

Synonyms: zealot, follower

PASSIVE

adjective (<u>pass</u> iv)

submissive, inactive

Chantalle cut in front of a group of passive-looking boys on line at the music store.

Synonyms: resigned, tolerant

. . .

PASTICHE

noun (pah steesh)

piece of literature or music imitating other works

The playwright's clever pastiche of the well-known fairy tale had the audience rolling in the aisles.

Synonyms: medley, spoof

. . .

PATENT

adjective (<u>paa</u> tehnt)

obvious, evident

Moe could no longer stand Frank's patent fawning over the boss and so confronted him.

Synonyms: unconcealed, clear

PATHETIC

adjective (puh <u>thet</u> ik)

arousing scornful pity

Timmy held in his laughter when he saw Josh's pathetic excuse for a home-work answer on the chalkboard.

Synonyms: miserable, piteous

. . .

PATHOGENIC

adjective (paa thoh <u>jehn</u> ihk)

causing disease

Bina's research on the origins of pathogenic microorganisms should help stop the spread of disease.

Synonyms: noxious, infecting

. . .

PATHOS

noun (<u>pay</u> thohs)

compassion

Shanna loved Shakespeare's plays because they contained both comedy and pathos.

Synonym: pity

PATRICIAN
adjective (puh <u>trih</u> shuhn)

aristocratic

*Though he really couldn't afford an expensive lifestyle, Claudius had **patrician** tastes.*

Synonym: high-class

. . .

PATRONIZE
verb (<u>pay</u> troh niez)

to act as patron of, to adopt an air of condescension toward, to buy from

*LuAnn **patronized** the students, treating them like simpletons, which they deeply resented.*

Synonym: condescend

. . .

PAUCITY
noun (<u>paw</u> suh tee)

scarcity, lack

*Because of the relative **paucity** of bananas in the country, their price was very high.*

Synonyms: dearth, deficiency, shortage

PECCADILLO
noun (pehk uh <u>dih</u> loh)

minor sin or offense

*Gabriel tends to harp on his brother's **peccadilloes** and never lets him live them down.*

Synonyms: failing, fault, lapse, misstep

. . .

PECULATE
verb (<u>pehk</u> yuh layt)

to embezzle

*These days in the news, we read more and more about workers **peculating** the system.*

Synonym: misappropriate

. . .

PECUNIARY
adjective (pih <u>kyoon</u> nee <u>ehr</u> ee)

relating to money

*Michelle's official title was office manager, but she ended up taking on a lot of **pecuniary** responsibilities such as payroll duties.*

Synonyms: fiscal, financial

PEDAGOGUE

noun (pehd uh gahg)

teacher

*The beloved professor was known as an influential **pedagogue** at the university.*

Synonym: instructor

. . .

PEDANT

noun (peh daant)

uninspired, boring academic

*The speaker's tedious commentary on the subject soon gained him a reputation as a **pedant**.*

Synonyms: pedagogue, scholar, schoolmaster

. . .

PEER

noun (peer)

contemporary, equal

*Ashley approached a group of her **peers** and asked them if they were going to the school dance on Saturday.*

Synonym: match

PEJORATIVE

noun (peh jaw ruh tihv)

having bad connotations, disparaging

*The teacher scolded Mark for his unduly **pejorative** comments about his classmate's presentation.*

Synonyms: belittling, dismissive, insulting

. . .

PELLUCID

adjective (peh loo sihd)

transparently clear in style or meaning, easy to understand

*Though she thought she could hide her ulterior motives, they were **pellucid** to everyone else.*

Synonym: apparent

. . .

PENCHANT

noun (pehn chehnt)

an inclination, a definite liking

*After Daniel visited the Grand Canyon, he developed a **penchant** for travel.*

Synonyms: leaning, predilection

PENITENT
adjective (peh nih tehnt)

expressing sorrow for sins or offenses, repentant

*Claiming the murderer did not feel **penitent**, the victim's family felt his pardon should be denied.*

Synonyms: remorseful, apologetic

. . .

PENURIOUS
adjective (peh noor ee us)

stingy, poverty-stricken

*Marisol swore that she would rather live a **penurious** life and be free to create art than get a job that would stifle her creativity.*

Synonym: poor

. . .

PENURY
noun (pehn yuh ree)

an oppressive lack of resources (as money), severe poverty

*Once a famous actor, he eventually died in **penury** and anonymity.*

Synonyms: destitution, impoverishment

PERCEPTION
noun (per sep shun)

act or ability to see or understand

*The students' **perception** of what was cool was often determined by the opinions of their peers.*

Synonym: comprehension

. . .

PERCIPIENT
adjective (puhr sihp ee uhnt)

discerning, able to perceive

*The **percipient** detective saw through the suspect's lies and uncovered the truth in the matter.*

Synonyms: insightful, perceptive

. . .

PERDITION
noun (puhr dihsh uhn)

complete and utter loss, damnation

*Faust brought **perdition** upon himself when he made a deal with the devil in exchange for power.*

Synonym: abyss

PEREGRINATE
verb (<u>pehr</u> ih gruh nayt)

to travel on foot

*It has always been a dream of mine to **peregrinate** from one side of Europe to the other with nothing but a backpack.*

Synonyms: walk, traverse

. . .

PERFIDIOUS
adjective (puhr <u>fih</u> dee uhs)

faithless, disloyal, untrustworthy

*The actress's **perfidious** companion revealed all of her intimate secrets to the gossip columnist.*

Synonyms: deceitful, devious, treacherous

. . .

PERFUNCTORY
adjective (puhr <u>fuhnk</u> tor ee)

done in a routine way, indifferent

*The machinelike bank teller processed the transaction and gave the waiting customer a **perfunctory** smile.*

Synonyms: careless, halfhearted, tepid

PERIODIC
adjective (pir ee <u>odd</u> ik)

recurring from time to time, cyclical

*Ashley **periodically** practiced different smiles in the mirror just in case someone wanted to take her picture.*

Synonym: intermittent

. . .

PERIPATETIC
adjective (peh ruh puh <u>teh</u> tihk)

moving from place to place

*Morty claims that his **peripatetic** hot dog stand gives him the opportunity to travel all over the city.*

Synonyms: itinerant, nomadic, vagabond

. . .

PERJURE
verb (<u>pir</u> joor)

to tell a lie under oath

*Paul **perjured** himself when he swore on his dead gerbil that he returned the overdue DVD to the video store.*

Synonyms: deceive, mislead

P

PERMEABLE
adjective (puhr mee uh buhl)

penetrable

Karen discovered that her raincoat was **permeable** *when she was drenched while wearing it in a rainstorm.*

Synonyms: pervious, porous

. . .

PERMEATE
verb (puhr mee ayt)

to penetrate

This miraculous new cleaning fluid is able to **permeate** *stains and dissolve them in minutes!*

Synonyms: imbue, infuse, pervade, suffuse

. . .

PERNICIOUS
adjective (puhr nih shuhs)

very harmful

Poor nutrition and lack of exercise has a **pernicious** *effect on the human body.*

Synonyms: deadly, destructive, evil, pestilent, wicked

PERPLEX
verb (pir pleks)

to confuse

Josh's explanation of a ground-rule double during the high school baseball game **perplexed** *Ashley.*

Synonyms: complicate, baffle

. . .

PERSEVERE
verb (pir suh veer)

to refuse to stop no matter how hard something is

Willow decided to **persevere** *with her yoga practice until she could twist herself into a pretzel shape.*

Synonym: persist

. . .

PERSISTENCE
noun (pir sis tuns)

the act, state, or quality of not giving up

Ashley's **persistence** *paid off when she convinced four hundred students to cheer for their home team.*

Synonyms: continuance, durability, endurance

PERSPICACIOUS

adjective (puhr spuh <u>kay</u> shuhs)

shrewd, astute, keen-witted

*Inspector Poirot used his **perspicacious** mind to solve mysteries.*

Synonyms: insightful, intelligent, sagacious

. . .

PERVADE

verb (puhr <u>vayd</u>)

to be present throughout, to permeate

*Four spices—cumin, turmeric, coriander, and cayenne—**pervade** almost every Indian dish, and give the cuisine its distinctive flavor.*

Synonyms: imbue, infuse, penetrate, permeate, suffuse

. . .

PESTILENCE

noun (<u>peh</u> stihl ehns)

epidemic, plague

*The country went into national crisis when it was plagued by both **pestilence** and floods at the same time.*

Synonyms: contagion, disease, illness, scourge, sickness

PERTINACIOUS

adjective (puhr tn <u>ay</u> shuhs)

persistent, stubborn

*Despite her parents' opposition, Tina was **pertinacious** in her insistence to travel alone.*

Synonym: obstinate

. . .

PERTINENT

adjective (<u>pir</u> tih nent)

applicable, appropriate

*Paul used index cards to make sure he included all the **pertinent** information in his oral report on the Civil War.*

Synonyms: relevant, material

. . .

PERVASIVE

adjective (pir <u>vay</u> siv)

tending to pervade, spreading throughout

*The delicious smell of cinnamon buns was so **pervasive** throughout the mall that Marisol felt compelled to buy one.*

Synonym: widespread

PESSIMISM
noun (<u>pes</u> uh mizm)

negativity

*No one could accuse Ashley of **pessimism** as she always looks on the bright side of things.*

Synonym: hopeless

• • •

PETRIFY
verb (<u>pe</u> tre fi)

to turn into stone, to paralyze with fear

*Marta was **petrified** when she was stopped by the security guard in the mall.*

Synonym: harden

• • •

PETULANCE
noun (<u>peh</u> chu luhns)

rudeness, peevishness

*The child's **petulance** annoyed the teacher, who liked her students to be cheerful and cooperative.*

Synonyms: fretfulness, irritability, querulousness, testiness

PHALANX
noun (<u>fay</u> laanks)

a compact or close-knit body of people, animals, or things

*A **phalanx** of guards stood outside the prime minister's home day and night.*

Synonyms: mass, legion

• • •

PHILANTHROPY
noun (fihl <u>aan</u> throh pee)

charity, a desire or effort to promote goodness

*The Metropolitan Museum of Art owes much of its collection to the **philanthropy** of private collectors who willed their estates to the museum.*

Synonyms: altruism, humanitarianism

• • •

PHILISTINE
noun (<u>fihl</u> uh steen)

a person who is guided by materialism and is disdainful of intellectual or artistic values

*The **philistine** never even glanced at the rare violin in his collection but instead kept an eye on its value and sold it at a profit.*

Synonyms: churl, vulgarian

PHILOLOGY
noun (fih <u>lahl</u> uh jee)

the study of ancient texts and languages

Philology was the predecessor to modern-day linguistics.

. . .

PHLEGMATIC
adjective (fleg <u>mat</u> ik)

calm in temperament, sluggish

George's phlegmatic work ethic was evident when he took four hours to stack a pile of sweaters for his boss.

Synonym: impassive

. . .

PHYSIOLOGICAL
adjective (phys i o <u>log</u> i cal)

related to the functions and activities of living organisms

The doctor determined that Ka Vang's pain had a physiological cause and ordered more tests.

PIGMENT
noun (<u>pig</u> ment)

substance used for coloring

Marisol created a gorgeous shade of green by mixing yellow and blue pigments into her white paint.

Synonyms: dye, stain

. . .

PILFER
verb (<u>pihl</u> fuhr)

to steal

Marianne did not pilfer the money for herself but rather for her sick brother, who needed medicine.

Synonyms: arrogate, embezzle, filch, poach, purloin

. . .

PIOUS
adjective (<u>pi</u> es)

religiously devout or moral

The preist gave his congregation a pious speech on the value of honesty.

Synonyms: spriritual, holy

PIQUE
verb (peek)

to arouse anger or resentment in, provoke

*His continual insensitivity **piqued** my anger.*

Synonyms: irritate, rouse

• • •

PITHY
adjective (pih thee)

profound, substantial, concise, succinct, to the point

*Martha's **pithy** comments during the interview must have been impressive, because she got the job.*

Synonyms: brief, compact, laconic, terse

• • •

PITTANCE
noun (piht ns)

meager amount or wage

*Zack felt sure he would not be able to buy food for his family with the small **pittance** the government gave him.*

Synonyms: insufficiency, scrap

PLACATE
verb (play cayt)

to soothe or pacify

*The burglar tried to **placate** the snarling Doberman by saying, "Nice doggy," and offering it a treat.*

Synonyms: appease, conciliate, mollify

• • •

PLACEBO
noun (plu see boh)

a substance with no medical value that is given as medication

*Lisa said she felt much smarter after swallowing one of Shanna's coveted smart pills, she had no idea that it was a **placebo**.*

Synonyms: fake, inactive

• • •

PLAGIARIZE
verb (play ju riyz)

to pass off another's ideas as one's own

*George got an F on a paper when the teacher realized that he'd **plagiarized** another student's work.*

Synonym: copy

PLAINTIVE

adjective (<u>playn</u> tihv)

expressive of suffering or woe, melancholy

*The **plaintive** cries from the girl trapped in the tree were heard by all.*

Synonyms: mournful, sorrowful

. . .

PLASTIC

adjective (<u>plaa</u> stihk)

able to be molded, altered, or bent

*The new material was very **plastic** and could be formed into products of vastly different shapes.*

Synonyms: adaptable, ductile, malleable, pliant

. . .

PLATITUDE

noun (<u>plaa</u> tuh tood)

overused and trite remark

*Instead of the usual **platitudes**, the comedian gave a memorable and inspiring speech to the graduating class.*

Synonym: cliché

PLAUDITS

noun (<u>plaw</u> ditz)

enthusiastic praise

*Marisol received **plaudits** from her art teacher when she displayed her magnificent painting.*

Synonym: applause

. . .

PLAUSIBLE

adjective (<u>plaw</u> z bl)

seeming to be true

*Debbie said she was late because she was stuck in traffic, which seemed like a **plausible** story.*

Synonym: valid

. . .

PLEBEIAN

adjective (plee <u>bee</u> uhn)

crude or coarse, characteristic of commoners

*After five weeks of rigorous studying, the graduate settled in for a weekend of **plebeian** socializing and television watching.*

Synonyms: unrefined, conventional

PLENTIFUL

adjective (<u>plen</u> tih ful)

abundant

*Josh was psyched to find a **plentiful** supply of nachos, his favorite snack, on a tray in the fridge.*

Synonym: bountiful, ample

• • •

PLETHORA

noun (<u>pleh</u> thor uh)

excess

*Assuming that more was better, the defendant offered the judge a **plethora** of excuses.*

Synonyms: glut, overabundance, superfluity, surfeit

• • •

PLOY

noun (<u>ploy</u>)

maneuver, plan

*George's **ploy** to butter up his teacher so that she'd give him an A was unsuccessful.*

Synonym: trick

PLUCKY

adjective (<u>pluh</u> kee)

courageous, spunky

*The **plucky** young nurse dove into the foxhole, determined to help the wounded soldier.*

Synonym: brave

• • •

PLY

verb (plie)

to join together, to use diligentily, to engage

*The weaver **plied** the fibers together to make a blanket.*

Synonyms: handle, manipulate

• • •

POIGNANT

adjective (<u>poi</u> gnant)

emotionally moving in a way that is touching

*It was a **poignant** moment when Gerald's father finally admitted to him that he'd been wrong.*

Synonyms: heartbreaking, profound

POLARIZE
verb (<u>poh</u> lu ryz)

to tend toward opposite extremes

*The school was **polarized** over the issue of pass/fail grading.*

Synonym: divide

. . .

POLEMIC
noun (puh <u>leh</u> mihk)

controversy, argument, verbal attack

*The candidate's **polemic** against his opponent was vicious and small-minded rather than well reasoned and convincing.*

Synonyms: denunciation, refutation

. . .

POLITIC
adjective (<u>pah</u> luh tihk)

shrewd and crafty in managing or dealing with things

*She was wise to curb her tongue and was able to explain her problem to the judge in a respectful and **politic** manner.*

Synonym: tactful

POLYGLOT
noun (<u>pah</u> lee glaht)

a speaker of many languages

*Ling's extensive travels have helped her to become a true **polyglot**.*

Synonym: multilingual

. . .

POMP
noun (<u>pomp</u>)

dignified display

*Ashley waved graciously as she accepted her title and took in the **pomp** of the pageant's crowning ceremony.*

Synonym: splendor

. . .

POMPOUS
adjective (<u>pom</u> pus)

pretentious

*Chantalle wondered if admitting how glad she was to be so beautiful and talented was a bit **pompous**, even if it was totally true.*

Synonyms: arrogant, conceited

PONTIFICATE
verb (pahn <u>tih</u> fih kayt)

to speak in a pretentious manner

*She **pontificated** about the virtues of being rich until we all left the room in disgust.*

Synonyms: declaim, lecture, orate, preach, sermonize

• • •

PORE
verb (pohr)

to read studiously or attentively

*I've **pored** over this text, yet I still can't understand it.*

Synonym: fix attention on

• • •

PORTENTOUS
adjective (pohr <u>tehn</u> tuhs)

foreshadowing, ominous, eliciting amazement and wonder

*Everyone thought the rays of light were **portentous** until they realized a nine-year-old was playing a joke on them.*

Synonym: premonitory

POSIT
verb (<u>pohz</u> iht)

to assume as real or conceded, propose as an explanation

*Before proving the math formula, we needed to **posit** that x and y were real numbers.*

Synonym: suggest

• • •

POSTPONE
verb (post <u>pohn</u>)

to delay

*Shanna **postponed** her date for an hour so that she could get her hair just right.*

Synonyms: defer, shelve

• • •

POTABLE
adjective (<u>poh</u> tuh buhl)

suitable for drinking

*Though the water was **potable**, it tasted terrible.*

Synonym: unpolluted

POTENTATE
noun (<u>poh</u> tehn tayt)

a ruler, one who wields great power

*Alex was much kinder before he assumed the role of **potentate**.*

Synonyms: leader, dominator

. . .

PRAGMATIC
adjective (prag <u>mat</u> ik)

practical, moved by facts rather than abstract ideals

*Timmy's **pragmatic** approach to saving money helped him purchase a new motorcycle.*

Synonym: realistic

. . .

PRANK
noun (<u>prank</u>)

practical joke

*Paul promised his mom that he'd stop playing mean **pranks** on the kids at school.*

Synonyms: antic, caper, trick

PRATTLE
noun (<u>praa</u> tuhl)

meaningless, foolish talk

*Her husband's mindless **prattle** drove Heidi insane, sometimes she wished he would just shut up.*

Synonyms: babble, blather, chatter, drivel, gibberish

. . .

PREAMBLE
noun (<u>pre</u> am bul)

introductory passage

*The **preamble** to the student bylaws was so boring that Derek skipped right over it.*

Synonym: opening

. . .

PRECARIOUS
adjective (prih <u>caa</u> ree uhs)

lacking in security or stability, dependent on chance or uncertain conditions

*Given the **precarious** circumstances, I chose to opt out of the deal completely.*

Synonyms: doubtful, chancy

PRECEDENT
noun (<u>press</u> uh dent)

earlier example of a similar situation

*Josh's older brother set a **precedent** for athletic achievement in their family.*

Synonym: previous

• • •

PRECEPT
noun (<u>pree</u> sept)

principle

*Timmy eventually realized that there was no **precept** that states geniuses had to dress like dorks.*

Synonym: rule

• • •

PRECIOUS
adjective (<u>presh</u> us)

valuable, beloved

*Willow couldn't resist the **precious** little puppy at the pound, so she took it home.*

Synonyms: darling, lovable

PRECIPITATE
adjective (preh <u>sih</u> puh tayt)

sudden and unexpected

*Because the couple wed after knowing each other only a month, many expected their **precipitate** marriage to end in divorce.*

Synonyms: abrupt, headlong, impetuous, rash, reckless

• • •

PRECIPITATE
verb (preh <u>sih</u> puh tayt)

to cause to happen, to throw down from a height

*It's fairly certain that Lloyd's incessant smoking **precipitated** his early death from emphysema.*

Synonym: hurl

• • •

PRECIPITOUS
adjective (pree <u>sih</u> puh tuhs)

steeply, hastily

*At the sight of the approaching helicopters, Private Johnson **precipitously** shot a flare into the air.*

Synonyms: impetuous, headlong, reckless

PRECIS
noun (<u>pray</u> see) (pray <u>see</u>)

short summary of facts

*Fara wrote a **précis** of her thesis on the epic poem to share with the class.*

Synonym: summary

. . .

PRECLUDE
verb (pre <u>klood</u>)

prevent, exclude

*Ashley was **precluded** from cheering at the game because she forgot her uniform.*

Synonym: avert

. . .

PRECOCIOUS
adjective (pri <u>koh</u> shiss)

unusually advanced or talented at an early age

*Lisa, Shanna's **precocious** little sister, has developed advanced blackmailing skills.*

Synonyms: bright, developed

PREDETERMINE
verb (pree deh <u>ter</u> min)

to decide in advance

*Timmy had **predetermined** that he wouldn't show anyone the scar on his stomach.*

Synonym: predestined

. . .

PREDICAMENT
noun (pre di ke ment)

a difficult situation

*The boys knew that they were in a **predicament** when they were caught throwing eggs—holding the carton in their hands.*

Synonyms: corner, jam, pickle

. . .

PREDICTABLE
adjective (pre <u>dikt</u> uh bul)

expected beforehand

*Timmy's weekend routine was always so **predictable**, every Saturday night he played mini-golf with his friends.*

Synonym: obvious

PREDILECTION
noun (preh dih _lehk_ shuhn)

preference, liking

The old woman's **predilection** for candy was evident from the chocolate bar wrappers strewn all over her apartment.

Synonyms: bias, leaning, partiality, penchant, proclivity

. . .

PREDOMINANT
adjective (pre _dom_ ih nunt)

most important or conspicuous

The **predominant** feature on Marisol's face was her rather large nose.

Synonym: foremost

. . .

PREPOSSESSING
adjective (pree pu _zes_ ing)

attractive, engaging

Josh thought that Chantalle was the most **prepossessing** right after exercising.

Synonym: appealing

PRESAGE
noun (_preh_ sihj)

something that foreshadows, a feeling of what will happen in the future

The demolition of the Berlin Wall was a **presage** to the fall of the Soviet Union.

Synonym: premonition

. . .

PRESCIENT
adjective (_preh_ shuhnt)

having foresight

Jonah's decision to sell the apartment turned out to be a **prescient** one, as its value soon dropped by half.

Synonyms: augural, divinatory, mantic, oracular, premonitory

. . .

PRESERVE
verb (pre _zurv_)

to protect, to keep unchanged

Timmy slathers on sunscreen every morning to **preserve** his youthful appearance as long as possible.

Synonym: maintain

PRESTIDIGITATION
noun (<u>prehs</u> tih <u>dihj</u> ih <u>tay</u> shuhn)

a cleverly executed trick or deception, sleight of hand

*My hunch was that he won the contest not so much as a result of real talent, but rather through **prestidigitation**.*

Synonym: conjuration

. . .

PRETENSE
noun (<u>pre</u> tenss)

false appearance or action

*Shanna entered the furrier's shop under the **pretense** of browsing, but she really wanted to buy a new coat.*

Synonym: masquerade

. . .

PRETENTIOUS
adjective (pri <u>ten</u> shus)

pretending to be important, intelligent or cultured

*Derek hated clubs, he felt that the people who go to them act snobby and **pretentious**.*

Synonyms: affected, grandiose, highfalutin

PRETERNATURAL
adjective (pree tuhr <u>naach</u> uhr uhl)

existing outside of nature, extraordinary, supernatural

*We were all amazed at her **preternatural** ability to recall smells from her early childhood.*

Synonyms: psychic, abnormal

. . .

PREVARICATE
verb (prih <u>vaar</u> uh cayt)

to lie, evade the truth

*Rather than admit that he had overslept again, the employee **prevaricated**, claiming that traffic had made him late.*

Synonyms: equivocate, fabricate, fib, hedge, palter

. . .

PRIMARY
adjective (<u>pry</u> meh ree)

main, first, earliest

*The **primary** reason that Shanna won the election for class president is that she is popular.*

Synonym: foremost

PRIMEVAL
adjective (priem <u>ee</u> vuhl)

ancient, primitive

*The archaeologist claimed that the skeleton was of **primeval** origin, though in fact it was the remains of a modern-day monkey.*

Synonyms: primordial, original

. . .

PRISTINE
adjective (prih <u>steen</u>)

fresh and clean, uncorrupted

*Because concerted measures had been taken to prevent looting, the archeological site was still **pristine** when researchers arrived.*

Synonyms: innocent, undamaged

. . .

PRIVATION
noun (prih <u>vay</u> shuhn)

lack of usual necessities or comforts

*The convict endured total **privation** while locked up in solitary confinement for a month.*

Synonyms: deprivation, forfeiture, loss, poverty

PROBITY
noun (<u>proh</u> buh tee)

honesty, high-mindedness

*The conscientious witness responded with the utmost **probity** to all the questions posed to her.*

Synonyms: honor, integrity, rectitude, uprightness, virtue

. . .

PROCLAIM
verb (pro <u>klaym</u>)

announce officially

*Timmy wanted to approach the girl who worked at the coffeehouse and **proclaim** that he liked her, but he kept chickening out.*

Synonym: declare

. . .

PROCLIVITY
noun (proh <u>clih</u> vuh tee)

tendency, inclination

*His **proclivity** for speeding got him into trouble with the highway patrol on many occasions.*

Synonyms: partiality, penchant, predilection, predisposition, propensity

PROCRASTINATE
verb (pro <u>kras</u> tih nayt)

to put off doing work

*Rather than study for finals, Shanna **procrastinated** by taking her little sister to the park.*

Synonyms: **stall, delay**

• • •

PROCURE
verb (pro <u>kyoor</u>)

to acquire, obtain, to get

*Marisol showed her friend the new acrylic paints that she had **procured** at the art store.*

Synonym: **earn**

• • •

PROD
verb (<u>prahd</u>)

poke, nudge, in the literal and figurative sense

*Derek's friends **prodded** him to graffiti the handball wall at the high school.*

Synonyms: **goad, spur**

PRODIGAL
adjective (<u>prah</u> dih guhl)

recklessly extravagant, wasteful

*The **prodigal** expenditures on the military budget during a time of peace created a stir in the Cabinet.*

Synonym: **lavish**

• • •

PRODIGIOUS
adjective (pruh dih juhs)

vast, enormous, extraordinary

*The musician's **prodigious** talent made her famous all over the world.*

Synonyms: **gigantic, huge, impressive, marvelous**

• • •

PRODIGY
noun (<u>prahd</u> ih jee)

person with exceptional talents

*When Josh was two years old his parents thought he was a **prodigy** because he could count from one to ten in Spanish.*

Synonym: **wonder**

PROFANE

adjective (pro <u>fayn</u>)

impure, contrary to religion, sacrilegious

*Timmy's mom heard him utter some **profane** comments and made him wash his mouth out with soap.*

Synonym: irreverant

. . .

PROFFER

verb (<u>prahf</u> uhr)

to offer for acceptance

*The deal **proffered** by the committee satisfied all those at the meeting, ending a month-long discussion.*

Synonym: propose

. . .

PROFLIGATE

adjective (<u>praa</u> flih guht)

corrupt, degenerate

*Some historians claim that it was the Romans' decadent, **profligate** behavior that led to the decline of the Roman Empire.*

Synonyms: dissolute, extravagant, improvident, prodigal, wasteful

PROFOUND

adjective (pro <u>fownd</u>)

deep, meaningful, far-reaching

*Paul's determination to improve his writing skills had a **profound** effect on his college applications.*

Synonym: intense

. . .

PROFUSION

noun (pro <u>fyoo</u> zhin)

abundance, extravagance

*The walls of Marisol's room were covered with a **profusion** of posters and photos.*

Synonyms: load, heap

. . .

PROGENITOR

noun (proh <u>jehn</u> uh tuhr)

an ancestor in the direct line, forefather, founder

*Though his parents had been born here, his **progenitors** were from India.*

Synonym: inventor

PROHIBIT
verb (pro <u>hib</u> it)

to forbid, prevent

*Shanna's parents **prohibited** her from dating older boys, but that didn't stop her.*

Synonyms: ban, bar

• • •

PROLIFERATE
verb (proh <u>lih</u> fuhr ayt)

to grow by rapid production of new parts, increase in number

*The cancer cells **proliferated** so quickly that even the doctor was surprised.*

Synonym: multiply

• • •

PROLIFIC
adjective (pro <u>lif</u> ik)

productive, fertile

*Marisol was a **prolific** artist, who had so far produced two hundred and forty-seven paintings.*

Synonym: fruitful

PROMINENCE
noun (<u>prom</u> ih nence)

importance

*Shanna will be given great **prominence** at graduation because she had the highest GPA in the senior class.*

Synonym: eminence

• • •

PROMOTE
verb (pru <u>moht</u>)

to contribute to the progress of

*Willow did her best to **promote** the clothing drive at school and make it a success.*

Synonym: publicize

• • •

PROMULGATE
verb (<u>prah</u> muhl gayt)

to make known by open declaration, proclaim

*The publicist **promulgated** the idea that the celebrity had indeed gotten married.*

Synonyms: announce, broadcast

PROPAGANDA
noun (pra pe gan de)

the spreading of information, true or false, to achieve a specific pupose

*Jerry began spewing **propaganda** about why he was a better candidate for class president than Marcia.*

Synonyms: disinformation, indoctrination

• • •

PROPAGATE
verb (prop uh gayt)

to spread out, to have offspring

*The rumor about Chantalle sending herself roses **propagated** around school.*

Synonym: circulate

• • •

PROPEL
verb (pro pel)

to cause to move forward

*Timmy watched in awe as the cannon in the main ring of the circus **propelled** the man to the other side of the tent.*

Synonym: push

PROPENSITY
noun (proh pehn suh tee)

A natural inclination or preference

*She has a **propensity** for lashing out at others when stressed, so we leave her alone when she's had a rough day.*

Synonym: tendency

• • •

PROPHETIC
adjective (pro fet ik)

foretelling events by divine means

*Derek's horoscope about having a hot date this weekend proved **prophetic** when his ex asked him out.*

Synonym: predictive

• • •

PROPINQUITY
noun (pruh pihng kwih tee)

nearness

*The house's **propinquity** to the foul-smelling pig farm made it impossible to sell.*

Synonym: proximity

PROPITIATE
verb (proh pih shee ayt)

to conciliate, to appease

Because their gods were angry and vengeful, the Vikings propitiated them with many sacrifices.

Synonyms: appease, conciliate, mollify, pacify, placate

. . .

PROPITIOUS
adjective (pruh pih shuhs)

favorable, advantageous

"I realize that I should have brought this up at a more propitious moment, but I don't love you," said the bride to the groom in the middle of their marriage vows.

Synonyms: auspicious, benign, conducive

. . .

PROPONENT
noun (pruh poh nent)

advocate, defender

Ashley was a strong proponent of treating others the way she wanted to be treated.

Synonym: supporter

PROPRIETY
noun (pro pry ih tee)

correct behavior, appropriateness

Because George did not have a tissue, propriety demanded that he wait until he found one to blow his nose.

Synonym: decency

. . .

PROSAIC
adjective (proh say ihk)

relating to prose (as opposed to poetry), dull, ordinary

Simon's prosaic style bored his writing teacher to tears, though he thought he had an artistic flair.

Synonyms: unimaginative, everyday

. . .

PROSCRIBE
verb (proh skrieb)

to condemn or forbid as harmful or unlawful

Consumption of alcohol was proscribed in the country's constitution, but the ban was eventually lifted.

Synonyms: prohibit, ban

PROSELYTIZE
verb (prah <u>suhl</u> uh tiez)

to convert to a particular belief or religion

*The religious group went from door to door in the neighborhood, **proselytizing** enthusiastically.*

Synonyms: convince, missionize, move, preach, sway

• • •

PROSPECT
noun (<u>pross</u> pekt)

possibility

*Shanna's college counselor told her that the **prospect** of attaining a scholarship to her first-choice college was very real.*

Synonym: chance

• • •

PROSPERITY
noun (pross <u>per</u> ih tee)

wealth or success

*Timmy hoped he'd attain **prosperity** in adulthood by becoming a famous inventor.*

Synonym: accomplishment

PROSTRATE
adjective (<u>prah</u> strayt)

lying face downward in adoration or submission

*Lying **prostrate** awaiting the Pope, a car splashed me with water.*

Synonym: submissive

• • •

PROTAGONIST
noun (pro <u>tag</u> uh nist)

main character in a play or story

*Marisol often fantasized about dating an author who would make her the **protagonist** in his novel.*

Synonym: hero

• • •

PROTEAN
adjective (<u>proh</u> tee uhn)

readily assuming different forms or characters

*The **protean** actor could play a wide variety of different characters convincingly.*

Synonym: versatile

PROTÉGÉ
noun (<u>pro</u> tuh zhay)

one receiving personal direction and care from a mentor

*Josh took on a **protégé** from the JV football team and taught him new throwing techniques.*

Synonym: disciple

. . .

PROTOTYPE
noun (<u>pro</u> to tiyp)

early, typical example

*Finally, Timmy was ready to test the **prototype** of his automatic toilet paper dispenser.*

Synonym: original

. . .

PROVINCIAL
adjective (pruh <u>vihn</u> shuhl)

limited in outlook, narrow, unsophisticated

*Having grown up in the city, Anita sneered at the **provincial** attitudes of her country cousins.*

Synonyms: unpolished, unrefined

PROVOCATIVE
adjective (proh <u>vok</u> uh tiv)

tending to provoke a response, usually anger or disagreement

*The history teacher began class with a **provocative** statement about war in order to begin a debate in class.*

Synonyms: instigating, piquing

. . .

PROXIMITY
noun (prok <u>sim</u> ih tee)

nearness

*Shanna was bummed when a blue car grabbed the only parking spot in **proximity** to her favorite store.*

Synonyms: closeness, contiguity, immediacy

. . .

PROXY
noun (<u>prahk</u> see)

a person authorized to act for someone else

*In the event the stock shareholder can't attend the meeting, he'll send a **proxy**.*

Synonyms: representative, alternate

PRUDENCE
noun (<u>proo</u> dehns)

wisdom, caution or restraint

*The college student exhibited **prudence** by obtaining practical experience along with her studies, which greatly strengthened her résumé.*

Synonyms: astuteness, circumspection, discretion

. . .

PRUDENT
adjective (<u>prood</u> int)

careful, cautious

*Willow felt it **prudent** to walk the long way home rather than take a dangerous shortcut.*

Synonym: discreet

. . .

PRUNE
verb (<u>proon</u>)

to trim or make shorter

*Paul helped his mother with the gardening by **pruning** the bushes in the backyard.*

Synonym: clip

PSEUDONYM
noun (<u>soo</u> duh nihm)

a fictitious name, used particularly by writers to conceal identity

*Though George Eliot sounds as though it's a male name, it was the **pseudonym** that Marian Evans used when she published her classic novel* Middlemarch.

Synonym: pen name

. . .

PUERILE
adjective (<u>pyoo</u> ruhl)

childish, immature, silly

*His **puerile** antics are really annoying, sometimes he acts like a five-year-old!*

Synonyms: infantile, jejune, juvenile

. . .

PUGILISM
noun (<u>pyoo</u> juhl ih suhm)

boxing

***Pugilism** has been defended as a positive outlet for aggressive impulses.*

Synonyms: fighting, sparring

PUGNACIOUS
adjective (pug <u>nay</u> shus)

quarrelsome, eager and ready to fight

*The serene eighty-year-old used to be a **pugnacious** troublemaker in her youth, but she's softer now.*

Synonyms: **bellicose, belligerent, contentious**

. . .

PUISSANT
adjective (<u>pwih</u> sihnt) (<u>pyoo</u> sihnt)

powerful

*His memoir was full of descriptions of **puissant** military heroics, but most were exaggerations or outright lies.*

Synonym: **strong**

. . .

PULCHRITUDE
noun (<u>puhl</u> kruh tood)

beauty

*The mortals gazed in admiration at Venus, stunned by her incredible **pulchritude**.*

Synonyms: **comeliness, gorgeousness, handsomeness, loveliness, prettiness**

PUN
noun (<u>pun</u>)

play on words

*Paul thought the **pun** he made about homework was funny, but everyone else thought it was just corny.*

Synonym: **joke**

. . .

PUNCTILIOUS
adjective (puhngk <u>tihl</u> ee uhs)

concerned with precise details about codes or conventions

*The **punctilious** student never made spelling errors on her essays.*

Synonyms: **precise, scrupulous, meticulous**

. . .

PUNCTUAL
adjective (<u>punk</u> shoo ull)

on time

*Because Willow is a **punctual** person, she thinks it's rude when someone arrives late to an event.*

Synonym: **prompt**

P

PUNDIT
noun (puhn diht)

one who gives opinions in an authoritative manner

The **pundits** on television are often more entertaining than the sitcoms.

Synonym: critic

. . .

PUNITIVE
adjective (pyoo nih tiv)

having to do with punishment

Josh received **punitive** action by the referee when he pushed a player on the opposing team.

Synonyms: correctional, disciplinary

. . .

PUNGENT
adjective (puhn juhnt)

sharp and irritating to the senses

The smoke from the burning tires was extremely **pungent**.

Synonyms: acrid, caustic, piquant, poignant, stinging

PURLOIN
verb (puhr loyn)

to steal

The amateur detective Dupin found the **purloined** letter for which the police had searched in vain.

Synonyms: pilfer, embezzle

. . .

PURPORT
verb (puhr pohrt)

to profess, suppose, claim

Brad **purported** to be an opera lover, but he fell asleep at every performance he attended.

Synonyms: pretend, purpose

. . .

PURSUIT
noun (pur soot)

the act of chasing or striving

George likes watching movies that end up with the good guy in hot **pursuit** of the bad guy.

Synonyms: track, trail

PUSILLANIMOUS

adjective (pyoo suh <u>laa</u> nih muhs)

cowardly, without courage

*The **pusillanimous** man would not enter the yard where the miniature poodle was barking.*

Synonyms: cowardly, timid

QUAGMIRE
noun (<u>kwaag</u> mier)

marsh, difficult situation

*Oliver realized that he needed help to get himself out of this **quagmire**.*

Synonyms: bog, fen, mire, morass, swamp

• • •

QUAINT
adjective (<u>kwaynt</u>)

charmingly strange

*Chantalle thought the accessories store on Main Street was **quaint** in comparison to the mall.*

Synonyms: odd, old-fashioned

QUANDRY
noun (<u>kwan</u> du ree)

predicament

*Derek was in a **quandary** when his band was called onstage for an encore—what should they play?*

Synonym: dilemma

• • •

QUELL
verb (<u>kwell</u>)

to pacify, to suppress

*There was nothing Ashley could do to **quell** the arguing of the two girls who fought over the last brownie.*

Synonyms: quash, squash

QUERULOUS
adjective (<u>kwehr</u> yoo luhs)

inclined to complain, irritable

*Curtis's complaint letter received prompt attention after the company labeled him a **querulous** customer.*

Synonyms: peevish, puling, whiny, sniveling

. . .

QUERY
verb (<u>kweh</u> ree)

to question

*Timmy **queried** Derek about how to get girls to like him.*

Synonym: challenge

. . .

QUIESCENCE
noun (kwie <u>eh</u> sihns)

inactivity, stillness

*Bears typically fall into a state of **quiescence** when they hibernate during the winter months.*

Synonyms: calm, dormancy, idleness, repose

QUIESCENT
adjective (kwie <u>eh</u> sihnt)

motionless

*Many animals are **quiescent** over the winter months, minimizing activity in order to conserve energy.*

Synonyms: dormant, latent

. . .

QUIP
noun (<u>kwip</u>)

clever, witty joke

*Paul thought his **quip** about the teacher's hairstyle was pretty funny until he got in trouble.*

Synonyms: jest, pun

. . .

QUIXOTIC
adjective (kwihk sah tihk)

overly idealistic, impractical

*The practical Danuta was skeptical of her roommate's **quixotic** plans to build an amphitheater in their yard.*

Synonyms: capricious, impulsive, romantic, unrealistic

QUIZZICAL

adjective (<u>kwiz</u> ih kul)

expression of puzzlement

*Timmy gave Derek a **quizzical** look when Derek said that girls would like him if he played the guitar.*

Synonym: baffled

QUOTIDIAN

adjective (kwo <u>tih</u> dee uhn)

occurring daily, commonplace

*The sight of people singing on the street is so **quotidian** in New York that passersby rarely react to it.*

Synonyms: everyday, normal, usual

RACONTEUR
noun (raa cahn <u>tuhr</u>)

witty, skillful storyteller

*The **raconteur** kept all the passengers entertained with his stories during the six-hour flight.*

Synonyms: anecdotalist, monologist

• • •

RADIANT
adjective (<u>ray</u> dee unt)

glowing, beaming, emitting heat

*Marisol looked **radiant** as she walked the catwalk at the school fashion show.*

Synonyms: aglow, sunny

RADICAL
adjective (<u>rad</u> ih kul)

marked departure from the norm

*Ashley tried to gently tell Willow that her boycott of deodorant was a **radical** assault on her senses.*

Synonym: extreme

• • •

RAIL
verb (<u>rayl</u>)

to scold with bitter or abusive language

*Josh laughed when he caught the coach **railing** at an imaginary football ref in the mirror.*

Synonyms: berate, castigate

RAMBLE
verb (<u>ram</u> bl)

to roam, wander, to babble, digress

*Timmy **rambled** aimlessly through the mall looking for his best friend.*

Synonyms: **maunder, stray**

. . .

RANCOR
noun (<u>raan</u> kuhr)

bitter hatred

*Having been teased mercilessly for years, Herb became filled with **rancor** toward those who had humiliated him.*

Synonym: **deep-seated ill will**

. . .

RANCOROUS
adjective (<u>rank</u> o russ)

bitter, hateful

*A **rancorous** argument erupted between the coach and the referee after a close call.*

Synonyms: **resentful, embittered**

RANKLE
verb (<u>raang</u> kuhl)

to cause anger and irritation

*At first the kid's singing was adorable, but after 40 minutes it began to **rankle**.*

Synonyms: **embitter, annoy**

. . .

RAPACIOUS
adjective (ruh <u>pay</u> shuhs)

taking by force, driven by greed

*Sea otters are so **rapacious** that they consumer ten times their body weight in food every day.*

Synonyms: **ravenous, voracious**

. . .

RAPT
adjective (raapt)

deeply absorbed

*The story was so well performed that the usually rowdy children were **rapt** until the final word.*

Synonyms: **engrossed, immersed**

RAREFY
verb (<u>rayr</u> uh fie)

to make rare, thin, or less dense

*The atmosphere **rarefies** as altitude increases, so the air atop a mountain is too thin to breathe.*

Synonyms: attenuate, prune

• • •

RASCAL
noun (<u>ras</u> kul)

playful, mischievous person, a scoundrel

*Although George was a **rascal** at times, the principal still liked the boy.*

Synonym: scamp

• • •

RASPY
adjective (<u>ras</u> pee)

rough, grating

*Ashley's high-pitched voice turned low and **raspy** when she contracted bronchitis.*

Synonym: hoarse

RATIFY
verb (<u>ra</u> te fie)

to approve formally

*The principal called for an administrative vote to **ratify** the new school dress code.*

Synonyms: authorize, sanction

• • •

RAUCOS
adjective (<u>raw</u> kus)

harsh sounding

*The **raucous** senior carnival caused a lot of damage to the school's football field.*

Synonym: boisterous

• • •

RAVENOUS
adjective (<u>ra</u> ve nes)

wldly eager to eat

*After a long practice the football team was **ravenous** when they arrived at the pizzeria.*

Synonym: voracious

RAZE
verb (rayz)

to tear down, demolish

*The house had been **razed**, where it once stood, there was nothing but splinters and bricks.*

Synonyms: level, destroy

. . .

REACTIONARY
adjective (ree aak shuhn ayr ee)

marked by extreme conservatism, especially in politics

*The former radical hippie had turned into quite a **reactionary**, and the press tried to expose her as a hypocrite.*

Synonyms: ultraconservative, right-wing, orthodox

. . .

REAP
verb (reep)

to obtain a return, often a harvest

*Ashley **reaped** a reward of twenty bucks after she found the man's lost wallet.*

Synonym: gather

REBATE
noun (ree bayt)

deduction in amount to be paid

*Paul received a 30 percent **rebate** on the new stereo that he bought.*

Synonym: discount

. . .

REBUFF
verb (re buff)

to bluntly reject

*Ashley **rebuffed** her classmate's offer to go on a date.*

Synonyms: deny, decline

. . .

RECALCITRANT
adjective (ree kaal sih truhnt)

resisting authority or control

*The **recalcitrant** mule refused to go down the treacherous path, however hard its master pulled at its reins.*

Synonyms: defiant, headstrong, stubborn, unruly, willful

RECALL
verb (re <u>kawl</u>)

cancel, revoke, take back

*Marisol **recalled** some purses that she'd designed due to a defective clasp.*

Synonym: rescind

. . .

RECANT
verb (ree <u>kant</u>)

to retract a statement or opinion

*The statement was so damaging that the politician had no hopes of recovering his credibility, even though he tried to **recant** the words.*

Synonyms: disavow, disclaim, disown, renounce, repudiate

. . .

RECAPITULATE
verb (<u>ree</u> kuh <u>pihch</u> yoo layt)

to review by a brief summary

*After the long-winded president had finished his speech, his assistant **recapitulated** for the press the points he had made.*

Synonyms: synopsize, condense, digest

RECIDIVISM
noun (rih <u>sihd</u> uh vih zihm)

a tendency to relapse into a previous behavior, especially criminal behavior

*According to statistics, the **recidivism** rate for criminals is quite high.*

Synonyms: return, backslide, relapse

. . .

RECKLESS
adjective (<u>rek</u> lis)

careless, rash

*Derek's **reckless** behavior onstage at the school rock concert cost him a week of detention.*

Synonym: irresponsible

. . .

RECOIL
verb (<u>re</u> koi el)

to pull back physically or emotionally

*Stacy **recoiled** in horror when she saw the spider in her gym locker.*

Synonyms: flinch, wince

R

RECONCILIATION
noun (reh con sil ee <u>ay</u> shun)

the resolution of a dispute

*Sometimes Chantalle picked small fights with Shanna because their **reconciliations** were so much fun.*

Synonym: rapprochement

• • •

RECONDITE
adjective (<u>rehk</u> uhn diet) (rih <u>kahn</u> diet)

relating to obscure learning, known to only a few

*The ideas expressed in the ancient philosophical treatise were so **recondite** that only a few scholars could appreciate them.*

Synonym: esoteric

• • •

RECRIMINATION
noun (<u>ree</u> kri mi nay shun)

counter accusation

*When Willow said that Marisol lacked any artistic talent, Marisol retorted with the **recrimination** that Willow lacked personality.*

Synonym: criticism

RECTITUDE
noun (<u>rehk</u> tih tood)

moral uprightness

*Young women used to be shipped off to finishing schools to teach them proper manners and **rectitude**.*

Synonyms: honesty, honor, integrity, probity, righteousness

• • •

REDRESS
noun (<u>rih</u> drehs)

relief from wrong or injury

*Seeking **redress** for the injuries she had received in the accident, Doreen sued the driver of the truck that had hit her.*

Synonyms: amends, indemnity, quittance, reparation, restitution

• • •

REDUNDANCY
noun (ri <u>dun</u> din see)

unnecessary repetition

*Josh handed in a five-page report, but after his teacher marked all of the **redundancies**, he ended up with only two paragraphs.*

Synonyms: verboseness, wordiness

REFINEMENT
noun (ri fiyn ment)

improvement, elegance

Chantalle showed her lack of refinement by chewing her food like a cow at dinner.

Synonym: culture

• • •

REFRACT
verb (rih fraakt)

to deflect sound or light

The crystal refracted the rays of sunlight so they formed a beautiful pattern on the wall.

Synonyms: bend, slant

• • •

REFRACTED
adjective (ri frak tid)

sharply bent

Marisol loved it when the refracted rays of sunlight made the clouds look bright pink.

Synonym: deflected

REFURBISH
verb (re fur bish)

to renovate

Paul helped his father refurbish his mother's old coffee table and made it look brand-new.

Synonym: repair

• • •

REFUTE
verb (rih fyoot)

to contradict, discredit

She made such a persuasive argument that nobody could refute it.

Synonym: deny

• • •

REGALE
verb (re gayl)

amuse

Timmy regaled his friends room with tales about his summer vacation.

Synonym: entertain

REGURGITATE
verb (re <u>gur</u> juh tayt)

rush, surge, or throw back

*Most teachers prefer that their students truly understand a subject rather than just **regurgitate** a bunch of facts.*

Synonyms: heave, expel

. . .

REHASH
verb (re <u>hash</u>)

bring forth again with no real change

*When their mother asked what the problem was, Shanna and Lisa **rehashed** their argument for her.*

Synonym: retell

. . .

REITERATE
verb (re <u>it</u> uh rayt)

to say or do again

*The coach **reiterated** the importance of the big football game to the team.*

Synonym: repeat

REJOINDER
noun (rih <u>joyn</u> duhr)

response

*Patrick tried desperately to think of a clever **rejoinder** to Marcy's joke, but he couldn't.*

Synonyms: retort, riposte

. . .

RELAPSE
noun (ree <u>laps</u>)

regress

*Paul thought he had recovered from the flu, but suffered a **relapse** and got sick again.*

Synonym: backslide

. . .

RELEGATE
verb (<u>reh</u> luh <u>gayt</u>)

to send into exile, banish, assign

*Because he hadn't scored any goals during the season, Abe was **relegated** to the bench for the championship game.*

Synonyms: consign, classify, refer

RELEVANCE
noun (<u>rel</u> uh vens)

pertinence to the matter at hand, applicability

*Ashley hoped that a poor grade in chorus would not bear much **relevance** to a college acceptance.*

Synonym: pertinence

. . .

RELINQUISH
verb (re <u>lin</u> kwish)

to renounce or surrender something

*Chantalle would never willingly **relinquish** her seat at the popular lunch table.*

Synonym: abdicate

. . .

RELISH
verb (<u>reh</u> lish)

to enjoy greatly

*George **relished** the tasty hot dog, which was piled high with all the fixings.*

Synonyms: adore, revel

RELUCTANT
adjective (re <u>luk</u> tant)

unwilling, opposing

*Derek was **reluctant** to shave off his Mohawk, but he wanted to impress the college admissions officers.*

Synonym: hesitant

. . .

RELY
verb (re <u>liy</u>)

be dependant, have confidence

*Shanna knows that she can **rely** on her good study habits to get through college successfully.*

Synonyms: hang, hinge

. . .

REMEDIABLE
adjective (rih <u>mee</u> dee uh buhl)

capable of being corrected

*In the belief that the juvenile delinquent was **remediable** and not a hardened criminal, the judge put him on probation.*

Synonym: fixable

REMISS
adjective (ri <u>miss</u>)

negligent or carelessness about a job

*Timmy was **remiss** in his job at his dad's office and accidentally threw out important files.*

Synonym: derelict

• • •

REMISSION
noun (rih <u>mih</u> shuhn)

a lessening of intensity or degree

*The doctor told me that the disease had gone into **remission**.*

Synonyms: abatement, subsiding

• • •

REMNANT
noun (rem nent)

something left over, surviving trace

*George ate the **remnants** of his potato chips that had spilled onto the carpet the day before.*

Synonyms: remainder, scraps

REMORSEFUL
adjective (re <u>mors</u> ful)

feeling sorry for sins

*Marisol felt **remorseful** for accidentally dripping some paint onto her mother's new couch.*

Synonym: contrite

• • •

REMOTE
adjective (re <u>moht</u>)

distant, isolated

*Paul knew there wasn't even a **remote** chance that Marisol would go out with him.*

Synonyms: slim, slight

• • •

REMUNERATION
noun (rih <u>myoo</u> nuh ray shuhn)

payment for goods or services or to recompense for losses

*You can't expect people to do this kind of boring work without some form of **remuneration**.*

Synonyms: recompense, pay

RENOVATION

noun (ren oh _vay_ shun)

making something new again

*The school's dingy old gym was in need of some major **renovation**.*

Synonym: repair

• • •

RENUNCIATION

noun (re nun see _ay_ shin)

rejection of beliefs or preferences

*Shanna's sudden **renunciation** of horror flicks was due to the nightmares she had experienced.*

Synonyms: abnegation, renouncement

• • •

REPARTEE

noun (re _par_ tee)

witty reply

*John's talent for **repartee** made him an effective debator.*

Synonym: retort

REPAST

noun (_rih_ paast)

meal or mealtime

*Ravi prepared a delicious **repast** of chicken tikka and naan.*

Synonyms: banquet, feast

• • •

REPEL

verb (re _pel_)

to rebuff, repulse, disgust, offend

*The idea of smoking cigarettes **repelled** Ashley because she thought they smelled bad.*

Synonyms: resist, reject

• • •

REPENTANT

adjective (re _pen_ tent)

apologetic, remorseful, guilty

*George was **repentant** for sneaking a bite of pizza from his friend's kitchen.*

Synonyms: contrite, guilty

REPLETE

adjective (rih <u>pleet</u>)

abundantly supplied, complete

*The gigantic supermarket was **replete** with consumer products of every kind.*

Synonyms: abounding, full

• • •

REPLICATE

verb (<u>rep</u> lih kayt)

to duplicate, repeat

*According to Marisol, the good thing about abstract art is that you can never **replicate** the same piece twice.*

Synonym: copy

• • •

REPOSE

noun (rih <u>pohz</u>)

relaxation, leisure

*After working hard every day in the busy city, Mike finds his **repose** on weekends playing golf with friends.*

Synonyms: calmness, tranquility

REPREHENSIBLE

adjective (rehp ree <u>hehn</u> suh buhl)

blameworthy, disreputable

*Lowell was thrown out of the bar because of his **reprehensible** behavior toward the other patrons.*

Synonyms: culpable, deplorable

• • •

REPRESS

verb (re <u>press</u>)

to restrain or hold in

*Chantalle **repressed** the urge to check her email because she had just checked it five minutes ago.*

Synonyms: quell, supress

• • •

REPRIEVE

noun (re <u>preev</u>)

postponement of a punishment

*Shanna was given a **reprieve** from her loss of phone privileges so that she could call her grandmother on her birthday.*

Synonym: relief

REPRIMAND
verb (<u>rep</u> rih mand)

rebuke, admonish

*Willow **reprimanded** her puppy for having an accident in the kitchen.*

Synonym: reprove

. . .

REPROBATE
noun (reh <u>pruh</u> bayt)

morally unprincipled person

*If you ignore your society's accepted moral code, you will be considered a **reprobate**.*

Synonyms: knave, rake, rogue, scoundrel, sinner

. . .

REPROVE
verb (rih <u>proov</u>)

to criticize or correct, usually in a gentle manner

*Mrs. Hernandez **reproved** her daughter for staying out late and not calling.*

Synonyms: rebuke, admonish, reprimand

REPUDIATE
verb (rih <u>pyoo</u> dee ayt)

to reject as having no authority

*The old woman's claim that she was Russian royalty was **repudiated** when DNA tests showed she was not related to them.*

Synonyms: abjure, disclaim, disown, forswear, renounce

. . .

REPUTABLE
adjective (<u>reh</u> pyoo tu bul)

honorable

*Shanna heard from a very **reputable** source that she was going to be voted prom queen.*

Synonym: respectable

. . .

REQUISITION
verb (re kwi <u>zih</u> shun)

to demand the use of

*Josh **requisitioned** the freshman's pencil and the kid quickly handed it over.*

Synonym: commandeer

R

REQUITE
verb (rih kwiet)

to return or repay

Thanks for offering to lend me $1,000, but I know I'll never be able to requite your generosity.

Synonyms: reciprocate, compensate

• • •

RESCIND
verb (rih sihnd)

to repeal, cancel

After the celebrity was involved in a scandal, the car company rescinded its offer of an endorsement contract.

Synonyms: void, annul, revoke

• • •

RESERVE
noun (re zerv)

something put aside for future use

Chantalle put her favorite movie on reserve at the video store because she intended to rent it over the weekend.

Synonyms: bespeak, book

RESILIENT
adjective (rih sihl yuhnt)

able to recover quickly after illness or bad luck, able to bounce back to shape

Psychologists say that being resilient in life is one of the keys to success and happiness.

Synonyms: flexible, elastic

• • •

RESOLUTE
adjective (reh suh loot)

marked by firm determination

Louise was resolute: She would get into medical school no matter what.

Synonyms: firm, unwavering, intent

• • •

RESOURCE
noun (ree sors)

something that can be used

Willow wanted to buy a puppy, but she didn't have the financial resources to do so.

Synonym: fund

RESPLENDENT
adjective (rih <u>splehn</u> dihnt)

splendid, brilliant

*The bride looked **resplendent** in her gown and sparkling tiara.*

Synonyms: dazzling, bright

• • •

RESTIVE
adjective (<u>reh</u> stihv)

impatient, uneasy, restless

*The customers became **restive** after having to wait in line for hours, and began to shout complaints at the staff.*

Synonyms: agitated, anxious, fretful

• • •

RESTORE
verb (reh <u>stor</u>)

reestablish, revive

*In an effort to **restore** his abs to the six-pack he once had, Josh began a regimen of two hundred sit-ups a day.*

Synonyms: return, renew

RESTRAINED
adjective (ri <u>stray</u> nd)

controlled, repressed

*Shanna took a **restrained** breath before she told her parents that she lost their car in the mall's parking lot.*

Synonyms: quiet, restricted

• • •

RETAIN
verb (ri <u>tayn</u>)

keep possession of

*Ashley's mother had **retained** the memory of every birthday since Ashley was born.*

Synonyms: have, hold

• • •

RETICENT
adjective (<u>reh</u> tih suhnt)

not speaking freely, reserved

*Physically small and **reticent**, Joan Didion often went unnoticed by those upon whom she was reporting.*

Synonyms: restrained, secretive, silent, taciturn

R

RETINUE
noun (<u>reht</u> noo)

group of attendants with an important person

The nobleman had to make room in his mansion not only for the princess, but also for her entire **retinue**.

Synonyms: entourage, following

• • •

RETIRING
adjective (rih <u>tier</u> ihng)

shy, modest, reserved

A shy and **retiring** *man, Chuck was horrified at the idea of having to speak in public.*

Synonym: timid

• • •

RETORT
verb (ri <u>tort</u>)

to answer quickly

Glenn refused to **retort** *when his teacher asked him "What's your problem?"*

Synonyms: comeback, quip

RETRACT
verb (re <u>trakt</u>)

to take back or draw in

Josh **retracted** *his statement that roller-blading was easy when he tried it and fell down multiple times.*

Synonym: abjure

• • •

RETRENCH
verb (rih <u>trehnch</u>)

to cut down, to reduce

The most recent round of layoffs **retrenched** *our staff to only three people.*

Synonyms: excise, remove, shorten

• • •

RETROACTIVE
adjective (ret roh <u>ak</u> tiv)

applying to an earlier time

Willow was psyched that her raise was **retroactive**, *which meant that she would get extra money for working last month, too.*

REVELRY

noun (<u>reh</u> vuhl ree)

boisterous festivity

*An atmosphere of **revelry** filled the school after its basketball team's surprising victory.*

Synonyms: cavorting, frolic, gaiety, jollity, merrymaking

. . .

REVERE

verb (ri <u>veer</u>)

regard with awe

*Timmy the chess prodigy was **revered** by the other players at the teen chess tournament.*

Synonym: worship

. . .

REVILE

verb (rih <u>veye</u> uhl)

to criticize with harsh language, verbally abuse

*The artist's new installation was **reviled** by critics who weren't used to the departure from his usual work.*

Synonyms: vituperate, scold, assail

REVIVE

verb (reh <u>viyv</u>)

bring back to life, restore to use

*When Ashley is feeling blah, she likes to **revive** herself with an ice cream cone.*

Synonym: resuscitate

. . .

REVOKE

verb (ri <u>vohk</u>)

to annul, call back

*Paul's public library card was **revoked** because he forgot to return some books he had borrowed years ago.*

Synonym: cancel

. . .

RHAPSODY

noun (<u>rap</u> su dee)

a state of overwhelming emotion

*Derek was in **rhapsody** whenever he thought about his childhood.*

Synonym: ecstasy

RHETORIC

noun (<u>reh</u> tuhr ihk)

the art of speaking or writing effectively, skill in the effective use of speech

*Lincoln's talent for **rhetoric** was evident in his beautifully expressed Gettysburg Address.*

Synonyms: eloquence, articulateness

• • •

RHETORICAL
adjective (ri <u>tor</u> ih kul)

related to using language effectively

*"Do you think I'm stupid or something?" is generally a **rhetorical** question.*

Synonym: oratorical

• • •

RIBALD
adjective (<u>rih</u> buhld)

humorous in a vulgar way

*The court jester's **ribald** brand of humor delighted the rather uncouth king.*

Synonyms: coarse, gross, indelicate, lewd, obscene

RIDDLE
verb (<u>rih</u> duhl)

to make many holes in, permeate

*The gunfired **riddled** the helicopter with thousands of holes.*

Synonyms: honeycomb, perforate, pierce, prick, punch

• • •

RIFE
adjective (rief)

abundant prevalent especially to an increasing degree, filled with

*The essay was so **rife** with grammatical errors that it had to be rewritten.*

Synonyms: numerous, prevailing

• • •

ROCOCO
adjective (ruh <u>koh</u> koh) (roh kuh <u>koh</u>)

very highly ornamented, relating to an 18th century artistic style of elaborate ornamentation

*The ornate furniture in the house reminded Tatiana of the **rococo** style.*

Synonyms: intricate, ornate

ROSTER
noun (ros ter)

a record of names

*Josh's name appears at the top of the high school football **roster** because he is the team captain.*

Synonym: list

. . .

ROSTRUM
noun (rahs truhm)

an elevated platform for public speaking

*Though she was terrified, the new member of the debate club approached the **rostrum** with poise.*

Synonyms: stage, podium

. . .

ROUSE
verb (rowz)

provoke, excite, stir

*Ashley's job as head cheerleader is to **rouse** the fans and cheer on the home team.*

Synonym: wake

ROUT
verb (raut)

to conquer, chase off

*The baseball team cheered after they successfully **routed** the opposition.*

Synonym: defeat

. . .

RUDE
adjective (rood)

crude, primitive, uncouth

*Willow found George's sloppy eating habits **rude**, yet strangely captivating.*

Synonyms: rough, unrefined

. . .

RUMINATE
verb (roo muh nayt)

to contemplate, reflect upon

*The scholars spent days at the retreat **ruminating** upon the complexities of the geopolitical situation.*

Synonyms: deliberate, meditate, mull, muse, ponder

RUSTIC
adjective (<u>ruh</u> stihk)

rural

*The **rustic** cabin was an ideal setting for a vacation in the country.*

Synonyms: bucolic, pastoral

RUTHLESS
adjective (<u>rooth</u> less)

merciless, compassionless

*The AP World History teacher was infamous for giving **ruthless** exams.*

Synonyms: callous, heartless

SACCHARINE
adjective (<u>saa</u> kuh ruhn)

excessively sweet or sentimental

*Geoffrey's **saccharine** poems nauseated Lucy, and she wished he'd stop sending them.*

Synonyms: maudlin, fulsome

• • •

SACRILEGIOUS
adjective (<u>saak</u> rih <u>lihj</u> uhs)

impious, irreverent toward what is held to be sacred or holy

*It's considered **sacrilegious** for one to enter a mosque wearing shoes.*

Synonyms: profane, blasphemous

SACROSANCT
adjective (<u>saa</u> kroh saankt)

extremely sacred, beyond criticism

*Many people considered Mother Teresa to be **sacrosanct** and would not tolerate any criticism of her.*

Synonyms: holy, inviolable, off-limits

• • •

SAFEGUARD
noun (<u>sayf</u> gard)

precautionary measure

*Josh asked his buddy to spot him in the weight room as a **safeguard**.*

Synonym: defense

SAGACIOUS

adjective (suh _gay_ shuhs)

shrewd

Owls have a reputation for being **sagacious,** _perhaps because of their big eyes, which resemble glasses._

Synonyms: astute, judicious, perspicacious, sage, wise

. . .

SALACIOUS

adjective (suh _lay_ shuhs)

appealing to sexual desire

His television character was wholesomely funny so audiences who saw his stand-up comedy routine were shocked by how **salacious** _his jokes were._

Synonym: lustful

. . .

SALIENT

adjective (_say_ lee uhnt)

prominent, of notable significance

His most **salient** _characteristic is his tendency to dominate every conversation._

Synonyms: noticeable, marked, outstanding

SALUBRIOUS

adjective (suh _loo_ bree uhs)

healthful

Rundown and sickly, Rita hoped that the fresh mountain air would have a **salubrious** _effect on her health._

Synonyms: bracing, curative, medicinal, therapeutic, tonic

. . .

SALVAGE

verb (_sal_ vij)

to recover

In an effort to **salvage** _his chance of graduating on time, George tried to attend all his classes._

Synonym: save

. . .

SANCTIMONIOUS

adjective (_saangk_ tih _moh_ nee uhs)

hypocritically devout, acting morally superior to another

The **sanctimonious** _columnist turned out to have been hiding a gambling problem that cost his family everything._

Synonyms: holier-than-thou, self-righteous

SANGUINE
adjective (<u>saan</u> gwuhn)

ruddy, cheerfully optimistic

*A **sanguine** person thinks the glass is half full, while a depressed person thinks it's half empty.*

Synonyms: confident, hopeful, positive, rosy, rubicund

. . .

SARDONIC
adjective (sahr <u>dah</u> nihk)

cynical, scornfully mocking

*Denise was offended by the **sardonic** way in which her date made fun of her ideas and opinions.*

Synonyms: acerbic, caustic, sarcastic, satirical, snide

. . .

SATIATE
verb (<u>say</u> shee ayt)

to satisfy (as a need or desire) fully or to excess

*After years of journeying around the world with nothing but backpacks, the friends had finally **satiated** their desire to travel.*

Synonym: gorge

SATURATE
verb (<u>sa</u> che rayt)

to fill completely

*Sally **saturated** her daisy patch with water.*

Synonym: soak

. . .

SATURNINE
adjective (<u>saat</u> uhr nien)

cold and steady in mood, gloomy, slow to act

*Her **saturnine** expression every day made her hard to be around.*

Synonyms: sullen, bitter

. . .

SAVANT
noun (suh <u>vahnt</u>)

a person of learning, especially one with knowledge in a special field

*The **savant** so impressed us with his knowledge that we asked him to come speak at our school.*

Synonym: scholar

SAVVY
noun (<u>sav</u> vy)

practical understanding, intelligence

*Morgan is known as a **savvy** and intelligent individual.*

Synonym: shrewdness

• • •

SCAMPER
verb (<u>skam</u> per)

run off quickly

*Willow hurried to keep up as her puppy **scampered** down the road.*

Synonym: scurry

• • •

SCAPEGOAT
noun (<u>skayp</u> goht)

someone blamed for every problem

*Paul spilled a glass of juice on the rug and used his dog, Muffin, as a **scapegoat**.*

Synonym: patsy

SCATHING
adjective (<u>skay</u> theng)

extremely critical

*Trisha couldn't forgive Chantelle for her **scathing** comments.*

Synonym: harsh

• • •

SCHISM
noun (<u>ski</u> zem)

a division or separation

*The team members agreed to stop arguing amongst themselves to avoid a permanent **schism**.*

Synonyms: division, separation

• • •

SCHOLARLY
adjective (<u>skol</u> ur lee)

related to higher learning

*Timmy was looking forward to leaving high school behind in favor of more **scholarly** pursuits.*

Synonym: academic

SCINTILLA

noun (sihn <u>tihl</u> uh)

trace amount

*This poison is so powerful that no more of a **scintilla** of it is needed to kill a horse.*

Synonyms: atom, iota, mote, spark, speck

• • •

SCINTILLATE

verb (<u>sihn</u> tuhl ayt)

to sparkle, flash

*The society hostess was famous for throwing parties that **scintillated** and impressed every guest.*

Synonyms: gleam, glisten, glitter, shimmer, twinkle

• • •

SCORN

noun (<u>scorn</u>)

contempt, derision

*Josh's teammates regarded him with **scorn** when he drank all the Gatorade the team had planned to dump over the coach's head.*

Synonym: disdain

SCOUNDREL

noun (<u>skown</u> drul)

villain, rogue

*To Timmy, Josh is just a bully and a **scoundrel**.*

Synonym: rascal

• • •

SCOUR

verb (<u>skower</u>)

to scrub clean

*Marisol had to **scour** her paint-stained fingernails with soap before she could get them clean.*

• • •

SCRUPULOUS

adjective (<u>skroop</u> yuh luhs)

acting in strict regard for what is considered proper, punctiliously exact

*After the storm had destroyed their antique lamp, the Millers worked to repair it with **scrupulous** care.*

Synonyms: painstaking, meticulous

SCRUTINIZE

verb (<u>skroo</u> tin iyz)

to observe carefully

*Paul **scrutinized** the three hairs growing on his chin, wondering if he should shave them.*

Synonym: inspect

• • •

SCURRILOUS

adjective (<u>skuh</u> ruh luhs)

vulgar, low, indecent

*The decadent aristocrat took part in **scurrilous** activities every night, unbeknownst to his family.*

Synonyms: abusive, coarse, foul-mouthed

• • •

SCURRY

verb (<u>skur</u> ree)

scamper, run lightly

*Marisol screamed when she spotted a mouse **scurrying** across the tiles in the girls' bathroom at school.*

Synonym: hurry

SEAMY

adjective (<u>see</u> mee)

morally degraded, unpleasant

*The tour guide avoided the **seamy** parts of town.*

Synonyms: sordid, sleazy

• • •

SECRETE

verb (se <u>kreet</u>)

to release fluids from a body

*Timmy was scared by the weird pus **secreting** from the scab on his knee.*

Synonym: hide

• • •

SECTARIAN

adjective (sehk <u>tayr</u> ee uhn)

narrow-minded, relating to a group or sect

*Since the fall of Communism in the former Yugoslavia, its various ethnic groups have plunged into **sectarian** violence.*

Synonym: schismatic

SECULAR

adjective (<u>seh</u> kyoo luhr)

not specifically pertaining to religion, relating to the world

*Although his favorite book was the Bible, the archbishop also read **secular** works such as mysteries.*

Synonyms: temporal, material

• • •

SEDATIVE

noun (<u>sed</u> uh tiv)

something that calms

*Willow uses ginger tea as a **sedative** for her stomach when it feels upset.*

Synonym: soothing

• • •

SEDITION

noun (seh <u>dih</u> shuhn)

behavior that promotes rebellion or civil disorder against the state

*Li was arrested for **sedition** after he gave a fiery speech in the main square.*

Synonyms: insurrection, conspiracy

SEEP

verb (<u>seep</u>)

to slowly flow or pass through a small opening

*Dana's pen exploded in her purse, causing ink to **seep** all over it.*

Synonym: ooze

• • •

SEETHE

verb (<u>seethe</u>)

to experience great agitation

*The class **seethed** when they heard about all of the homework they had.*

Synonyms: boil, churn, roil

• • •

SEMINAL

adjective (<u>seh</u> muhn uhl)

influential in an original way, providing a basis for further development, creative

*The scientist's discovery proved to be **seminal** in the area of quantum physics.*

Synonyms: original, generative

SENESCENT
adjective (sih <u>nehs</u> uhnt)

aging, growing old

*Fearful of becoming **senescent**, Jobim worked out several times a week and ate only healthy foods.*

Synonyms: aged, mature

• • •

SENTENTIOUS
adjective (sehn <u>tehn</u> shuhs)

having a moralizing tone

*The principal took on a **sententious** tone when he lectured the students on their inappropriate behavior during the school assembly.*

Synonyms: aphoristic, moralistic, pithy, pompous, terse

• • •

SENTIENT
adjective (<u>sehn</u> shuhnt)

aware, conscious, able to perceive

*Despite his complete lack of sleep, Jorge was still **sentient** when I spoke to him this morning.*

Synonyms: feeling, intelligent, thinking

SEQUEL
noun (<u>see</u> kwul)

literary or artistic work that continues a previous piece

*George was excited to learn that a **sequel** to his favorite move was being made.*

Synonym: continuation

• • •

SEQUESTER
verb (suh <u>kweh</u> stuhr)

to set apart, seclude

*When juries are **sequestered**, it can take days, even weeks, to come up with a verdict.*

Synonyms: segregate, isolate

• • •

SERAPHIC
adjective (seh <u>rah</u> fihk)

angelic, pure, sublime

*Selena's sweet, **seraphic** appearance belied her nasty, bitter personality.*

Synonyms: cherubic, heavenly

SERENDIPITY

noun (se ren dip ih tee)

habit of making fortunate discoveries
by chance

*Marisol thought it was **serendipity** that
she tripped over the backpack; the
owner later became her boyfriend.*

Synonym: providence

. . .

SERENE

adjective (se reen)

calm, peaceful

*Willow took a moment to enjoy the
serene beach during sunset.*

Synonym: tranquil

. . .

SERVILE

adjective (sur viyl)

overly submissive

*Chantalle's boyfriend was quite **servile**
and catered to her every whim.*

Synonym: obedient

SETBACK

noun (set back)

change from better to worse

*Ashley's pizza party had a minor
setback when the pizzas were delivered
hours late.*

Synonym: obstacle

. . .

SEVERE

adjective (se veer)

harsh, strict, extremely bad in degree

*Ashley had a **severe** case of the
heebie-jeebies when she approached
the haunted house.*

Synonyms: rigid, stern

. . .

SHABBY

adjective (sha bee)

worn-out, threadbare, deteriorated

*Marisol didn't think her clothes looked
shabby until Chantalle asked her if she
shopped in a dumpster.*

Synonyms: grungy, ratty

SHROUD
verb (shrowd)

to conceal or hide

*Willow **shrouded** her Tarot cards with a silk cloth so that their energy could not escape.*

Synonym: cloak

• • •

SHUN
verb (shun)

avoid deliberately

*Derek **shunned** Willow's blog, which talked about how unoriginal she thought his band was.*

Synonym: escape

• • •

SIGNPOST
noun (siyn post)

indication

*Derek felt that the **signposts** indicated that he would have a career in the music industry.*

Synonym: guide

SIMIAN
adjective (sih mee uhn)

apelike, relating to apes

*Early man was more **simian** in appearance than is modern man.*

Synonyms: anthropoid, primate

• • •

SIMPER
verb (sihm puhr)

to smirk, smile foolishly

*The spoiled girl **simpered** as her mother praised her extravagantly to the guests at the party.*

Synonyms: grin, smirk

• • •

SINECURE
noun (sien ih kyoor)

a well-paying job or office that requires little or no work

*The corrupt mayor made sure to set up all his relatives in **sinecures** within the administration.*

SINUOUS
adjective (<u>sihn</u> yoo uhs)

winding, intricate, complex

*Thick, **sinuous** vines wound around the trunk of the tree.*

Synonyms: curvilinear, devious, lithe, serpentine, supple

• • •

SKEPTICISM
noun (skep tih sizm)

disbelief, uncertainty

*Despite Josh's **skepticism**, his dad proved that he could get tickets to the Super Bowl.*

Synonym: doubt

• • •

SKIRT
verb (<u>skurt</u>)

to evade, pass close by, circle around

*For fun, Shanna sometimes asked her parents where babies came from, just to watch them **skirt** the issue.*

Synonym: avoid

SLAKE
verb (slayk)

to calm down or moderate

*In order to **slake** his curiosity, Bryan finally took a tour backstage at the theater.*

Synonyms: moderate, quench, satisfy

• • •

SLEW
noun (<u>slew</u>)

A large amount of something

*Michelle said it would just take a minute to check her email, but a **slew** of new messages kept her busy for nearly an hour.*

Synonym: bunch

• • •

SLUGGISH
adjective (<u>slug</u> ish)

lazy, inactive

*After eating a huge turkey dinner, Timmy felt so **sluggish** that he took a nap.*

Synonym: slow

SMUG
adjective (<u>smug</u>)

excessively self-satisfied

*Shanna felt **smug** after she found out that Chantalle had paid twice as much as she had for the same pair of jeans.*

Synonym: conceited

• • •

SOBRIQUET
noun (<u>soh</u> brih <u>kay</u>) (<u>soh</u> brih <u>keht</u>)

a nickname

*One of former president Ronald Reagan's **sobriquets** was The Gipper.*

Synonyms: alias, pseudonym

• • •

SOCIABLE
adjective (<u>so</u> shu bul)

friendly, gracious

*Derek thinks it's easier to be **sociable** at the pool hall than at school.*

Synonym: convivial

SOJOURN
noun (<u>soh</u> juhrn)

a temporary stay

*After graduating from college, Iliani embarked on a **sojourn** to China.*

Synonym: visit

• • •

SOLACE
noun (<u>sol</u> is)

comfort in distress

*Ashley took **solace** in the fact that the sun would come out tomorrow.*

Synonym: consolation

• • •

SOLECISM
noun (<u>sahl</u> ih sihz uhm) (<u>sohl</u> ih sihz uhm)

grammatical mistake

*The applicant's letter was filled with embarrassing **solecisms**, such as "I works here at 20 years."*

Synonym: language blunder

SOLICITOUS

adjective (suh <u>lih</u> sih tuhs)

anxious, concerned, full of desire, eager

*Overjoyed to see the pop idol in her very presence, the **solicitous** store owner stood ready to serve.*

Synonyms: considerate, careful

• • •

SOLILOQUY

noun (so <u>lil</u> o quy)

a dramatic monologue

*Shakespeare featured at least one **soliloquy** in most of his plays.*

Synonym: speech

• • •

SOLIPSISM

noun (<u>sahl</u> ihp sihz uhm) (<u>sohl</u> ihp sihz uhm)

belief that oneself is the only reality

*Arthur's **solipsism** annoyed others, because he treated them as if they didn't exist.*

Synonym: self-interest

SOLITARY

adjective (<u>sol</u> ih ter ee)

alone, remote

*George felt as though he were in **solitary** confinement whenever he was grounded.*

Synonyms: secluded, isolated

• • •

SOLUBLE

adjective (<u>sol</u> yu bul)

capable of being solved or dissolved

*Timmy licked his lips watching the **soluble** hot cocoa mix dissolve in his cup as he added hot water.*

Synonym: resolvable

• • •

SOMNOLENT

adjective (<u>sahm</u> nuh luhnt)

drowsy, sleepy, inducing sleep

*Carter became **somnolent** after he ate a huge meal.*

Synonyms: sluggish, slumberous, somniferous, soporific

SONOROUS
adjective (sah <u>nuhr</u> uhs)

producing a full, rich sound

The **sonorous** blaring of the foghorn woke up Lily at 4:30 in the morning.

Synonyms: orotund, resonant, vibrant

. . .

SOOTHE
verb (<u>sooth</u>)

to calm, placate, comfort

After a tough day, Willow practiced yoga to **soothe** her nerves and bring her back to a happy place.

Synonyms: help, relax

. . .

SOPHISTRY
noun (<u>sahf</u> ih stree)

deceptive reasoning or argumentation

The politician used **sophistry** to cloud the issue whenever he was asked a tough question in a debate.

Synonym: cogitation

SOPHOMORIC
adjective (sahf <u>mohr</u> ihk)

exhibiting great immaturity and lack of judgment

After Sean's **sophomoric** behavior, he was grounded for weeks.

Synonym: juvenile

. . .

SOPORIFIC
adjective (sahp uhr <u>ihf</u> ihk)

sleepy or tending to cause sleep

The movie proved to be so **soporific** that soon loud snores were heard throughout the theater.

Synonyms: drowsy, narcotic, somniferous, somnolent

. . .

SPARTAN
adjective (<u>spahr</u> tihn)

highly self-disciplined, frugal, austere

When he was in training, the athlete preferred to live in a **spartan** room, so he could shut out all distractions.

Synonyms: restrained, simple

SPECIOUS
adjective (spee shuhs)

having the ring of truth but actually being untrue, deceptively attractive

*After I followed up with some research on the matter, I realized that the charismatic politician's argument had been **specious**.*

Synonyms: misleading, untrue, captious

. . .

SPLICE
verb (spl ice)

to join or bind

*Julia tried to **splice** the cable wires in order to get free service, but when she broke her TV she wished she hadn't.*

Synonym: attach

. . .

SPONTANEOUS
adjective (spon tay nee us)

on the spur of the moment, impulsive

*In an effort to be more **spontaneous**, Paul serenaded Marisol in the middle of the lunchroom.*

Synonym: automatic

SPORTIVE
adjective (spohr tihv)

frolicsome, playful

*The lakeside vacation meant more **sportive** opportunities for the kids than the wine tour through France.*

Synonyms: frisky, merry

. . .

SPRINT
verb (sprint)

dash, run quick for short distances

*George **sprinted** across the schoolyard like lightning when he was late for class.*

Synonym: race

. . .

SPROUT
verb (sprowt)

emerge and develop rapidly

*Shanna's cousin had **sprouted** six inches since the last time she had seen her.*

Synonym: grow

SPURIOUS

adjective (<u>spyoor</u> ee uhs)

lacking authenticity, counterfeit, false

*Quoting from a **spurious** document, the employee declared that all profits should be signed over to him.*

Synonyms: ersatz, fake, fraudulent, mock, phony

• • •

SPURN

verb (<u>spern</u>)

to turn away or reject with scorn

*Marta **spurned** the idea of having class on Saturdays.*

Synonym: decline

• • •

SQUALID

adjective (<u>skwa</u> lihd)

filthy and degraded as the result of neglect or poverty

*The **squalid** living conditions in the building outraged the new tenants.*

Synonyms: unclean, foul

SQUANDER

verb (<u>skwan</u> der)

to waste

*George's parents think he **squanders** away all his time perusing the Internet.*

Synonym: misuse

• • •

SQUELCH

verb (<u>skwelch</u>)

to suppress, to put down with force

*Derek **squelched** the drummer's idea that the band should change their name.*

Synonym: quell

• • •

STAGNANT

adjective (<u>stag</u> nent)

immobile

*George realized the awful smell in his apartment was coming from the **stagnant** water in the sink.*

Synonym: stale

STAID
adjective (stayd)

self-restrained to the point of dullness

The lively young girl felt bored in the company of her staid, conservative date.

Synonyms: grave, sedate, serious, sober, solemn

• • •

STALWART
adjective (stahl wuhrt)

marked by outstanding strength and vigor of body, mind, or spirit

The 85-year old went to the market every day, impressing her neighbors with her stalwart routine.

Synonyms: strong, bold

• • •

STASIS
noun (stay sihs)

a state of static balance or equilibrium, stagnation

The rusty, ivy-covered World War II tank had obviously been in stasis for years.

Synonyms: inertia, standstill

STATUTE
noun (sta choot)

law

Willow was outraged when a new town statute stated that starting tomorrow all kids under eighteen would have a ten o'clock curfew.

Synonym: edict

• • •

STEALTHILY
adverb (stelth ih lee)

covertly

Paul stealthily approached Marisol's locker and slipped a rose inside it when she wasn't looking.

Synonym: secretly

• • •

STENTORIAN
adjective (stehn tohr ee yehn)

extremely loud

Cullen couldn't hear her speaking over the stentorian din of the game on TV.

Synonyms: clamorous, noisy

STERN
adjective (<u>sturn</u>)

strict, harsh

*Josh's mom gave him a **stern** look and told him to take his feet off the coffee table.*

Synonym: severe

. . .

STIFLE
verb (<u>sty</u> ful)

to smother or suffocate

*Paul **stifled** a laugh when he saw the principal chasing his toupee across the school parking lot.*

Synonym: suppress

. . .

STIGMA
noun (<u>stihg</u> mah)

a mark of shame or discredit

In The Scarlet Letter *Hester Prynne was required to wear the letter 'A' on her clothes as a public **stigma** for her adultery.*

Synonyms: blemish, blot, opprobrium, stain, taint

STIMULATE
verb (<u>stim</u> yu layt)

to excite, provoke

*Timmy desperately hoped he could **stimulate** an interesting conversation on his upcoming date.*

Synonyms: arouse, encourage, excite

. . .

STINT
verb (stihnt)

to be sparing or frugal, to restrict with respect to a share or allowance

*Don't **stint** on the mayonnaise, because I don't like my sandwich too dry.*

Synonyms: skimp, scrimp

. . .

STIPULATE
verb (<u>stihp</u> yuh <u>layt</u>)

to specify as a condition or requirement of an agreement or offer

*The contract **stipulated** that if the movie was never filmed, the actress got paid anyway.*

Synonyms: specifize, detail, designate

STOIC

adjective (<u>stoh</u> ihk)

indifferent to or unaffected by emotions

While most of the mourners wept, the dead woman's husband kept up a **stoic,** *unemotional facade.*

Synonyms: impassive, stolid

• • •

STOLID

adjective (<u>stah</u> lihd)

having or showing little emotion

The prisoner appeared **stolid** *and unaffected by the judge's harsh sentence.*

Synonyms: impassive, stoic

• • •

STOMP

verb (<u>stahmp</u>)

step heavily

Shanna **stomped** *into her sister Lisa's room and accused her of taking her strawberry lip gloss.*

Synonym: trample

STRADDLE

verb (<u>stra</u> del)

be on both sides of something

Willow finds it infuriating when politicians **straddle** *issues rather than take stands.*

Synonyms: bestride, hedge

• • •

STRATEGEM

noun (<u>straa</u> tuh juhm)

trick designed to deceive an enemy

The Trojan Horse must be one of the most successful military **stratagems** *used throughout history.*

Synonyms: artifice, feint, maneuver, ruse, while

• • •

STRATIFY

verb (<u>straa</u> tuh fie)

to arrange or divide into layers

Schliemann **stratified** *the numerous layers of Troy, an archeological dig that remains legendary.*

Synonyms: grade, separate

STRIDENT
adjective (<u>strie</u> dehnt)

loud, harsh, unpleasantly noisy

*The traveler's **strident** manner annoyed the flight attendant, but she managed to keep her cool.*

Synonyms: grating, shrill, discordant

• • •

STRINGENT
adjective (<u>strihn</u> guhnt)

imposing severe, rigorous standards

*Many people found it difficult to live up to the **stringent** moral standards imposed by the Puritans.*

Synonyms: restricted, tight, demanding

• • •

STULTIFY
verb (<u>stuhl</u> tuh fie)

to impair or reduce to uselessness

*The company's leadership was **stultified** by its practice of promoting the owner's incapable children to powerful positions.*

Synonyms: damage, mar

STUMP
verb (<u>stump</u>)

to challenge, to baffle

*Timmy spent the entire day trying to solve the puzzle, but he was totally **stumped**.*

Synonyms: frustrate, disconcert

• • •

STURDY
adjective (<u>stur</u> dee)

firm, well built, stout

*Shanna prefers strappy sandals to the **sturdy** loafers that her mother wears.*

Synonyms: substantial, hardy

• • •

STYMIE
verb (<u>stie</u> mee)

to block or thwart

*The police effort to capture the bank robber was **stymied** when he escaped through a rear window.*

Synonyms: stump, baffle, foil

SUBJUGATE

verb (<u>suhb</u> juh gayt)

to conquer, subdue, to enslave

*The Romans **subjugated** all the people they conquered, often enslaving them.*

Synonyms: defeat, enthrall, vanquish, yoke

. . .

SUBLIME

adjective (suh <u>bliem</u>)

lofty or grand

*The music was so **sublime** that it transformed the rude surroundings into a special place.*

Synonyms: august, exalted, glorious, grand

. . .

SUBMISSIVE

adjective (sub <u>miss</u> iv)

tending to meekness, to submit to the will of others

*Josh was **submissive** when the officer pulled him over for speeding.*

Synonym: obedient

SUBSIST

verb (sub <u>sist</u>)

stay alive

*No matter how delicious chocolate bars are, one cannot **subsist** on chocolate alone.*

Synonym: survive

. . .

SUBSTANTIATE

verb (sub <u>stan</u> she ayt)

to verify, confirm, provide supporting evidence

*Timmy camped in his backyard all night, determined to **substantiate** his theory that aliens really were hovering nearby.*

Synonym: prove

. . .

SUBTERFUGE

noun (<u>suhb</u> tuhr fyooj)

trick or tactic used to avoid something

*Spies who are not skilled in the art of **subterfuge** are generally exposed before too long.*

Synonyms: ruse, stratagem

SUBTERRANEAN
adjective (<u>suhb</u> tuh <u>ray</u> nee uhn)

hidden, secret, underground

Subterranean tracks were created for the trains after it was decided they had run out of room above ground.

Synonyms: buried, concealed, sunken

. . .

SUBVERT
verb (sub <u>vurt</u>)

to undermine or corrupt

*Chantalle tried to **subvert** Shanna's diet by eating a hot fudge sundae in front of her.*

Synonym: debase

. . .

SUCCUMB
verb (su <u>kum</u>)

to give in to a stronger power

*Shanna **succumbed** to her desire for hot fudge and ice cream and ordered a sundae.*

Synonym: yield

SUFFICE
verb (suh <u>fiys</u>)

meet requirements, be capable

*Josh really wanted to date Belinda, but her twin sister, Brenda, would **suffice**.*

Synonym: serve

. . .

SULLY
verb (<u>suh</u> lee)

to tarnish, taint

*With the help of a public-relations firm, he was able to restore his **sullied** reputation.*

Synonyms: defile, besmirch

. . .

SUPERANNUATED
adjective (soo puhr <u>aan</u> yoo ay tihd)

too old, obsolete, outdated

*The manual typewriter has become **superannuated**, although a few loyal diehards still swear by it.*

Synonyms: disused, outworn

SUPERCILIOUS
adjective (soo puhr <u>sihl</u> ee uhs)

arrogant, haughty, overbearing,
condescending

*She was a shallow and scornful society
woman with a **supercilious** manner.*

Synonyms: disdainful, patronizing,
proud

. . .

SUPERFICIAL
adjective (soo per <u>fish</u> ul)

hasty, shallow and phony

*Most people think Chantalle is
superficial because all she cares about
are clothes and parties.*

Synonym: facile

. . .

SUPERFLUOUS
adjective (soo <u>puhr</u> floo <u>uhs</u>)

extra, more than necessary

*The extra recommendations Jake
included in his application were
superfluous, as only one was required.*

Synonyms: excess, surplus

SUPERSEDE
verb (<u>soo</u> puhr <u>seed</u>)

to cause to be set aside, to force out of
use as inferior, replace

*Her computer was still running version
2.0 of the software, which had long
since been **superseded** by at least three
more versions.*

Synonym: supplant

. . .

SUPERSTITIOUS
adjective (soo per <u>stish</u> iss)

one irrationally believes that completely unrelated circumstances can
influence an event

*Willow is a little **superstitious**, but not
enough to carry around a little rabbit's
foot for good luck.*

. . .

SUPPLANT
verb (suh <u>plaant</u>)

to replace (another) by force, to take
the place of

*The overthrow of the government
meant a new leader to **supplant** the
tyrannical former one.*

Synonyms: displace, supersede

SUPPLE
adjective (supl)

flexible, pliant

*Willow brushed the soft and **supple** leaf across her cheek, before she realized that it was poison ivy.*

Synonym: elastic

. . .

SUPPRESS
verb (suh press)

to end an activity or subdue

*Derek could not **suppress** his smile when he saw the huge crowd who had come to hear his band.*

Synonyms: censor, silence, repress

. . .

SURFEIT
noun (suhr fiht)

excessive amount

*Because of the **surfeit** of pigs, pork prices have never been lower.*

Synonyms: glut, plethora, repletion, superfluity, surplus

SURLY
adjective (suhr lee)

rude and bad-tempered

*When asked to clean the windshield, the **surly** gas station attendant tossed a dirty rag at the customer and walked away.*

Synonyms: gruff, grumpy, testy

. . .

SURMISE
verb (ser mize)

to guess or infer

*John **surmised** that he should write his paper on mold, because he had so much of it growing in his bedroom.*

Syonyms: assume, presume

. . .

SURMOUNT
verb (suhr mownt)

to conquer, overcome

*The blind woman **surmounted** great obstacles to become a well-known trial lawyer.*

Synonyms: clear, hurdle, leap

SURPLUS

noun (<u>sir</u> plus)

excess

*The lunch lady slid the **surplus** mystery meat into the refrigerator after the lunch period was over.*

Synonym: **extra**

• • •

SURREPTITIOUS

adjective (<u>suh</u> rehp <u>tih</u> shuhs)

characterized by secrecy

*The queen knew nothing of the **surreptitious** plot being hatched against her at court.*

Synonyms: **clandestine, covert, furtive**

• • •

SURROGATE

noun (<u>sir</u> uh git)

one filling in for someone else

*Paul acted as a **surrogate** for his friend when he went onstage during open-mic night at the comedy club.*

Synonym: **substitute**

SUSCEPTIBLE

adjective (sus <u>cep</u> ti ble)

impressionable to a fault

*Vern remembered being **susceptible** to ear infections as a kid.*

Synonym: **vulnerable**

• • •

SUSPEND

verb (su <u>spend</u>)

to defer, interrupt

*Shanna **suspended** her extracurricular activities in order to study for finals.*

Synonym: **adjourn**

• • •

SWARM

noun (<u>swarm</u>)

a large number traveling in a group

*Chantalle was inundated by a **swarm** of mosquitoes after spraying herself with perfume.*

Synonym: **crowd**

SYBARITE

noun (sih buh riet)

a person devoted to pleasure and luxury

*A confirmed **sybarite**, the nobleman fainted at the thought of having to leave his palace and live in a small cottage.*

Synonym: hedonist

• • •

SYCOPHANT

noun (sie kuh fuhnt)

self-serving flatterer, yes-man

*Dreading criticism, the actor surrounded himself with admirers and **sycophants**.*

Synonyms: bootlicker, fawner, lickspittle, toady

• • •

SYMBIOSIS

noun (sihm bee oh sihs)

cooperation, mutual helpfulness

*The rhino and the tick-eating bird live in **symbiosis**, the rhino gives the bird food in the form of ticks, and the bird rids the rhino of parasites.*

Synonyms: association, interdependence

SYMMETRY

noun (sim eh tree)

equality and balance in objects

*For the school art show, Marisol hung an all-black canvas next to an all-white one and titled them "Perfect **Symmetry**."*

Synonym: harmony

• • •

SYNCHRONICITY

noun (syn chro ni ci ty)

the occurrence of related events that cannot be explained conventionally

*Jed believed that **synchronicity** was at work the day that he won $400 in the lottery.*

Synonyms: coincidence

• • •

SYNERGY

noun (sin er jee)

cooperative interaction producing greater results

*The coach complemented the team's amazing **synergy**, which led them to win the game.*

Synonym: teamwork

SYNCOPATION

noun (sihn cuh _pay_ shun)

temporary irregularity in musical rhythm

*A jazz enthusiast will appreciate the use of **syncopation** in this musical genre.*

· · ·

SYNOPSIS

noun (sy _nop_ sis)

a short outline

*Groans could be heard after Professor Barrington handed out her **synopsis** of the material that would be on the test.*

Synonym: summary

SYNTHESIZE

verb (_sin_ thi siyz)

to produce artificially

*Derek preferred going to a live rock concert, as opposed to listening to a **synthesized** imitation on a CD.*

S

TACIT
adjective (<u>taa</u> siht)

silently understood or implied

*Although not a word had been said, everyone in the room knew that a **tacit** agreement had been made about which course of action to take.*

Synonyms: implicit, unspoken

• • •

TACITURN
adjective (<u>taa</u> sih tuhrn)

silent, not talkative

*The clerk's **taciturn** nature earned him the nickname Silent Bob.*

Synonyms: laconic, reticent

• • •

TACT
noun (<u>takt</u>)

consideration in dealing with others, skill in not offending others

*Chantalle could have commented on her friend's weird outfit with more **tact**, rather than pointing and laughing.*

Synonyms: courtesy, delicacy

TACTILE
adjective (<u>taak</u> tihl)

producing a sensation of touch

*The Museum of Natural History displays objects for people to touch so that they have a **tactile** understanding of how different people and animals lived.*

Synonyms: perceptible, tangible

• • •

TALISMAN
noun (<u>tal</u> iss man)

magic object that offers supernatural protection

*Ashley's mom hung a **talisman** in her family car to protect it from accidents.*

Synonym: charm

TALON
noun (<u>taa</u> luhn)

claw of an animal, especially a bird of prey

*A vulture holds its prey in its **talons** while it dismembers it with its beak.*

Synonyms: claw, nail

• • •

TANGENTIAL
adjective (taan <u>jehn</u> shuhl)

digressing, diverting

*Your argument is interesting, but it's **tangential** to the matter at hand, so I suggest we get back to the point.*

Synonyms: digressive, extraneous, inconsequential, irrelevant, peripheral

• • •

TANGIBLE
adjective (<u>tan</u> ji bul)

able to be sensed, perceptible, measurable

*Shanna had **tangible** evidence of her sister reading her diary to show her parents.*

Synonyms: palpable, touchable

TANTAMOUNT
adjective (<u>taan</u> tuh mownt)

equal in value or effect

*If she didn't get concert tickets to see her favorite band, it would be **tantamount** to a tragedy.*

Synonyms: commesurate, equivalent

• • •

TAUNT
verb (<u>tawnt</u>)

to ridicule, mock, insult

*George **taunted** the monkeys at the zoo by shoving bananas in his mouth while they were watching.*

Synonym: tease

• • •

TAUTOLOGICAL
adjective (<u>tawt</u> uh <u>lah</u> jih kuhl)

having to do with needless repetition, redundancy

*I know he was only trying to clarify things, but his **tautological** statements confused me even more.*

Synonyms: verbose, wordy

TAWDRY
adjective (<u>taw</u> dree)

gaudy, cheap, showy

*The performer changed into her **tawdry**
costume and stepped onto the stage.*

Synonyms: flashy, chintzy

. . .

TEMERITY
noun (<u>teh</u> mehr ih tee)

unreasonable or foolhardy disregard
for danger, recklessness

*I offered her a ride since it was late at
night, but she had the **temerity** to say
she'd rather walk.*

Synonym: boldness

. . .

TEMPERANCE
noun (<u>tem</u> per unss)

restraint, self-control

*Marisol showed great **temperance**
when she passed the table packed with
delicious desserts and took only one.*

Synonym: moderation

TEMPESTUOUS
adjective (tehm <u>pehs</u> choo uhs)

stormy, turbulent

*Our camping trip was cut short when
the sun shower we were expecting
turned into a **tempestuous** downpour.*

Synonyms: tumultuous, blustery

. . .

TEMPORAL
adjective (<u>tehmp</u> ore uhl)

having to do with time

*The story lacked a sense of the
temporal, so we couldn't figure out if
the events took place in one evening
or over the course of a year.*

Synonym: chronological

. . .

TENABLE
adjective (<u>tehn</u> uh buhl)

defensible, reasonable

*His decision to quit his job and
travel around the world was **tenable**
only because he inherited millions
of dollars.*

Synonyms: maintainable, rational

TENACIOUS
adjective (teh <u>nay</u> shuhs)

tending to persist or cling, persistent in adhering to something valued or habitual

*For years, against all odds, women **tenaciously** fought for the right to vote.*

Synonyms: stubborn, dogged, obstinate

. . .

TENET
noun (<u>teh</u> niht)

a principle, belief, or doctrine accepted by members of a group

*One of the **tenets** of Islam is that it is not acceptable to eat pork.*

Synonym: canon

. . .

TENTATIVE
adjective (<u>ten</u> tu tiv)

not fully worked out, uncertain

*Shanna made a **tentative** agreement to go out with her friends on Friday night, but had to check her calendar to confirm that she was free.*

Synonym: conditional

TENUOUS
adjective (<u>tehn</u> yoo uhs)

having little substance or strength, flimsy, weak

*Francine's already **tenuous** connection to her cousins was broken when they moved away and left no forwarding address.*

Synonyms: thin, shaky

. . .

TEPID
adjective (<u>teh</u> pid)

neither hot or cold, lacking spirit

*Marnie had a **tepid** reaction to tonight's bland homework assignments.*

Synonyms: halfhearted, lukewarm, uneager, unenthusiastic

. . .

TERRESTRIAL
adjective (tuh <u>reh</u> stree uhl)

earthly, down-to-earth, commonplace

*Many "extraterrestrial" objects turn out to be **terrestrial** in origin, as when flying saucers turn out to be normal airplanes.*

Synonyms: earthbound, mundane, sublunary, tellurian, terrene

TERSE
adjective (tuhrs)

concise, brief, free of extra words

*Her **terse** style of writing was widely praised by the editors, who had been used to seeing long-winded material.*

Synonyms: succinct, brusque

• • •

TERTIARY
adjective (<u>ter</u> ti ary)

of third rank or value

*Because the Stratocaster was Johnny's third-best guitar, he nicknamed it "**Tertiary** Terry."*

• • •

TESTIMONY
noun (<u>tess</u> ti moh nee)

statement made under oath

*George was glued to the television as he watched the witness's damning **testimony** on his favorite law show.*

Synonym: account

THERAPEUTIC
adjective (ther uh <u>pyoo</u> tik)

medicinal

*Josh gulped down the nasty herbal drink thinking it was **therapeutic**, but it didn't make him feel any better.*

Synonym: curative

• • •

THICKET
noun (<u>thick</u> et)

dense bushes

*Paul watched the squirrels chase each other across the grass, then into a nearby **thicket**.*

Synonym: coppice

• • •

THRESHOLD
noun (<u>thresh</u> old)

the point of entering

*Once Chester had reached his **threshold** for pain, he told the team's trainer to call in the doctor.*

Synonym: beginning

THRONG
noun (throng)

a large group of people

*Every Saturday a **throng** of kids gathered for a bonfire on the beach.*

Synonym: crowd

. . .

THWART
verb (thwahrt)

to block or prevent from happening, frustrate, defeat the hopes or aspirations of

***Thwarted** in its attempt to get at the bananas inside the box, the chimp began to squeal.*

Synonyms: oppose, foil, frustrate

. . .

TIMELESS
adjective (tiym les)

eternal

*Marisol considers her bell-bottoms and cotton ponchos **timeless**, not retro.*

Synonym: ageless

TIMOROUS
adjective (tih muhr uhs)

timid, shy, full of apprehension

*A **timorous** woman, Lois relied on her children to act for her whenever aggressive behavior was called for.*

Synonyms: anxious, fearful, frightened

. . .

TIRADE
noun (tie rayd)

long, harsh speech or verbal attack

*Observers were shocked at the manager's **tirade** over such a minor mistake.*

Synonyms: diatribe, fulmination, harangue, obloquy

. . .

TITULAR
adjective (tihch yoo luhr)

existing in title only, having a title without the functions or responsibilities

*The **titular** king did little more than sit on his throne all day.*

Synonyms: honorary, named

TOADY
noun (<u>toh</u> dee)

one who flatters in the hope of gaining favors

*The king was surrounded by **toadies** who rushed to agree with whatever outrageous thing he said.*

Synonyms: sycophant, parasite

. . .

TOLERATE
verb (<u>tol</u> uh rayt)

to endure, permit, to respect others

*Shanna's little sister often drives her crazy, but she **tolerates** it because she loves her.*

Synonym: bear

. . .

TOME
noun (tohm)

book, usually large and academic

*The teacher was forced to refer to various **tomes** to find the answer to the advanced student's question.*

Synonyms: codex, volume

TORPID
adjective (<u>tohr</u> pihd)

lethargic, unable to move, dormant

*After surgery, the patient was **torpid** until the anesthesia wore off.*

Synonyms: apathetic, benumbed, hibernating, inactive, inert

. . .

TORPOR
noun (<u>tohr</u> puhr)

extreme mental and physical sluggishness

*After surgery, the patient's **torpor** lasted several hours until the anesthesia wore off.*

Synonyms: apathy, languor

. . .

TORRID
adjective (<u>tore</u> id)

extremely hot or passionate

*The prom queen's **torrid** relationship with her boyfriend was all anyone could talk about.*

Synonym: scorching

TORTUOUS
adjective (<u>tohr</u> choo uhs)

having many twists and turns, highly complex

*To reach the remote inn, the travelers had to negotiate a **tortuous** path.*

Synonyms: winding, circuitous

• • •

TOUCHSTONE
noun (<u>tuch</u> stohn)

something used to test the excellence of others

*Ashley, who is warm, bright, and enthusiastic, is the **touchstone** for a happy student.*

Synonym: standard

• • •

TOUT
verb (towt)

to praise or publicize loudly or extravagantly

*She **touted** her skills as superior to ours, though in fact, we were all at the same level.*

Synonyms: acclaim, proclaim

TRACTABLE
adjective (<u>traak</u> tuh buhl)

obedient, yielding

*Though it was exhausted, the **tractable** workhorse obediently dragged the carriage through the mud.*

Synonyms: acquiescent, compliant, docile, governable, malleable

• • •

TRAJECTORY
noun (truh <u>jehk</u> tuh ree)

the path followed by a moving object, whether through space or otherwise, flight

*The **trajectory** of the pitched ball was interrupted by an unexpected bird.*

Synonyms: path, route, course

• • •

TRANSCRIBE
verb (tran <u>skriyb</u>)

to reproduce, record

*Willow got a cramp in her hand as she **transcribed** every word the teacher said into her notebook.*

Synonym: copy

TRANSIENT
adjective (<u>traan</u> see uhnt)

passing with time, temporary, short-lived

*The reporter lived a **transient** life, staying in one place only long enough to cover the current story.*

Synonyms: brief, transitory

• • •

TRANSITORY
adjective (<u>traan</u> sih <u>tohr</u> ee)

short-lived, existing only briefly

*The actress's popularity proved **transitory** when her play folded within the month.*

Synonyms: transient, ephemeral, momentary

• • •

TRAPEZOID
noun (<u>trap</u> e zoid)

a shape having two parallel and two nonparallel sides

*Today's geometry class focused on **trapezoids**.*

TRAVESTY
noun (<u>tra</u> ves tee)

parody, exaggerated imitation, caricature

*Timmy thought getting detention for the one prank he played on the school bully was a **travesty** of justice.*

Synonym: mockery

• • •

TREMULOUS
adjective (<u>treh</u> myoo luhs)

trembling, timid, easily shaken

*The **tremulous** kitten had been separated from her mother.*

Synonyms: shaking, timorous, anxious

• • •

TRENCHANT
adjective (<u>trehn</u> chuhnt)

acute, sharp, incisive, forceful, effective

*Dan's **trenchant** observations in class made him the professor's favorite student.*

Synonyms: biting, caustic, cutting, keen

TREPIDATION

noun (treh pih <u>day</u> shuhn)

fear and anxiety

*Alana approached the door of the principal's office with **trepidation**.*

Synonyms: alarm, apprehension, dread, fright

. . .

TRIANGULATION

noun (tri an gu <u>la</u> tion)

a technique for establishing the distance between any two points

*The researchers used **triangulation** in an effort to locate the missing artifacts.*

. . .

TRIFLING

adjective (<u>trie</u> fling)

of slight worth, trivial, insignificant

*That little glitch in the computer program is a **trifling** error, in general, it works very well.*

Synonyms: frivolous, idle, paltry, petty, picayune

TRITE

adjective (triet)

shallow, superficial

*Lindsay's graduation speech was the same **trite** nonsense we have heard hundreds of times in the past.*

Synonyms: banal, hackneyed, shopworn, stale, threadbare

. . .

TROUNCE

verb (trowns)

to beat severely, defeat

*The inexperienced young boxer was **trounced** in a matter of minutes.*

Synonyms: vanquish, conquer

. . .

TRUCULENT

adjective (<u>truhk</u> yuh lehnt)

disposed to fight, belligerent

*The bully was initially **truculent** but eventually stopped picking fights at the least provocation.*

Synonyms: antagonistic, combative

TRUNCATE

verb (<u>truhnk</u> ayt)

to cut off, shorten by cutting

*The mayor **truncated** his standard lengthy speech when he realized that the audience was not in the mood to listen to it.*

Synonyms: crop, curtail, lop

. . .

TUMULT

noun (<u>tuh</u> muhlt)

state of confusion, agitation

*The **tumult** of the demonstrators drowned out the police chief's speech.*

Synonyms: commotion, chaos, din, disturbance, turmoil

. . .

TURGID

adjective (<u>tuhr</u> jihd)

swollen as from a fluid, bloated

*In the process of osmosis, water passes through the walls of **turgid** cells, ensuring that they never contain too much water.*

Synonym: distended

TURPITUDE

noun (<u>tur</u> pi tood)

inherent vileness, foulness

*Timmy's mother felt that television is to blame for most of the **turpitude** in society.*

Synonym: depravity

. . .

TUTELAGE

noun (<u>toot</u> uh lihj)

guardianship, guidance

*Under the **tutelage** of her older sister, the young orphan was able to persevere.*

Synonym: supervision

. . .

TYRO

noun (<u>tie</u> roh)

beginner, novice

*An obvious **tyro** at salsa, Millicent received no invitations to dance.*

Synonyms: apprentice, fledgling, greenhorn, neophyte, tenderfoot

UBIQUITOUS
adjective (yoo <u>bihk</u> wih tuhs)

being everywhere simultaneously

*Fast food franchises are **ubiquitous** in the United States, and are common in foreign countries as well.*

Synonyms: inescapable, omnipresent

• • •

UMBRAGE
noun (<u>uhm</u> brihj)

offense, resentment

*The businessman took **umbrage** at the security guard's accusation that he had shoplifted a packet of gum.*

Synonyms: asperity, dudgeon, ire, pique, rancor

UNCANNY
adjective (uhn <u>kaa</u> nee)

so keen and perceptive as to seem supernatural, peculiarly unsettling

*Though they weren't related, their resemblance was **uncanny**.*

Synonyms: weird, eerie

• • •

UNCONSCIONABLE
adjective (uhn <u>kahn</u> shuhn uh buhl)

unscrupulous, shockingly unfair or unjust

*After she promised me the project, the fact that she gave it to someone else is **unconscionable**.*

Synonyms: dishonorable, indefensible

UNCTUOUS
adjective (<u>ungk</u> choo uhs)

greasy, oily, smug and falsely earnest

*The **unctuous** salesman showered the rich customers with exaggerated compliments.*

Synonyms: fulsome, phony, smarmy

• • •

UNFETTER
verb (un <u>fet</u> er)

to free from restrictions

*The dog owners believed they should have the right to **unfetter** their dogs occasionally, rather than keep them on leashes at all times.*

Synonym: free

• • •

UNFROCK
verb (uhn <u>frahk</u>)

to dethrone, especially of priestly power

*Any priest caught sullying the good name of his profession would certainly be **unfrocked**.*

Synonyms: demote, degrade

UNHERALDED
adjective (un <u>her</u> ul did)

unexpected, not publicized

*The gallant knight's arrival was **unheralded**, so the princess was surprised to discover him in the castle.*

Synonym: unannounced

• • •

UNIVERSAL
adjective (yoo ni <u>ver</u> sal)

applicable to anything

*Because of her **universal** appeal, the actress was the perfect spokeswoman for the charity auction.*

Synonym: worldwide

• • •

UNKEMPT
adjective (un <u>kempt</u>)

sloppily maintained

*Eli whipped out a comb and fixed his **unkempt** hair in time for the year-book photo.*

Synonym: messy

UNPARALLELED
adjective (un par uh leld)

having no equal or match

*To many, Michael Jordan was an **unparalleled** athlete who redefined basketball stardom.*

Synonym: peerless

• • •

UNSCRUPULOUS
adjective (un scroop yu luss)

devoid of honor

*Dr. Moreau's **unscrupulous** experiments revolved around trying to mutate animals and humans together.*

Synonym: unethical

• • •

UNTENABLE
adjective (un ten uh bul)

indefensible

*Too late, the captain realized that he ordered his men into an **untenable** position in the battle.*

Synonym: uninhabitable

UNYIELDING
adjective (un yeel ding)

firm, resolute

*Despite her son's desperate pleas, Mrs. Young was **unyielding**: under no circumstances could he stay out after midnight.*

Synonyms: determined, implacable

• • •

UPBRAID
verb (uhp brayd)

to scold sharply

*The teacher **upbraided** the student for scrawling graffiti all over the walls of the school.*

Synonyms: berate, chide, reproach, rebuke, tax

• • •

URBANE
adjective (uhr bayn)

courteous, refined, suave

*The **urbane** teenager sneered at the mannerisms of his country-bumpkin cousin.*

Synonyms: cosmopolitan, debonair, elegant, polite, soigné

USURP
verb (yoo <u>suhrp</u>)

to seize by force

*The vice-principal was power-hungry, and threatened to **usurp** the principal's power.*

Synonyms: appropriate, arrogate, assume, preempt

• • •

USURY
noun (<u>yoo</u> zuh ree)

the practice of lending money at exorbitant rates

*The moneylender was convicted of **usury** when it was discovered that he charged 50 percent interest on all his loans.*

Synonyms: loan-sharking, interest

UTILITARIAN
adjective (yoo tih lih <u>teh</u> ree uhn)

efficient, functional, useful

*The suitcase was undeniably **utilitarian**, with its convenient compartments of different sizes.*

Synonyms: practical, pragmatic

VACILLATE
verb (<u>vaa</u> sihl ayt)

to waver, show indecision

The customer held up the line as he vacillated between ordering chocolate or coffee ice cream.

Synonyms: **falter, hesitate, oscillate, sway, waffle**

. . .

VACUOUS
adjective (<u>vaa</u> kyoo uhs)

empty, void, lacking intelligence, purposeless

The congresswoman's vacuous speech angered the voters, who were tired of hearing empty platitudes.

Synonyms: **idle, inane, stupid, vacant**

VAPID
adjective (<u>vaa</u> pihd)

tasteless, dull

Todd found his blind date vapid and boring, and couldn't wait to get away from her.

Synonyms: **inane, insipid, vacuous**

. . .

VARIEGATED
adjective (<u>vaar</u> ee uh <u>gayt</u> ehd)

varied, marked with different colors

The variegated foliage of the jungle allows it to support thousands of animal species.

Synonym: **diversified**

. . .

VAUNTED
adjective (<u>vawnt</u> ehd)

boasted about, bragged about

The vaunted new computer program turned out to have so many bugs that it had to be recalled.

Synonyms: **acclaimed, celebrated**

VEER
verb (veer)

to change direction or course

*The car **veered** off the narrow gravel road and drove into a nearby ditch.*

Synonym: swerve

. . .

VEHEMENTLY
adverb (vee ih mehnt lee)

marked by extreme intensity of emotions or convictions

*She **vehemently** opposed the closing of the neighborhood garden, and was even arrested for protesting when the bulldozers came.*

Synonyms: vociferously, unequivocally

. . .

VELOCITY
noun (ve lah se tee)

quickness of motion

*The sudden **velocity** of the locomotive startled the passengers on board.*

Synonym: speed

VENERABLE
adjective (veh nehr uh buhl)

respected because of age

*All of the villagers sought the **venerable** old woman's advice whenever they had a problem.*

Synonyms: distinguished, elderly, respectable

. . .

VENERATE
verb (vehn uhr ayt)

to respect deeply

*In a traditional Confucian society the young **venerate** their elders, deferring to the elders' wisdom and experience.*

Synonyms: adore, honor, idolize, revere

. . .

VERACITY
noun (vuhr aa sih tee)

accuracy, truth

*The **veracity** of the statement "all guys are dogs" is highly debatable.*

Synonym: precision

VERBATIM

adverb (ver <u>bay</u> tem)

in the exact words

*Rosa followed her teacher's instructions **verbatim** and got an A on her project.*

Synonyms: directly, exactly

• • •

VERBOSE

adjective (vuhr <u>bohs</u>)

wordy

*Shanna wondered if her two-hour valedictorian speech was a bit too **verbose**.*

Synonyms: rambling, long-winded

• • •

VERBOTEN

noun (ver <u>bo</u> ten)

forbidden, especially by rule or law

*Kyle often used a German accent when giving a friendly reminder and used words like **verboten**.*

Synonym: prohibited

• • •

VERDANT

adjective (<u>vuhr</u> dnt)

green with vegetation, inexperienced

*He wandered deep into the **verdant** woods in search of mushrooms and other edible flora.*

Synonyms: grassy, leafy, wooded

VERISIMILITUDE

noun (vehr uh sih <u>mihl</u> ih tood)

quality of appearing true or real

*The TV show's **verisimilitude** led viewers to believe that the characters it portrayed were real.*

Synonym: reality

• • •

VERITABLE

adjective (<u>vehr</u> iht uh buhl)

being without question, often used figuratively

*Josh thought the all-girl's high school down the block was a **veritable** gold mine for dates.*

Synonym: virtual

• • •

VERNACULAR

noun (vuhr <u>naa</u> kyoo luhr)

everyday language used by ordinary people, specialized language of a profession

*Preeti could not understand the **vernacular** of the south, where she had recently moved.*

Synonyms: dialect, patois, lingo

VERNAL
adjective (<u>vuhr</u> nuhl)

related to spring, fresh

*Bea basked in the balmy **vernal** breezes, happy that winter was coming to an end.*

Synonyms: springlike, youthful

• • •

VESTIGE
noun (<u>veh</u> stihj)

trace, remnant

***Vestiges** of the former tenant still remained in the apartment, although he hadn't lived there for years.*

Synonyms: relic, remains, sign

• • •

VEX
verb (vehks)

to annoy, irritate, puzzle, confuse

*The old man who loved his peace and quiet was **vexed** by his neighbor's loud music.*

Synonyms: annoy, bother, chafe, exasperate, irk, nettle, peeve, provoke

VICARIOUSLY
adverb (vie <u>kaar</u> ee uhs lee)

felt or undergone as if one were taking part in the experience or feelings of another

*She lived **vicariously** through the characters in the adventure books she was always reading.*

Synonyms: substitute, delegated

• • •

VICISSITUDE
noun (vih <u>sih</u> sih tood)

change or variation, ups and downs

*Investors must be prepared for **vicissitudes** in the market and not panic when stock prices fall occasionally.*

Synonyms: inconstancy, mutability

• • •

VIE
verb (vi)

to strive for superiority

*The team captain would often **vie** for game MVP by trying to score more points than anyone else.*

Synonyms: content, compete

VILIFY
verb (<u>vih</u> lih fie)

to slander, defame

*As gossip columnists often **vilify** celebrities, they're usually held in low regard.*

Synonym: malign

. . .

VIM
noun (vihm)

vitality and energy

*The **vim** with which she worked so early in the day explained why she was so productive.*

Synonyms: power, force

. . .

VINDICATE
verb (<u>vihn</u> dih kayt)

to clear of blame, support a claim

*Tess felt **vindicated** when her prediction about the impending tornado came true.*

Synonyms: justify, exonerate

VIRTUOSO
noun (vihr choo <u>oh</u> soh)

someone with masterly skill, expert musician

*He is a **virtuoso** conductor and has performed in all the most prestigious concert halls.*

Synonyms: genius, master

. . .

VIRULENT
adjective (<u>veer</u> yuh luhnt)

extremely poisonous, malignant, hateful

*Alarmed at the **virulent** press he was receiving, the militant activist decided to go underground.*

Synonyms: infectious, toxic

. . .

VISCERAL
adjective (<u>vihs</u> uhr uhl)

instinctive, not intellectual, deep, emotional

*When my twin was wounded many miles away, I, too, had a **visceral** reaction.*

Synonyms: gut, earthy

VISCID
adjective (vih sid)

being of a thick, adhesive consistency

*The **viscid** honey took forever to pour from the jar.*

Synonym: sticky

• • •

VISCOUS
adjective (<u>vih</u> skuhs)

thick and adhesive, like a slow-flowing fluid

*Most **viscous** liquids, like oil or honey, become even thicker as they are cooled down.*

Synonyms: gelatinous, glutinous, thick

• • •

VITIATE
verb (<u>vi</u> she ate)

to make faulty or defective

*The malfunctioning machine **vitiated** all the tennis rackets until it was fixed.*

Synonym: impair

VITRIOLIC
adjective (vih tree <u>ah</u> lihk)

burning, caustic, sharp, bitter

*Given the opportunity to critique his enemy's new book, the spiteful critic wrote an unusually **vitriolic** review of it for the newspaper.*

Synonyms: acerbic, scathing

• • •

VITUPERATE
verb (vie <u>too</u> puhr ayt)

to abuse verbally, berate

***Vituperating** someone is never a constructive way to effect change.*

Synonyms: scold, reproach, castigate

• • •

VOCIFEROUS
adjective (voh <u>sih</u> fuhr uhs)

loud, noisy

*Amid the **vociferous** protests of the members of parliament, the prime minister continued his speech.*

Synonym: vocal

VOLATILE
adjective (<u>vah</u> luh tuhl)

easily aroused or changeable, lively or explosive

*His **volatile** personality made it difficult to predict his reaction to anything.*

Synonyms: capricious, erratic, fickle, inconsistent, inconstant, mercurial, temperamental

. . .

VOLITION
noun (vo <u>li</u> shen)

the power to make a choice or decision

*Emelia made the decision to have tacos for dinner under her own **volition**.*

Synonym: will

. . .

VOLLEY
noun (<u>vah</u> lee)

a flight of missiles, round of gunshots

*The troops fired a **volley** of bullets at the enemy, but they couldn't be sure how many hit their target.*

Synonyms: discharge, barrage

VOLUBLE
adjective (<u>vahl</u> yuh buhl)

talkative, speaking easily, glib

*The **voluble** man and his reserved wife proved the old saying that opposites attract.*

Synonyms: loquacious, verbose

. . .

VORACIOUS
adjective (vo rae shes)

having a huge appetite

*The **voracious** jogger thought about running over to the closest pizzeria.*

Synonym: ravenous

. . .

VOUCHSAFE
verb (<u>vau</u> ch safe)

to furnish as a special favor

*The bishop **vouchsafed** the request to hold a fair on the church grounds.*

Synonym: grant

. . .

VULGARIAN
noun (vel <u>ger</u> e an)

a vulgar person

*Barry was considered a **vulgarian** by his classmates and no one wanted to sit with him at lunch.*

Synonym: plebian

WAN
adjective (wahn)

sickly pale

*The sick child had a **wan** face, in contrast to her rosy-cheeked sister.*

Synonyms: ashen, sickly

• • •

WANTON
adjective (<u>wahn</u> tuhn)

undisciplined, unrestrained, reckless

*The order of the school was a much needed change from her former, **wanton** ways.*

Synonyms: capricious, lewd, licentious

• • •

WARY
adjective (<u>wayr</u> ee)

careful

*The dog was **wary** at first, only gradually letting its guard down.*

Synonym: cautious

WATERSHED
noun (<u>wot</u> er shed)

critical turning point

*The invention of sound in movies was a **watershed** in the development of modern cinema.*

Synonym: important

• • •

WAVER
verb (<u>way</u> vuhr)

to fluctuate between choices

*If you **waver** too long before making a decision about which testing site to register for, you may not get your first choice.*

Synonyms: dither, falter

• • •

WAX
verb (waaks)

to increase gradually, to begin to be

*The moon was **waxing**, and would soon be full.*

Synonyms: enlarge, expand

WEAN
verb (<u>ween</u>)

to stop being dependent upon

Desperate to lose weight, Janice **weaned** *herself off of chocolate cake.*

Synonym: **detach**

• • •

WEATHERED
verb (<u>we</u> therd)

to bear up against and come safely through

Jonas **weathered** *the storm under his tiny umbrella.*

Synonym: **survive**

• • •

WHEEDLE
verb (<u>weed</u> l)

to obtain through coaxing

Frank was an expert at **wheedling** *other students into doing his work for him.*

Synonym: **flatter**

• • •

WHET
verb (weht)

to sharpen, stimulate

The delicious odors wafting from the kitchen **whet** *Jack's appetite, and he couldn't wait to eat.*

Synonyms: **hone, grind, strop**

WHIMSICAL
adjective (<u>wihm</u> sih cuhl)

playful or fanciful idea

The ballet was **whimsical,** *delighting the children with its imaginative characters and unpredictable sets.*

Synonyms: **capricious, chameleonic, erratic, fickle, mutable**

• • •

WHISK
verb (<u>whisk</u>)

to brush off lightly

Charles **whisked** *the cookie crumbs off the table and put them in the garbage.*

Synonym: **wipe**

• • •

WHITTLE
verb (<u>wit</u> l)

shape wood with a knife

The skilled craftsman **whittled** *a crest onto the old oak door.*

Synonym: **carve**

WIDGET
noun (<u>wi</u> jet)

an unidentified article used for hypothetical examples

*Don always joked around that he worked at the **widget** factory down the road.*

Synonym: gadget

• • •

WIELD
verb (weeld)

to exercise authority or influence effectively

*For such a young congressman, he **wielded** a lot of power.*

Synonym: exert

• • •

WILY
adjective (<u>wie</u> lee)

clever, deceptive

*Yet again, the **wily** coyote managed to elude the ranchers who wanted it dead.*

Synonyms: cunning, tricky, crafty

WINSOME
adjective (<u>wihn</u> suhm)

charming, happily engaging

*Dawn gave the customs officers a **winsome** smile, and they let her pass without searching her bags.*

Synonyms: attractive, delightful

• • •

WITHHOLD
verb (with <u>hold</u>)

to restrain

*In order to ensure that people pay their taxes, many companies **withhold** the money from their employees' paychecks directly.*

Synonym: keep

• • •

WIZENED
adjective (<u>wih</u> zuhnd)

withered, shriveled, wrinkled

*The **wizened** old man was told that the plastic surgery necessary to make him look young again would cost more money than he could imagine.*

Synonyms: atrophied, desiccated, gnarled, mummified, wasted

WORST
verb (wuhrst)

to gain the advantage over, defeat

*The North **worsted** the South in America's Civil War.*

Synonyms: beat, vanquish

. . .

WRAITH
noun (rayth)

a ghost or specter, a ghost of a living person seen just before his or her death

*Gideon thought he saw a **wraith** late one night as he sat vigil outside his great uncle's bedroom door.*

Synonyms: apparition, bogeyman, phantasm, shade, spirit

. . .

WRATH
noun (<u>rath</u>)

forceful anger

*Hillary feared her father's **wrath** when she told him that she wrecked his car.*

Synonym: hostility

WRITHE
verb (<u>rie</u> th)

to squirm or twist as if in pain

*Jenny watched the crowd of **writhing** bodies on the dance floor.*

Synonyms: wiggle, wriggle

. . .

WRY
adjective (rie)

bent or twisted in shape or condition, dryly humorous

*Every time she teased him, she shot her friends a **wry** smile.*

Synonyms: askew, sardonic

XENOPHOBIA
noun (zee noh <u>foh</u> bee uh)

fear or hatred of foreigners or
strangers

*Countries in which **xenophobia** is
prevalent often have more restrictive
immigration policies than countries
which are more accepting of foreign
influences.*

Synonyms: bigotry, chauvinism,
prejudice

YEN
noun (yehn)

a strong desire, craving

*Pregnant women commonly have a **yen** for pickles.*

Synonym: desire

• • •

YEOMAN
noun (yo men)

one that performs a great and loyal service

*Dan did a **yeoman's** job as editor of the acclaimed school newspaper.*

Synonym: supporter

YIELD
verb (yeeld)

surrender, be productive

*Despite my initial pessimism about it, our staff meeting **yielded** a number of constructive suggestions.*

Synonym: concede

• • •

YOKE
verb (yohk)

to join together

*As soon as the farmer had **yoked** his oxen together, he began to plow the fields.*

Synonyms: bind, harness, pair

• • •

YURT
noun (yurt)

a domed Asian tent

*Vanessa spent her summer backpacking and living in a **yurt**.*

ZEAL
adjective (zeehl)

passion, excitement

*She brought her typical **zeal** to the project, sparking enthusiasm in the other team members.*

Synonyms: ardency, fervor, fire, passion

. . .

ZEALOT
noun (<u>zeh</u> luht)

someone passionately devoted to a cause

*The **zealot** had no time for those who failed to share his strongly held beliefs.*

Synonyms: enthusiast, fanatic, militant, radical

ZEALOUS
adjective (<u>zel</u> us)

enthusiastic, filled with passion

*The **zealous** members of the debate team couldn't wait to face their opponents.*

Synonym: eager

. . .

ZENITH
noun (<u>zee</u> nihth)

the point of culmination, peak

*The diva considered her appearance at the Metropolitan Opera to be the **zenith** of her career.*

Synonyms: acme, pinnacle

. . .

ZEPHYR
noun (<u>zeh</u> fuhr)

a gentle breeze, something airy or unsubstantial

*The **zephyr** from the ocean made the intense heat on the beach bearable for the sunbathers.*

Synonyms: breath, draft